The Watch at Peaked Hill

The Watch at Peaked Hill

Outer Cape Cod Dune Shack Life

1953–2003

Frenchie's Shack at Night by Salvatore Del Deo, 2015, oil on canvas, 14" x 20"

Josephine Breen Del Deo

4880 Lower Valley Road • Atglen, PA 19310

Dedicated to "Frenchie" and to "Schatzi"
Who gave us their universe

Library of Congress Control Number: 2015940137

Type set in Adobe Caslon

ISBN: 978-0-7643-4978-2
Printed in the United States of America

Published by Schiffer Publishing, Ltd.
4880 Lower Valley Road
Atglen, PA 19310
Phone: (610) 593-1777; Fax: (610) 593-2002
E-mail: Info@schifferbooks.com

Contents

Preface

THE NATURAL BEAUTY and isolation of the long curve of the Great Outer Beach of Cape Cod has been increasingly celebrated over the last three centuries. Only occasionally and minimally inhabited, it excited the first famous walking enthusiast, Henry David Thoreau, and has given countless others the confidence to become part of the eternal patterns of life exampled there, not just physical but philosophical and spiritual. This precious legacy generated the inspiration to create the Cape Cod National Seashore and has maintained the dedication to the dream of preservation and the idea that man could inhabit nature with intelligent accommodation to the ancient patterns of species other than his own. In the course of time, the earlier rhythms of usage became subject to an increasing necessity not only to preserve what was essentially present at the inception of such an idea, but to allow reasonable access to that legacy to each new generation of inhabitants and visitors alike. This task is daunting in scope and continues to present many challenges. It is, however, likely to succeed in almost every sense but one, which is, perhaps, the most important of all: to preserve a "way of life" perfected by minimal expectations in regard to society's material advantages and by confining perennial patterns of use to a kind of "survivalist relationship with nature."

The experience of living seasonally in a dune shack at Peaked Hill, over a period of more than fifty years, may reveal the rapture of solitude's gifts obtainable only at the price of consistent dedication to the principle that "less is better." Persons from all walks of life have clung tenaciously to these small, simple structures known as dune shacks with astonishing devotion, and, in the process, have exampled habitation, in general, that may serve to move humanity toward saner solutions for preserving the shrinking resources of our increasingly overwhelmed earthly domain.

The essence of the life I describe has been experienced now by every member of my immediate family. This has happened not through random encounters, but by repeated contact, over time, with an impulse that has always resided in man and which is sometimes deeply felt and often openly expressed. What we call the "creative spirit" lives in all these dune shacks, but the breath of that spirit must be nourished by love and, not so exceptionally, by attention to the oracles of nature that are in and about these spiritual temples. May the reader, therefore, discover in these pages both the exultation and the anguish of maintaining *The Watch at Peaked Hill.*

—Josephine Breen Del Deo

Acknowledgments

MANY PERSONS HAVE contributed, in particular and significant ways, to *The Watch at Peaked Hill.* To all of them, I have offered my sincere appreciation for their contribution in the Appendix Acknowledgments, Part I and Part II which follow the text of the book. What remains to express is my gratitude to several friends and members of my family who have given me constant spiritual support throughout an extended creative process:

Berta Walker, my dear friend, who has sponsored and supported so many activities within the full spectrum of the arts community in Provincetown and who has so enthusiastically endorsed *The Watch at Peaked Hill* in its long journey to publication.

Dune-dwelling neighbors and friends Marianne Benson and Peter Clemons, who have shared with me and my family the way of life in the dune shacks at Peaked Hill and who have given freely of their time and resources to assist me in the collection and organization of many important elements of my book.

Romolo Del Deo, my son, who has had the immense task of transposing my entire manuscript to the framework of today's publishing technology. His devotion can only be appreciated by those who have experienced the same difficult passage between the millennial succession from one generation to the next.

Salvatore Del Deo, my husband, who has shared all that I have been privileged to experience in our habitation at Peaked Hill. During the process of expressing its metaphor and meaning, he has been both advocate and mentor without whom it would have been impossible to bring this memoir to a successful conclusion.

— *The Author*

CHAPTER I

Between the Sand And Stars

1953-1959

AS WE DRIFTED off to sleep in the hammock of a bed that completely filled the supposititious bedroom of Frenchie's dune shack at Peaked Hill, the flutterings and cooing of Joseph, her dove, sounded muted and soft in our ears, lulling us to tranquility and, eventually, to sleep. Joseph's own special cage was sagaciously placed above our heads at the exact level where his companionship could sooth us at night and awaken us softly in the morning without an accompanying rain of feathers. The privilege of a private room in Frenchie's shack was based on her romantic credo, which honored lovers above all other earthly creatures. It was enough for her that we were in love, and, therefore, the whole of her universe between the sand and stars was turned over to us, momentarily, as a domain of heavenly bliss. Outside, on that memorable evening, the ocean added to the lulling of Joseph with the hypnotic rhythm of a full-moon tide. Here, where the land ended and eased itself to sea, one could imagine eternity as a blissful repetition of the same peaceful repose. We turned to each other and quickly forgot all earthly complaints, falling asleep in each other's arms.

Frenchie awakened us the next morning with the scrape of the screen door against the sandy floor, for the boards that lifted her but a bare inch above the settled dune of her abode were always loaded with the sand of daily traffic in and out of the tarpaper shack, no matter how carefully she swept the place. A cup of coffee was brewing on the three-burner kerosene stove, which was a model of functional efficiency: three tall chambers bearing the circle of wicks which demanded cleaning, trimming and meticulous attention, but which, when so attended, gave off a bluish light and a satisfactory heat on any day, rain or shine. The reservoir of a heavy glass receptacle for kerosene made periodic gurgles as it allocated the kerosene, on demand, to the base of its three settlements of circular wicks. When they burned "clean," they gave off a blue flame that indicated they were at peak performance.

So it was that Frenchie's ideal dune life became ours, and it has maintained its influence on our lives to the present day. As I write, the remembrance of her laughter, her stories, and her directions for dune living fill the shack not a bit less joyously and clearly than they did fifty years ago:

Always keep Fels Naptha soap in the shack; it is the best defense against poison ivy and moreover a helpful treatment.

Use the sand to sharpen your saw, sawing back and forth in the sand.

Scrub the bottom of your pots with sand before the final washing, as the sand is a perfect abrasive.

Leave a bar of soap for the mice in winter; they need the fat, you know.

There were many more rules of life at Peaked Hill, such as the observance of the diurnal tide changes to catch the peak of the high tide for pumping water.

Sometimes, Frenchie would complain slightly about the sand fleas, her arms covered with bites, but then she would light a cigarette for solace and begin to tell us about her life in the streets of Paris, dancing and singing with the band of gypsies for her living. We never questioned those stories about surviving in the sewers of Paris, as these were such romantic scenarios. Who would not be struck dumb with nostalgia for another time by this hauntingly provocative femme fatale, a beauty from *George White's Scandals* who came here, so she said, with Bette Davis and proceeded to bury her life in a shack that she built out of scraps of driftwood from the beach and from other salvaged materials that the ocean serendipitously provided at her doorstep?

Frenchie outside her dune shack on the edge of the ocean beach at sunset on the evening of July 25, 1953, *The Provincetown Advocate*, (summer), 1970. *Photo by John Bell*

What emerged was a magic moment of architecture perfectly suited to her eccentricity and her romanticism. No one but an artist, which she was in every fiber of her being, could have reinvented habitation in such way to fit into the natural element as she did. She cajoled the Atlantic to stay at a respectable distance from her door, but she could do nothing with the sea of sand which advanced relentlessly to the very threshold of her paradise each year. She annually bribed Warren "Pinky" Silva to bulldoze that ever-encroaching sand away from the shack so that her dune life could commence for another season.

Frenchie was a one-of-a-kind woman. Nothing of an external nature ever unduly inflicted itself on her internal and personal sense of place; she was herself at all times. She lived, in every respect, as a truly free spirit. Her unique character occasionally overwhelmed a few who wandered into her aura, but she always elicited awe for the intrepid persistence of her own particular interpretation of life. She had easily re-enscribed her name "Chanel" from her surname Schnell. Somehow, it suited her without the least proof of a connection to the great perfumery of Chanel. Although this would seem to create a challenging disjunct between truth and fiction, there was just enough convincing fiction, in Frenchie's case, to completely prioritize its presence in her stories and also just enough truth reverberating through certain clearly established facts of her history to promote doubt in the doubters and turn the rest of us into mystics like Frenchie, who firmly believed that "art" is life.

As a visual artist, Frenchie, today, might have been hailed as an exciting naif, not just an eccentric choosing to live an obscure life on the back shore of America's closest reach to the European continent. In one of her unique works of art, painted boldly on the boards at the head of her bed, a Haitian "Adam and Eve" continually raised the issue of the "Apple," while an invidiously twining serpent sized up the situation with obvious malintent.

Frenchie's Haitian "Adam and Eve" in the original shack. *Photo by Arthur Cohen*

The nude figures are evocative, erotic, and very unusual, and we carefully transferred this fresco-like painting on the old wall over her bed to a new location in the reconstructed shack more than twenty-five years after it was painted. As I regard these startling figures every day when we are in residence, they brazenly pose the eternal retelling of the ancient dilemma of man with as much biblical force as ever. [1]

Long before the plovers and the terns were determined to be a species worthy of protection by the Cape Cod National Seashore, Frenchie trotted out to protect them in the section of the universe directly in front of her shack which was the epicenter of the dangerous Peaked Hill Bars, known to all seafaring men as the "graveyard" of the Atlantic." She would mark every tern nest with signposts of driftwood and heaps of impedimenta, which surrounded the nesting mothers and warned away intruders. In this way, she spared hundreds of newborns over the years. She was indefatigably devoted to bird life in general, and, to injured birds, she was the St. Francis of Provincetown. Dr. Daniel Hebert, our legendary medical man who presided over the birth of over three thousand Provincetown babies in his lifetime and who could sew up a seaman or a cat with equal indifference to the discomfort of both, consigned to Frenchie the only other permit in town to administer chloroform, so adept was she at operating on animals of every kind, but especially on birds. I recall that, on one occasion, she neatly removed the infected eye of a suffering pigeon, restoring it to health. She would judge carefully the condition of her patients, putting to sleep permanently only those she deemed incurable, but to Frenchie, however, few were incurable, whether broken-winged or broken-spirited. Many a gull on the back shore survived a devastating tussle with the elements because of her compassionate ministrations.

John Bell, journalist and reporter for the *Provincetown Advocate* described Frenchie's character concerning her love of wildlife, birds especially:

> Delightful for her ready laughter, her wind-blown hair and weathered clothing, her independent spirit. She lived in a shack she had built in the dunes, neighbor to the late Harry Kemp, and she walked almost daily from Peaked Hill Bars to Provincetown to shop and get her mail. Eccentric, because she carried with her at all times, either in a fishnet-covered basket or tucked into the neck of her jacket, a pigeon named Joseph. Joseph died aged 28, a centenarian by human scale. He has been succeeded by Mabel, a herring gull, that two small boys picked up on Long Point five years ago and brought it to Frenchie It was two days old, helpless and featherless. [2]

Activities at Frenchie's birdhouse, which Sal built for her when we spent our first days at the shack and which he has refurbished and propped up and re-staked as a firm signpost along the Atlantic coast for many years, are very intense in the spring. The birdhouse perches on a dune rise a little northeast by east of the shack. Weathered now by wind from every quarter for more than fifty years, it still accommodates the next generation of swallows each year as regularly as the moon rises and the sun sets upon its silhouette. To see the mamma and papa swallows swoop and glide in and out of their double-door residence, bringing, first, grass for the nest and, later, sustenance to a newly hatched brood on a non-stop basis, day after day, is to believe in the miracle of life and in the overpowering determination of species to survive. Observing these glistening purple, blue-winged swallows slicing the warm, westerly wind, perching briefly on their front stoop, then ducking into the birdhouse to deposit freshly gathered provender for their offspring is an hypnotic experience. You watch and wait for the next run, then fall

Sal's drawing of Frenchie's bird house, September 1954

asleep and presently awake to find these parents still at it in the same fervent routine. Eventually, young fledglings stagger out into the open air, newly suited for their first space trip in their pin feathers, decide to dive into the unknown, totter on the vertiginous edge of a near crash landing, but, miraculously, fly, like their parents, and all is well with the world.

The chronicling of such annual miracles began and ended, for most of us, during the soft encouragement of spring weather, but there was one among us, for many years, whose devotion to the life cycle of the dune swallows received maximum year-round attention. That dune resident was known to us all as Dune Charlie, whom I dubbed "Birdman." Charlie Schmid had no peer when it came to bird watching, and his observations became legendary. His patient research finally earned him attention at an ornithological symposium in Switzerland, which he attended with his diaries in hand. Although perhaps not widely recognized in academic circles, such essential research in the field is an important contribution to the profession of inquiry, both amateur and expert, that characterizes any serious discipline.

Also in the spring, early house cleaning within the shack always began with the removal of the winter residences of the mouse population. Frenchie regularly left them a bar of soap to sustain their body fat through winter cold. She needn't have worried so much, for we discovered, in later years, that their perennial habit of snuggling down in huge wads of kapok stuffing garnered from an old rocker arm chair was the real reason they survived. We always found nests of kapok behind the bed, over the windowsills, in the open cupboard behind the milk crates which held the shingles for the wood stove, and everywhere in corners of the two-by-fours bracing the studding. Those remnants we cleaned out routinely as one does cobwebs in the house, but what was so surprising was that the chair, filled with holes in the seat that appeared like cave entrances to pueblo dwellings, always seemed to have sufficient remaining material to sit on after years of excavation.

Patrons of the Arts

Behind the closet door,
Back of the mirror
Range the patrons of the arts,
Serious purveyors of our letters, napkins, papers
To the gallery high up between the two-by-fours
Where landscapes are at once
Portrayal of, protection from the weather.
And when, in spring, the paintings are retrieved,
Each one reveals their true appreciators-
Mice softly nested and deceased in layers.

As to the presence of mice as opposed to other creatures, we preferred their company to weasels, who came in after the little fellows if we were careless enough to allow any small hole in the side walls or floor to go unplugged. Proof of their presence was always excrement coupled with the complete absence of our scurrying resident population, for a while, at least. In spite of the weasels' effectiveness as population control of the mice, they were definitely unwelcome visitors. We preferred mice.

Sometimes, we entertained uninvited guests such as the black racer that leisurely entered the shack one day through a loose board in the porch, slithering in at the French doors and rapidly racing across the room in front of us as we were having lunch. His cruising speed was quite impressive as he glided noiselessly to the screen door, found it ajar, and slid down the steps before our gasps had subsided. The length of these snakes can sometimes reach several feet and, although harmless to humans, they are menacing in appearance because of their size. This one was a permanent resident of the lumber pile at the outhouse and could be seen sunning itself occasionally on it, quite as content to stay away from us as we were from him. Subsequent visits were curtailed many years later by the demolition of the porch in an eighty-mile an-hour wind, which required the reconstruction of the porch free of the loose floor boards that had allowed the intrusion of the black racer seeking our resident mice.

In the quiet after-shock, when the sea has worn itself out attacking the shore in a heavy surf, sandpipers fill the beach with tiny drills, looking for a fresh delivery of the ocean's produce. Observing them in endless pursuit of the receding tide one day, I refined the behavioral elements of their *modus operandi*:

Sandpipers

Sandpipers chasing the pendulum hem of the tide,
Skirting the skirts of the sea, flouncing in, sweeping out,
Scurry to dine beneath petticoat ruffles of foam
Before life in their lacing unravels from sight.

Besides the tiny sandpipers, the ubiquitous gulls are perpetually present. These marvelous creatures, stalwart and beautiful in drifting flight over the dunes and across the currents of the wind, daily sailing close to the ocean's spray or high above the turbulence, are a certain reminder that some things will never change. Their presence in the air seems to be an eternal reality, always reminding us of a freedom we cannot achieve in kind. The gull is our refuse gatherer as well, a transfer station on wings, cleaning up the joint, which we continue to clutter with needless additions to our environment. Their best sense tells them to pluck the gurry from the wake of a fishing boat, trundle off with a dropped sandwich from a youngster's sticky hands, wait patiently to poke at the fish head severed by some bass fisherman, worry a drying skate relentlessly until some vestige of former flesh is ripped loose from the skeleton, and dive for the school fish beneath the surface of the broth of life just above the tide line.

Their life and death cycle is seldom made fully evident to man in any major way. In those weeks of autumn when the temperature begins to cool, the gannets can also be seen diving with the gull, and are often mistaken for the gull, swooping above the curling crests of white water at a targeting height and dive-bombing the trough of the waves with penetrating accuracy. Such a display can last for an hour when the school fish are running, but, whether lasting minutes or hours, their transfixing trajectories are always a breathtaking sight.

Frenchie's original shack was created as "found" architecture, but a few hundred yards away from Frenchie's is the shack of Harry Kemp, a small structure built in the immediate vicinity of the old Peaked Hill Life Saving station by a former Coast Guardsman by the name of Cadose, a link to the previous generation of structures with its descendants in very specific terms.[3] All of the shacks in the environs of the Peaked Hill stations, meaning the first Life Saving Station and the second Coast Guard Station, have given memorable life to that area since the turn of the twentieth century and remain today imbued with that determined individualism as to construction, which is adapted to defend against some of the most severe tests nature can provide except, of course, fire. Fire was a subject one didn't broach on the dunes. No fire department could reach the shacks, or, if they could, would not have been able to adequately provide the means of extinguishment.

Understandably, therefore, the dune residents kept their personal occupancy close to their chests. Newcomers to the scene were not often allowed visitation unsupervised by the presence of the owners. Each shack established its own system, watchful of its neighbor's welfare, but not intrusively so. Any fire that commenced in the compass grass or beach grass, for instance, was serious, for the roots were incredibly deep, and a smoldering fire in that fundamental element was a dreaded danger.[4] None of the "wild" bunch at Peaked Hill were, in this respect, "wild." They were sober as priests and priests of nature they all were and still are. Our first instructions to novitiates have always to do with fire protection and management. Water and sand are the two major elements of control, but prevention against carelessness is the most important of all. Stoves can fire hot on a windy day, and although Harry Kemp tried to prove that smoke could find its way outside through a hole in the roof that had been provided for its exit, the resultant smoke inhalation could be a deadly experience, as Sal recalls on more than one occasion. Harry was eventually persuaded to install a stove pipe for his dune stove, reluctantly abandoning his theory, which he claimed to have been inspired by the American Indians whose tepees never boasted a stove pipe either.

All of our stoves were made of cast iron or tin components of some sort. The most popular cast iron variety being the old Sears Roebuck model which was fairly light but

Harry Kemp at his shack on the dunes, c.1955. *Photo by John Bell*

strongly built and didn't occupy a huge amount of space. These stoves took driftwood and burned it beautifully, but, in doing so, did harm to their durability, the minerals and natural salts eventually wearing away at their innards. Of found driftwood, there was usually a modest supply, but it was, at times, tough to find, depending on the tides and the intensity and direction of the wind. If you walked far enough, however, you came back with a sufficiency to brew a pot of coffee. Frenchie's great kerosene special was, of course, peerlessly reliable at any hour of the day.

Harry Kemp, however, was a dune dweller of another stamp; he liked to live dangerously close to an uncomfortable paucity and to his collection of literary greats, especially Shakespeare, whom he kept damp and daily available in his tiny shack. A bed and books described his diocese. They sufficed to sustain his spirit for an entire lifetime. No romantic could have superceded his unconventional Bohemianism, and, to be sure, Harry Kemp was "The Last Bohemian."[5] Such things as swimming in the ocean in late fall or walking to the shack in a storm were not uncommon for him. On one of these occasions, he prompted Sal and his photographer friend Dan Bernstein to do the same. When they shivered and shook their way to rejoin Harry in the shack after an ocean plunge, he offered them a burlap gunny sack with which to dry off and then recited Shakespeare to fire up their spirits. This procedure, according to Harry, gave off a warmth no wood could provide.

Sal on the way to the shack, October 1,1957. *Written on the back of the photograph to his friend Dan Bernstein* "Beginning of Snail Road that takes one across the dunes. Jo packed food, books, paints and a pint of whiskey. Three days and 2 nights I saw not a soul. It was most beautiful and I managed to paint two pictures."

Sal often told me of his adventures with Harry, who called him "The Pope" and who loved him as a son. When the day came, in 1951, that Sal was drafted into the U.S. Army during the Korean War, he took leave of Provincetown and of Harry as if leaving his home, for indeed, Provincetown was his spiritual home. When he returned on leave, he drew a bead on Peaked Hill and he went back to see his mentor Harry Kemp. Harry combined literature and life with a rare, Byronic sense of the immensity of nature's influence and force. He lifted his mental plane to astounding levels of credulity and insisted on living at those levels in spite of the distracted monitoring of a number of his dear friends such as "Sunny" Rose Tasha. Sequestered once in the Cape Cod Hospital because of an aggravated diabetic condition, which threatened to instigate the removal of his toes on one foot, he escaped from the hospital and returned home to his beloved back shore, where he walked barefoot at the tide's edge for days and thus restored the circulation to his ailing extremity.

Sunny Tasha, who inherited the Kemp dune shack when Harry died in 1960, one year before the establishment of the Cape Cod National Seashore, kept the faith he willfully flaunted in the face of other people's reality. She never locked the door of his cloister on the dunes, leaving his sign in place: "There is nothing to steal here but solitude." She believed in the general decency of the human race, as he did, and in the unwritten code of all the dune dwellers, that should one have need of rest and food and a roof over one's head, you were welcome to all three, but you must leave the shack as you found it and replace what you had used, if possible.

The idea of a self-monitoring society was not new, of course, having occasionally been tried in many ways before, and always with mixed results. When, for instance, in the devastating years of the Vietnam War, during the sixties' social revolution of sorts, the few shack owners who kept to Harry and Sunny's credo were sadly disillusioned by the destructive and intrusive presence of drug users and general dereliction. It forced its way into a closed system of mutual respect and drove most of us to an ever-vigilant lookout for intruders. The protective policy was, again, largely the fear of carelessness, which could lead to fire and the loss of that intangible, illusive, and precious element—solitude.

Harry Kemp proselytized much in his lifetime, from the championing of women's suffrage in England in 1913[6] to his solitary walk to Washington, DC, to press for the banning of the atomic bomb in 1946,[7] to the never-ending attempt to secure universal recognition that Provincetown was the first landing place of the Pilgrims. After the dedication of the Pilgrim Monument by President William Howard Taft in 1910, it is hard to believe how anyone could miss the message of a 252-foot stone testimonial hugely proclaiming that fact for miles in every direction; it could even be seen from Plymouth, on a clear day. Established perception, no matter how flawed, was, more often than not, the "truth" for too many people in this matter, and far too few ever referred to the many sources of historical references in regard to the Pilgrims' first landfall. The facts remained unaltered, however: the Pilgrim's first landfall was Provincetown, Massachusetts, on November 11, 1620 (old-style calendar), where they drew up the "Mayflower Compact" in Provincetown Harbor.

John Van Arsdale, owner and founder of the Provincetown–Boston Airline and a dear friend of Harry's, used to shuttle Harry across Cape Cod Bay to Plymouth on occasion, so he could drop a small envelope of Provincetown sand on Plymouth Rock, thus giving it a modicum of authenticity, according to Harry. Early in the 1950s, I too became a consenting participant in an hilarious, but rather effective junket to Plymouth, outfitted as the "muse of true history" in a flowing bed-sheet and a pair of Roger Rilleau's sandals. Harry himself was wrapped in a poet's robe, wearing a wreath of bay leaves circling his brow as poet of the dunes, while Art Snader, Provincetown's official Town Crier at the time, was resplendent in full regalia, ringing a loud and sonorous bell to assist him in protesting the fact that Provincetown was the true landing place of the Pilgrims.

All this took place on the occasion of the preview for the movie *The Plymouth Adventure* at Plymouth. A large dinner for the cast and crew was sponsored by the D.A.R. of Plymouth as an assist to publicity. Our costumed trio made a ceremoniously grand entrance down an impressive long flight of stairs to the setting of the banquet tables already occupied by the movie crew and Plymouth dignitaries. We were promptly hailed by the press, always eager for bizarre events, and were eventually seated with due deference, but not much enthusiasm, by the Plymouth faithful next to the script writers.

Harry Kemp, Jo and Giovanna, with others, reenacting the first Pilgrim Monday Washday at the West End Breakwater in Provincetown. *Photo by Neil Nickerson for the* Cape Cod Times, *c. 1955–1957*

Reenactment of the signing of the Mayflower Compact at the bas relief depicting the Compact's signing by sculptor Cyrus Dalin, Provincetown, Massachusetts, November 22, c.1954. Seated centrally, Harry Kemp, without hat, immediately to his right with hat, Art Snader, Town Crier, to the right of Snader, "Sunny" Tasha, with her children, Paul and Paula, in her lap, Carl Tasha standing, looking out of the picture.

Regarded, once again, as another example of Provincetown's audacious high jinks brought off by a handful of Bohemian riffraff, we didn't really convince the powers that be, who had dutifully nurtured a tidy, golden economic goose by exploiting a skewing of historical fact. Harry's intent, however, lay beyond the merchandising of the myth and went to the heart of the matter, which was that the sequence of historic events should be universally acknowledged. Much later, the text has come to terms with the facts: Provincetown was the first landing place of the Pilgrims in 1620; Plymouth was the first permanent English colony.

Sunny Tasha and Harry Kemp reenacting the first Pilgrim Monday Washday at the West End Breakwater in Provincetown. *Photo by Neil Nickerson for the* Cape Cod Times, *c.1955–1957*

Harry did not stop at such "happenings" to convince the world of historical verities, however. He persisted in staging, on an annual basis, the re-enactment of the Pilgrim's first Monday washday in Provincetown Harbor, just at the point off the federal breakwater in the West End of the town contiguous to the Provincetown Inn. In this always strenuous tableau vivant, "Sunny" was the indomitable central figure. She pinned everyone together in their capes and breeches, topped off the women with white, seventeenth-century replicas of the Pilgrim headgear and saw to it that the men carried the iron pot for washing the clothes, shouldering the blunderbusses of olden days, which, in this case, were the family double-barreled shotguns. These enactments usually occurred on a bitter, cold November day and tested the fortitude of all our little band, much as similar circumstances had tested our predecessors. Harry thrived on such adversity, however, and came ashore with the rest of us in true Pilgrim fashion.

Publicity was, to Harry, the bread and butter of his life, and it remained the active ingredient of his still-adventurous last years as it had been in his first forays as a hobo and international tramp poet. Although he seldom gave over imagination to practicality, like many true visionaries, some of his ideas were immensely far-sighted and viable in the long run. The schemes he undertook needed financial backing, however, and this kind of support seemed always to be missing, or, at least, was half-hearted and insubstantial. He wanted to establish a memorial to that first washday in America, for instance, by commissioning a bronze statue for the spot where the Pilgrims conducted their first Monday washday. He found a sympathetic and skilled sculptress in Sheila Burlingame, whose excellent model for such a memorial was a strong and simple, but appropriate concept; however, no interested party could be found to back the idea. Neither national soap companies, local officials, nor private investors understood the imaginative possibilities of such an artistic and historical memorialization.[8]

Harry Kemp's most ambitious vision, however, was his insistent belief that Provincetown should have a full-scale model of the Mayflower berthed at the main wharf in Provincetown Harbor, thus establishing, once and for all, true history with true venture capitalism.

Though, incredibly, no one could be found to undertake, or even to theoretically endorse the project on Provincetown's behalf, the town of Plymouth, readily recognizing the enormous economic possibilities that a full-scale replica of the Mayflower would produce, took up the idea enthusiastically.

The impetus for the actual project of building the Mayflower II, however, was credited to the Englishman Warwick Charlton, who had served under Field Marshal Montgomery and wished to extend the very close and strong bonds that had developed between the two countries during the Second World War to the postwar era. Coincidentally, at that time, he obtained a copy of the American magazine *Neptune* in which the famous American naval architect William A. Baker showed plans he had developed for a Mayflower replica for the "blunder-buses Plantation." That conjoining of the momentum already in place at Plymouth, the plans far advanced by Baker, and a mutual agreement between the American home town and Charlton's small group of supporters, got the project underway. The vessel was built in Brixham Shipyard, Devon, England, by Stuart Upham and sailed from Plymouth, England, on April 20, 1957.[9]

Sheila Burlingame's statue of *The Pilgrim Housewife. Photo by John Bell* Provincetown Advocate, *1957–1958*

Her fifty-five day voyage to Plymouth was completed on June 13, 1957, but not before she stopped, as per her original voyage, in Provincetown Harbor on June 12th. Thanks to the strong friendship that Harry Kemp and Mayflower Captain Allan Villiers had established during Harry's pilgrimage to England in 1913 as the internationally notorious tramp poet, as well as to the urging of the Australian artist Mary Cecil Allen, who was also a close friend of the stalwart Australian Captain Villiers, and, most importantly, to his own personal integrity, Villiers honored the facts and brought the Mayflower II into Provincetown on her first landfall. My journal, regarding the event, reads as follows:

Arrival of Mayflower II:

This was Harry's day after many hopes and dreams and frustrations. He, at least, achieved the realization of seeing his "big idea" in actuality. He was one of the few to go aboard her, and I hope the distinction, in some way, compensated for the loss of the Mayflower II being berthed here. So go man's dreams and ambitions, too often thwarted by the world's stubborn baseness and lack of vision. We shall always feel, however, that the idea was first engendered here and that none other than Harry Kemp was originally responsible. As to her looks, she is a beauty-a picture-book boat with the bright, painted stripes on the hull and the incredibly high stern. She came into the harbor in tow, and this somewhat lessened her beauty, as she would have been great under full sail. Sal, however, saw her coming in at Race Point under sail. He claimed it was an unforgettable sight. Everyone in town profited by the historic day. Never has Provincetown seen more cars and people at one time, and the planes constantly scanning the place from the sky, made one feel as if we were under attack. The harbor was full of yachts and the fishermen were all in from the grounds, a sight truly not to be repeated. She is to leave for Plymouth early tomorrow, but we have had the first word on the signing of the "Compact" and the very first look at her upon her arrival in America.

The resultant publicity regarding all this was wonderful. The papers made the most of the Provincetown–Plymouth feud over such a skewing of the previously planned schedule that Villiers had upset by bringing the Mayflower to Provincetown first, but the captain had maintained his course: it was Provincetown or else. Harry was right in the middle of all this. He was escorted to the Mayflower II with full ceremonial honors, stepping on deck to congratulate his old friend and to receive a warm welcome himself from Captain Villiers and crew; they exchanged mutual greetings like seasoned shipmates. One of the few other Provincetown citizens to go aboard her was Dr. Daniel Hiebert, one of Harry's most dedicated supporters in our annual Pilgrim reenactment. Harry, of course, had written a poem for this grand occasion entitled: *The Mayflower II—A Painted Ship Upon a Painted Ocean —Coleridge The Ancient Mariner*, a lengthy eulogy, which, though commemorative of the formal occasion, could not possibly contain the fervor and excitement of the actual event.

Mayflower II in Provincetown Harbor, June 12, 1957. *Photo by Ross Moffett*

The last reliable information I have been able to obtain regarding the income produced by tourist visitation to the replica of the Mayflower was quite some time ago, but from a cursory and modest extrapolation of income over the ensuing time frame, it appears that the doughty replica, originally billed as an impossible pipe dream in Provincetown, has turned into another golden goose for Plymouth. In retrospect, therefore, acute business prognostication, leaving out any romantic or historical element in motivation, would have given the prize in practical economics to Harry Kemp.

The year 1957 turned out to be one of great joie de vivre for Sal and me in so many ways, as our daughter Giovanna was born in May, just three weeks before the June arrival of the Mayflower II in Provincetown Harbor. Aside from joining other Pilgrims in the reenactment of the first Monday washday six months after her birth, Giovanna also accompanied us everywhere on the dunes in that late fall. Our old, eight-cylinder Ford Mercury truck, stripped down to the bare chassis with a double set of mufflers, lacked many essential body parts, such as doors and a roof, and hardly provided a safe vehicle for family travel. Such minor considerations did not deter us from taking Giovanna to the back shore and the shack, she was cozily wrapped in layers of clothing topped off with one of my hand-woven shawls, which converted her into a papoose. The thought of a sudden unanticipated malfunction of our old wreck never occurred to us. It was largely a matter of astonishing youthful credulity, which always assumes nothing is going to happen. In our case, nothing ever did; we fearlessly drove that putative vehicle all over the dunes with unrestrained joy and abandonment.

Later on, in late 1959 and in 1960, that same vehicle served Sal well in his brief career as caretaker of several of the back shore shacks. Hazel Hawthorne Werner, for instance, frequently rented one or both of her shacks, Thalassa and Euphoria, as she herself was then fairly along in years and didn't always have the stamina to maintain her shacks or even to stay in them for any extended period without some assistance. From time to time, therefore, she hired Sal, occasionally assisted by his friend Eldred Mowery, to help her in the physical care and operation of her extraordinary domain. He spent numerous hours shuttling people and supplies back and forth and enjoying a tête-à-tête with Hazel. When the various tasks were done, he could sit down to relax over a pretty stiff cocktail and listen to the many accounts of Hazel's dune life in times past. Such a general routine, thus, greatly endangered the return voyage in a vehicle that offered no reassurances that one would not fall out at the first huge dip of an unexpected dune declivity, even if dead sober.

Sal, Jo, and Giovanna on the dunes in their Ford Mercury truck, fall, 1957. *Photo by Alice Palmer*

One of these routine shuttles involved picking up Norman Mailer and his (then) wife Adele for a trip into town from Hazel's shack Euphoria, where Norman was working assiduously on a current writing project. Sal and Eldred arrived that day unexpectedly, it seems, and found both Norman and Adele lounging outside the shack completely in the nude, thus emulating Adam and Eve in the Garden of Eden, so picturesquely transfixed on the wall of Frenchie's shack a few hundred yards away. Adele, ever mindful of Norman's right to privacy, screamed in surprise, jumped up and, with feminine instincts instantly in play, proceeded to cover Norman's private parts with both hands while they backed up hastily to gain the cover of the shack, Adele entirely oblivious to the fact that she herself was in her birthday suit. Needless to say, Sal and Eldred were highly amused at this family spectacle, and Norman, in order to mitigate the general embarrassment all around, brought out a bottle of Bordeaux which they promptly polished off before the return trip. That trip, therefore, began to materialize with further alarms, as Eldred, now fully ready for a little more amusement, suggested to Sal that they choose the "alternate route" back to town. Sal, entirely disposed to approve the plan, which both of them tacitly understood was a euphemism for freewheeling across the dunes, subjected his passengers to dune driving at its most daring best. The shrieks of Adele which ensued reverberated nonstop until they reached the level playing field of Commercial Street. After this unsolicited adventure, Norman and Adele swore off any further exposure to Sal's dune taxi service.

Although Hazel was a writer of some consequence in the heady, post-Eugene O'Neill life on the "back side," her chief claim to fame appears to lie more with the unique circle of friends she courted than with her writing. Her rather carefree, bohemian life on the dunes was common knowledge. For instance, she often rode a horse to and from the town in those days, and there are photographs of Hazel surrounded by such friends as the writer Edmund Wilson, the painter Peter Blume, and the art dealer Curt Valentin, among others. These notables were occasionally joined by local raconteur of note John Gaspie, whose ready wit and idiosyncratic character were a proven refreshment in any conversation.

In the early sixties, as previously described, she would open the bar in late afternoon and regale Sal and Eldred with stories of her exploits among the artists and writers whom she had loved and lost or loved and sent packing. Her extraordinary good looks, matched by a vibrant intelligence, did not help her concentration on literary achievement, but her talent was sufficient to establish a reputation that still lingers, even if not totally substantiated by an available body of evidence. Marion Haymaker, for instance, the eccentric and remarkable librarian of the Provincetown Public Library during the two decades after World War II, was not prone to allowing Hazel's well-known book, "The Salt Box," any conspicuous shelf space. I am told she routinely buried it somewhere in the stacks, where it could hardly be discovered by casual browsing, so disapproving was she of the contents. I know of only one person who has seen a copy of this work; however, some reference is usually made to it whenever her name comes up for discussion.

Hazel Hawthorne had the character of a diva and the physical presence to go with that description. She commanded respect and a great deal of awe, even in her later years, which were marred by the increasing debility of Parkinson's disease. It was an affliction she shared with her brother Roger Hawthorne, whose delightful narratives as a journalist chronicling people and events, especially in Provincetown, were a staple in that era. Both Hazel and Roger ended their days unable to hold a pencil; however, in Hazel's case, her remarkable physical strength lasted long after her limited capacity to communicate verbally, with great difficulty, the thoughts of her still able mind.

Giovanna and I with the town crier Art Snader, posed on the dunes for a front page story commemorating the Pilgrims landing in Provincetown, November 22, 1961. *The Christian Science Monitor*

On August 8, 1960, Harry Kemp died; nevertheless, Harry's small band of Pilgrims led by the indefatigable Sunny Tasha, carried on as always that November and celebrated the First Monday Washday at the Provincetown breakwater opposite the Provincetown Inn. The following year, Giovanna and I, with town crier Art Snader, posed on the dunes for a photograph of the Pilgrim presence on the historic occasion of the landing in Provincetown on November 21, 1620, (new calendar) which appeared on the front page of the November 22, 1961, edition of *The Christian Science Monitor*.

Frenchie in 1952, with Joseph in her basket. *Photo by John Bell*

Harry's ashes were symbolically scattered by Sunny Tasha at Peaked Hill and his other spiritual home in the heart of Greenwich Village.[10] There are those of us who believe he is still out there at his shack, writing poems in invisible ink with his perennial sea gull feather. Many of the poems he left us, that are still visible, are exultant with the celebration of life in the "Fishertown"[11] he adopted as his own and in his beloved back shore dune sanctuary.

Our early, carefree days in the dunes during the 1950s, moved inevitably into heavier seas where the idyls of youth meet the turbulence of events for which there is never adequate preparation, however, we remained confident, undaunted, and always sustained by the refuge of Frenchie's universe, which had been such an important part of our first few years together and would forever be a fixed star for us in the firmament at Peaked Hill.

With Frenchie at the Shack

Her birdhouse strong against the wind and riot of the dunes,
Marker for straying swallow, wandering heart,
Firmly finite in a vasty sea and sky—
What else has royalty to offer me
That equals half this crooked shack?
Her highness kneeling down to scrape the mounded sand
from sill and door
With hands that move the very dunes to serve her will,
gives grace to enter.
Tarpaper, sand, wind, rain and rusty nail
Have shaped the nave of this cathedral.
Oh, how it resounds to chords of liberated love,
Silvered by sun, each board runs to age more durable
than when its sap was fresh and green,
And like them, aging young, Frenchie puffs at her cigarette,
Laughs when I suggest a job cannot be done.
Sand brushed to crack, her yellow teapot shining,
The stove flares blue and steams the blackened pot.
Each match in place, and all the shack rides true
Like some fast clipper ship well-trimmed.
A pot of coffee, brewed so strong it strips the tongue of taste,
Turns sweet when just the two of us, odd cup in hand,
Sit down, without the slightest haste, to share the universe.

CHAPTER II

Prophecy and Fulfillment

1959–1962

ALL CAPE COD settlement, beginning with the native Indian civilization and proceeding through Viking, European, and, lastly, Pilgrim discoveries, has left us a natural environment that retained, through cyclical activities of rest and work, a certain balance. As population and commerce increased, however, and the seasonal pattern related more to tourism and less to fishing, the cycle offered diminishing time for recovery and presented ever more relentless stress to the environment. Seasonal dormancy, nevertheless, somewhat countered the pressures of development well into the middle of the twentieth century. The sea-saw was tipping, however, and soon began to plunge toward a year-round tourist and business economy of such density and complexity that the overall natural environment was unable to retain a reasonable resiliency.

Among those who saw this clearly was the Provincetown painter and archaeologist Ross Moffett. Long a familiar figure in those areas of the Cape where archaeological findings were abundant, especially in the towns of Truro, Wellfleet, and Eastham, Ross had spent years, together with fellow archaeologists, recording the history and nomenclature of previous Indian populations in our midst.[1] The careful scrutiny and analysis of men like Moffett in the same or related scientific disciplines, made clear the fragility of the present environment and pointed out the dangers to which it was becoming increasingly exposed.

On a Sunday in December 1959, therefore, just after the morning service at the Universalist Church in Provincetown, Ross Moffett and I discussed the recent hearings on the proposed Cape Cod National Seashore, which he had attended several days before in Eastham. His prognosis, at that moment, was bleak, as he had had an opportunity to see the forces ranged against the proposed park at close range. From that day forward, Ross Moffett and I began a mutual colloquy which extended for another two-and-a-half years. Six months prior to the Eastham hearings, however, Ross had written a letter to the *Provincetown Advocate*, which its editor, Paul Lambert, entitled "For Whom the Wild Swan." The letter opens with a few references to some important botanical features and to certain particularly beautiful geographical areas which would be preserved by the proposed park and concludes:

> A year ago, a wild swan chose this now sparsely populated section of the intended park for his winter quarters. Now, it may be asked what good is a wild swan? The answer, in this case, depends somewhat on one's point of view. This particular wild swan was a lot of good to those people who, in a considerable number, came from the mainland to see him swimming around or, preferably, rising in majestic flight. When the people trained their binoculars on the unusual visitor, I would suppose that they felt akin to the wild swan and thereby to nature and to the universe, that, to them this feeling was a variety of religious experience. At the same time, the bird watchers purchased food and lodging while on the Cape, so the wild swan was of benefit also to those of us who are of a strictly practical bent. Possibly, it is not too far-fetched to think that the proposed park as a whole may work out in the same way as the above incident for the benefit of those whose imaginations are quickened by the sight of a wild swan or by the kind of unspoiled nature that we would expect such a creature to alight in, and for the profit of those whose interests are more mundane. In the long run, doubtless everyone would be served. The National Seashore would be a national park of a nation in which there are probably far more people hankering for a figurative wild swan than most of us Cape Codders realize.[2]

This "Wild Swan" letter became the rallying cry, in a sense, for Provincetown's fight to preserve a large, virgin area in Provincetown known as the Province Lands. Within a short time, this cause would become not just Moffett's, but that of many of us who were drawn into one of the most unusual preservation efforts in the annals of recent American conservation history. The way in which the success of this effort came about, however, was due more to the foresight, the intelligence, and the endurance of Ross Moffett than to any other single individual or factor. He alone, in the very beginning, was the most outspoken visionary of a group of citizens, composed largely of writers and artists, calling ourselves the Emergency Committee for the Preservation of the Province Lands. The nucleus of this group had been active as the Provincetown Property Owner's Protective Association, and it included, in its original list of members, more than fifty artists and writers from an approximate membership of seventy-seven. On December 14, 1980, the Property Owner's Protective Association changed its name to the Emergency Committee for the Preservation of the Province Lands.

Jean Miller Cohen Burns's dune shack, July 1999. *Photo by Dilys Lewellyn Cowan* [4]

The case concerning the Province Lands was unique to our community. Of those slated to be included in the proposed Cape Cod National Seashore, no other town presented the same situation. The land in question, and over which a tug of war was to ensue that would last more than two and a half years, had existed in a virgin state since the arrival of the Pilgrims.[3]

At the time the Seashore was proposed, therefore, only about ten private dwellings had been built in the Province Lands, an area of slightly more than 3,000 acres, over a period which spanned 338 years. This statistic was extraordinary, and it did not escape the attention of the framers of the Park legislation. A complete summary of all aspects of the area to be included in the proposed National Seashore was put together by the Department of the Interior in 1958.[5] Rereading the text of this particular document now, and that of the Legislative Research Bureau of the Massachusetts State House (which has already been referred to in the footnote above), I am reminded of the thoughtful perusal of them given by Ross Moffett before he ever stepped forward to say:

> We in Provincetown have been much concerned lest the fine woodlands in the state-owned Province Lands be kept out of the Park. I would say that these unspoiled woodlands should not be turned over to developers for motels, hotels and so on, but that they should be included in the Park. They would constitute the Park's most valued northernmost feature.[6]

Such understated language belied the thoroughness of Ross's preparation on the subject. It also belied the intensity and strength of his commitment to conservation and to his lifelong concerns in the field of archaeology. No one knows better than I the numberless hours and the personal anguish that the controversy over the Province Lands cost him. The two of us worked together in a complementary relationship throughout this period; my frustration often boiled over the pot; his temperance always turned down the burner. An experienced vision made him careful and calm. My impatience often fired a new strategy. We never failed each other in mutual respect, and I look back now on the correspondence that reflects, but does not truly reveal, the daily decisions and the considerable involvement of time and am amazed that we prevailed. What we sought was seemingly unrealistic from the contemporary view: non-acquisition of land to develop; non-satisfaction of investment interests. Over and against this were the traditional forces of exploitation best represented by real estate investors and planners who argued, sometimes subtly, but always determinedly, against us. There was a veneer of reason and so-called common sense that sought to describe itself in "practical terms" and seemed logical to casual examination. It was the comfortable short view expressing itself in a society ever self-serving, no more so in Provincetown, than in any other community. The fact is that, eventually, Provincetown, of all the towns on the Cape, scheduled for inclusion in the National Seashore, was the only town to endorse the Cape Cod National Seashore Park unconditionally and to enter the Park exactly as the original first piece of legislation had suggested, without one acre being deleted from the promised land area. How did this happen? Certainly not by poetic pronouncements. Rather, it was through a carefully orchestrated and intense campaign that began in 1959 with Ross Moffett's "Wild Swan" letter.

Taking early initiative on behalf of the proposed legislation and soon becoming an indispensable part of the fight for the Province Lands, was artist and writer Miriam Hapgood DeWitt and her husband John DeWitt. The daughter of playwright Neith

Boyce and writer Hutchins Hapgood, Miriam Hapgood Dewitt's keen mind and political acumen were constantly ready for the contest in which we found ourselves from 1959 to 1962, when the Province Lands were finally deeded to the Seashore. Miriam and John, who summered in Provincetown but lived in Washington, DC, during the winter months, checked sequences of events at their source, attended hearings, and relayed up-to-the minute information on the progress of the Park legislation. In the April 23, 1959, *Provincetown Advocate*, appearing in the same column with Ross's "Wild Swan" letter, was one by Miriam that debunked the fantasy of self-zoning as a protection for the Province Lands area. Coincidentally, in the same column was a letter from the artist Edwin Dickinson making a plea for the Park and suggesting that if the National Seashore were not endorsed, people twenty years hence would say: "What were they thinking of?"

By September 1959, Miriam was writing to Ross to request his opinion about the forthcoming hearings on the proposed Park to be held in December in Eastham, Massachusetts. "What do you think ought to be done about presenting testimony at the hearings scheduled for December 9?" What Ross thought ought to be done was very simple: he presented a strong testimony on December 10, 1959, on behalf of the Park's establishment. With the exception of the statement of Wellfleet resident and well-known architect Serge Chermayeff, his was almost the only verbal presentation unreservedly in favor of the Park. Even the former U.S. Attorney General Francis Biddle expressed reservations concerning the pressures against private property that might be generated by excessive emphasis on recreation.

That hearing, as a matter of fact, was heavily weighted with views of local officials from the several towns on the Lower Cape whose selectmen, planning boards, etc., if not expressing downright opposition, voiced great skepticism about the workability of a Cape Cod National Seashore. Representing strong opposition from Provincetown, Mrs. Walter Chrysler, Jr., rather accurately stated the case for most persons who were vehemently against the establishment of the Park. The Chryslers had recently acquired a magnificent back shore cottage previously owned by an artist named Fenner Bridgham, who was the scion of a wealthy Providence family. His lovely oceanside retreat had been the scene of many happy artists' gatherings in the late forties and early fifties. The Chryslers feared the shadow of the Park on this dune residence, as well as the restriction on other of their ventures within the proposed Seashore Park area. Jean Chrysler said in her statement at the Eastham hearing in 1959:

> Any plan that permits the Federal Government to annex land on Cape Cod is deliberately and carefully devised to deprive each of the towns from Provincetown through Chatham of the possibility of any future expansion for any reason whatsoever and forever, a privilege which they should be able to enjoy from generation to generation.[7]

Chrysler's view that the Federal Government was depriving private citizens of the right to own land and dispose of it without interference was quite true, of course. The private citizen was being asked to compromise his ownership, in certain cases, and share certain privileges with the larger commonwealth of the country. Such a restriction on unlimited development was bound to create opposition at a local level. There was not, in the beginning, very much middle ground on this point. The opposition to the Park, however, gradually diminished as private ownership of improved property was assured, provided that it had been established prior to September 1, 1959. The serious restriction that remained was that unrestricted private development was frozen. Private ownership, on the other hand, was allowed, provided that it conformed to the legislation's stipulations. Those persons who foresaw development as an infinite privilege on a very finite piece of the planet, namely Cape Cod, were naturally incensed. This narrow vision in the world at large still prevails in spite of demonstrated hazards to humanity's survival that are incurred by unregulated entrepreneurship. The social contract necessarily tightens when license threatens to replace liberty. Chrysler's presentation appealed to a certain rationale of self-government and emphasized the hardship that land restriction would impose. It was, therefore, extremely difficult to counter that position.

It was a curious and interesting phenomenon of the field of players at the 1959 hearing on the Cape Cod National Seashore Park in Eastham that, of the 112 expressions about the proposed Park received in both oral and written communications, Ross documented the fact that 69 favored the Park unreservedly, 14 opposed it or suggested most serious modifications, and 19 objected to areas only in Chatham. This seeming edge of support, however, was very fragile and was largely contained in the written testimony, not the oral, and, therefore, was not delivered in person at the Eastham hearing. The prevailing "official" view in Eastham in December 1959 seemed to be largely ranged against the Seashore, and this was vocal and prominent.

Now, the full swing of the rounds over the creation of the Cape Cod National Seashore began in earnest. By June 1960, another hearing was held in Washington, DC, at which Miriam Hapgood DeWitt offered strong testimony. [8] Unfortunately, Representative Hastings Keith, one of the cosponsors of the original bill in Congress, S. 2636, began to waver and to reveal the political pressures for land grabbing that were upon him. An all-out effort had now to be made to stop the depletion of the Province Lands, a depletion which had been presented in tangible form to the Massachusetts Legislature as Bill #3258.[9] The majority of the citizens of the Provincetown community, however, knew nothing about this particular legislation. t was not until September 20, 1960, when a development plan for Provincetown drawn up by a Boston developer by the name of Van Ness Bates was exposed by accident, through a leak to the local press, that the full shock of the plan, which was surreptitiously underway, was revealed. This plan, which had innocently been requested by the town at a special town meeting in May 1960 and was entitled "Preliminary Survey Report Preparatory to Provincetown Master Plan" was compiled by Van Ness Bates Associates, Planning and Research Consultants of Boston. The bizarre details of this plan were presented in a twenty-seven page report covering the development of 1,500 acres of the then-State-owned Province Lands and just about everything else in Provincetown. It proposed, among other things, filling in the waterfront areas in the flats at Long Point and off Mayflower Heights, which, the report stated, would have to be modified by the installation of a trunk sewer line. It also proposed filling in valuable waterfront areas, removing historic landmarks, creating a heliport, and a triple-deck garage. Finally, it suggested the possibility of a bridge between Plymouth and Provincetown, bringing us exactly what we feared most, further inundation by tourism. In the same issue of the *New Beacon*, Miriam DeWitt's clarion rejoinder was printed:

> Do you want the woods where you gather blueberries and beach plums to be turned over to large developers for "improvements?" Do you want the ponds where you fish filled to make house lots or hemmed in by summer cottages? Do you want a country club and golf course in your back country?[10]

On November 17, 1960, Ross followed Miriam's letter with one in the *Provincetown Advocate* entitled "Some See Motels in Sunset Says Local Artist." Ross discoursed on the illogicity of reproducing urban sprawl on a uniquely beautiful strip of untouched landscape. He ended: "Someone has observed that this country is more interested in what is profitable than in what is good. While I do not think this is entirely true, I do think this observation applies neatly to the scheme for getting hold of the Province Land and for exploiting them, again, through outside interests. I greatly hope that the Province Lands are saved and incorporated into a National Park for the enjoyment and spiritual edification of future generations."

Fortunately for posterity, a bill filed in the General Court in September, which would have sliced 1,476 acres out of Provincetown's "back country," was defeated in the Massachusetts Legislature. Then, in October, State Senator Stone introduced yet another bill for cutting out the heart of the same "back country" and requesting 786 acres of the Province Lands be excluded from the Cape Cod Seashore Park. Under pressure, he backed down on this also, and the state did not pass this bill either. Stone then presented another bill, S. 742, which was a study for turning over a section of the Province Lands. His equivocal letters to me, to artist Fritz Bultman, and to Miriam DeWitt, at this time, did not help our sense of security in this matter. Although Stone claimed we would be given ample opportunity to testify on his speculative bill, the fact was that these plays for land acquisition were being made at a fast clip. Time was running out for the development interests and Senator Stone was clearly seeking a compromise position.[11]

The second and last hearings on the Park were to be conducted by the House Subcommittee on Public Lands of the Committee on Interior and Insular Affairs at Eastham on December 16 and 17, 1960; dates were given to all of us who wished to testify. This time, instead of only one person from Provincetown supporting the proposed legislation, there were ten of us presenting testimony and almost all were either artists or writers. [12] The eccentric Provincetown lawyer, S. Osborn Ball, affectionately known as Ozzie Ball, was categorically listed as the secretary of the Provincetown Civic Association, but he was truly a poet. His Balston Beach estate of some 200 acres in Truro fell squarely in the middle of the proposed land-takings of the National Seashore, yet his was the most forthright and one of the most impassioned pleas of all the testimony from Provincetown at the December 1960 hearings in Eastham:

> Now we come to Provincetown. If I would not be considered more ridiculous than I am, I would get down on my knees to your honorable committee and plead with you not to let the town of Provincetown take any portion of the Province Lands. This beautiful country—there is nothing like it in the whole United States—was taken for two purposes a century ago: to prevent those gigantic dunes from engulfing Provincetown in the northerly gales and to preserve for posterity one of the most beautiful places in the country. Provincetown doesn't need this bill they have filed. Don't let them have it. They talk about economy. I am going to die not knowing anything about economy. There isn't any such thing. That is a fancy word for builders who want to make money, for real estate men to develop it, for banks, for lawyers, people crazy to make money. If you add any more residences or businesses, you will choke it to death. I sincerely urge you to do all you can to save our little town, terribly maligned as it is and unjustly maligned. Save us from a fate much worse than anything the atomic bomb can do to us, because it will do it by degrees; it will choke us; it will finish us...[13]

It was at this point, just after the second hearing on the proposed Seashore Park legislation, that the Emergency Committee for the Preservation of the Province Lands assumed that name and coalesced the energies of all those opposed to the taking of the Province Lands with a unified voice. We were gathering strength for the approaching storm. Miriam DeWitt wrote often to Ross in December regarding the need for maps of the vacant land so that we could fend off the accusation that Provincetown had nowhere to go. She carefully developed her figures from contact with Park officials and from her own research, concluding that 452 acres of undeveloped land were still available as opposed to 572 that had been developed, 311 acres of which were roads. Both Ross and I sought to give this accurate picture of what was truly the viable case in Provincetown: i.e., that approximately as much land was left to build upon as had been built upon in the 233 years since Provincetown had been incorporated as a township. With the characteristic thoroughness that Ross Moffett approached any subject, he personally investigated all the pertinent areas of the town on foot and took a careful survey of available land. In terms of today's overdevelopment, both Miriam and Ross were prophetic: the development since the Park's establishment has probably doubled Provincetown's living space.

Closing arguments of both those in favor and those against the establishment of the Cape Cod National Seashore had now to be made. Heavily weighted, in the beginning, on the side of opposition, public statements in favor were starting to dominate the testimony. Real estate interests were flushed into the open and many pat phrases that had sounded the case for the various towns' opposition or reservations were coming under intelligent fire. In Provincetown, it was a tug of war between those of us who wanted to preserve the virgin area of the Province Lands and those who were attempting, in a last, desperate move, to delete a large portion of them before the Cape Cod National Seashore could be established.

In the days prior to Provincetown's annual town meeting in March 1961, the fierce exchange of letters in the *Provincetown Advocate* and elsewhere became a weekly cannonade. The case was coming to a furious finish, and the forces were ranged in ranks now clearly defined. We had run out of time. We knew that town meeting on March 13, 1961, was the last chance to hold the many natural treasures which Hazel Hawthorne Werner had so tenderly identified in an advertisement in the local press for the Emergency Committee, treasures which we had grown accustomed to seeing in our midst without fear of their destruction.

Our Emergency Committee for the Preservation of the Province Lands had widely circulated a flyer prior to the town meeting which posed the question: "If Provincetown Takes the Province Lands, Who Takes the Money?" This flyer which had been prepared by Miriam and John DeWitt, made very clear that the case for the Province Lands would be won as an economic brief as well as a conservation issue.

In advance of the meeting, Ross and I parsed out the questions that were to be answered by the voters there. The four questions phrased different propositions concerning the establishment of the Cape Cod National Seashore, but all four questions related directly to the fate of the Province Lands. Ross was to present the first three of the resolves and I, the last. On the night of the meeting, after an interminable discussion on a proposed new school addition, I moved the article on the Park questions forward. It was approximately 11:00 p.m. Would the interest of the voters hold?

The motion to move the article forward was approved and Ross began to speak in his gravely register. I still remember him at the microphone. Never before had he spoken at a town meeting. His nature was totally antipathetic to public speaking. Perhaps this is why, on that evening, there was a hushed attention in the audience. At that moment, the incredible commitment of Ross Moffett spoke better to the voters than the actual words. The questions were as follows:

1. *Are you in favor of the establishment of a Cape Cod National Seashore Park as specified in the Saltonstall Smith Bill, etc?* This bill, S. 857, would have deleted approximately 400 acres of the Province Lands. The vote came in and the measure was defeated.
2. The second question proposed by the Selectmen which would have deleted 1400 acres was also defeated by a larger margin.
3. This question asked if the voters favored the establishment of a National Seashore Park in general. There were only five dissenting votes, clearly establishing Provincetown's overwhelming approval of the Seashore Park

It was my turn. The fourth resolve had to do with the various proposals on the part of the Commonwealth of Massachusetts to delete a section of the Province Lands from the area of the Seashore Park:

4. *Are you in favor of legislation by the Commonwealth of Massachusetts which will enable the Town of Provincetown to acquire a portion of the State-owned or controlled lands for expansion purposes of a noncommercial nature?*[14]

I presented a careful summary of the case for retaining all of the more than 3,000 acres of the Province Lands and turning them over, intact, to the National Seashore. When I began to read my statement, Francis Steele, the Town Moderator, stepped away from the podium momentarily for some reason. At that point, John Snow, Chairman of the Board of Selectmen, rose to protest my remarks as being irrelevant, but Steele, quickly came back, countered by admitting that he had not heard the opening words of my statement and allowed me to continue. Regardless of his sentiments, pro or con, Francis Steele's quick and faithful adherence to the democratic and parliamentary process may have been a crucial moment for a great many Americans "hankering to see a wild swan."

When the vote on this last question came, it was 144 in favor and 61 against, retaining the entirety of the Province Lands as they were for inclusion in the National Seashore Park. [15] It was a moment which brought to fruition, as so few such moments have, a resolute stand on the environment, an intelligent plan to carry it out, and a final determination to see it through. No other town had so rallied to a view of the future. No other town on the Cape had supported the Park so wholeheartedly. We were, again, unique on the Cape. The input of the artists and writers throughout this entire effort had been crucial They represented the element of metaphor, and addressed, in their concise and beautiful statements, all the problems perennially posed by humanity in its predatory sojourn upon the earth, and yet were statements of hope through the intelligence of that very predator—the only hope we have—the firm conviction that the earth must not pass away.

The March 13 vote collapsed, in one stroke, the case for acquisition of the Province Lands, and from that moment on, the reverse process was set in motion. Ross Moffett phrased the position of the town for Washington officials, and we systematically informed the press and all others concerned. The *Cape Codder* newspaper picked up our victory: "Victory at Town Meeting," and described the event.[16] Malcom Hobbs, the editor, had consistently championed the Park from the very beginning, an editorial position that had been singular on the Cape. Thus, the pragmatism and the poetry of Ross Moffett had combined in a great conservation achievement that will perennially reaffirm, as he once did, that the sight of a wild swan is a religious experience that brings both spiritual satisfaction and economic well-being.

It would seem logical to assume that, after our decisive victory at the town meeting, the powers of "darkness," so to speak, would have been vanquished. Such was not the case, however. We had believed that the victory established a secure position from which no retreat was possible, but it did not. Those with designs to exploit the Province Lands, far from retreating, still threatened to advance. For instance, the developer Van Ness Bates regarded the town's vote to include all of the Province Lands in the Cape Cod National Seashore as merely a preliminary encounter in an unfinished engagement, as he would the vote to establish the park taken in Congress on August 7, 1961. His long letter in the *New Bedford Standard Times* only two days after the Seashore legislation was approved in Congress entitled "Not Appomatox but Bull Run," began immediately to worry the old bone of development.[17] This determined agent of exploitation continued to bedevil us with plans and arguments until the very moment when the Province Lands were legally ceded by the State of Massachusetts to the United States government a year and a half later.

Clearly, the energies required to manage the further fight to ensure the transfer of the Province Lands to the Seashore Park were considerable. In 1961, no less than three bills were filed in the Massachusetts Legislature attempting to develop the Province Lands. Although all these were successfully circumvented, there was a new issue that quickly became a serious threat.

It was an undisputed fact that a harbor of refuge for the fishing community had been badly needed for some time. Playing upon this need, the same interests that had wished to obtain major portions of the Province Lands now engaged in a propaganda campaign to obtain a critically important area of the clam flats and marshland, in back of Provincetown's West End Breakwater, for a marina, an area designated to be included in the Province Lands transfer.

On September 11, 1961, therefore, Ross Moffett and Captain Charles Mayo, Jr., a local captain with years of experience on sailing and sports fishing vessels, wrote a letter to the Provincetown Selectmen asking them for a definite position. They pointed out that the Board of Selectmen had promised to abide by the town's March 13 decision to set aside the entirety of the Province Lands for the National Park and also referred to the fact that the Chairman of the Board of Selectmen John Snow had, as late as August 6, 1961, one day before the enactment of the Park legislation in Congress, expressed a renewed demand to delete sections of the Province Lands from the proposed Park. The Selectmen's answer to this letter was curt. It simply referred to the recorded minutes of the Selectmen's minutes. Needless to say, Ross did not take kindly to this rebuff, and he did not let the matter rest there. In a second letter, sometime after October 1961, he and Mayo again wrote to the Selectmen, reviewing their previous request. They ended this letter with the statement that "in spite of the act of the National Congress, the

Province Lands will not be safe from exploitation until they are actually transferred by the General Court to the Federal Government." Indeed, they were not.

Meanwhile, the bill which was to transfer the Province Lands in their entirety to the National Seashore was, in November 1961, being prepared by Director of the Massachusetts Department of Natural Resources Charles Foster and others. On December 28, 1961, the *Provincetown Advocate* carried a long and emotional article about the need for a marina.[18] Ross Moffett and I, as well as many others, were not opposed to a harbor of refuge, per se, and never had been. Our stated position was that the West End marina proposal was largely a land-making "sweetheart" deal and not, in essence, a harbor of refuge proposal. In a report that Ross and I wrote for the Emergency Committee for the Preservation of the Province Lands, we outlined the threat to the environment that the West End proposal presented on at least seven counts. The fishermen deserved and needed a marina, but they had refused to investigate the alternative area many others endorsed, which was in the vicinity of the main pier, where the Army Corps of Engineers had already surveyed a harbor of refuge site between 1945 and 1948.

About this time, however, a new wrinkle in events occurred that had a material effect on the eventual creation of a harbor of refuge and the final composition of the National Park. A representative from Duxbury in the Massachusetts Legislature, Francis Perry, had begun a probe in the early summer of 1961 regarding the activities of Rodolphe Bessette, then director of the Division of Waterways, who was also, incidentally, responsible for the administration of the state-owned lands, the Province Lands included. Perry proved, in subsequent exposés, that Bessette had engaged in a number of "sweetheart" deals, one of which included land in Provincetown adjacent to the area being considered for a municipal marina. He pointed out that, in effect, the town was being manipulated to demand a marina/harbor of refuge at a site next to privately held interests, which would gain considerable advantage from such a location of boating facilities. [19] Perry's exposé was thoroughly documented and clearly stated, but the local backing for the marina was intense, and the bureaucratic protagonists were again the town manager and the chairman of the Board of Selectmen, who sought approximately 50 acres of land for the marina. As Ross Moffett emphasized in a statement prepared for the selectmen at the time, this constituted many more acres than were actually needed for a marina and smacked of speculation for selected private interests.

The eventual conviction of the Director of the Division of Waterways, Rodolph Bessette in connection with "sweetheart" deals in Provincetown and Wellfleet, and his subsequent dismissal by Governor John Volpe were due to the indefatigable efforts of Duxbury Representative Francis Perry. In spite of this, as the hearings on Provincetown's proposal to obtain a marina in the Province Lands approached in January 1962, we realized that some loss of land would probably occur. In this regard, John DeWitt had wisely written to Charles Olson, the chairman of the Commission on Harbors and Public Lands, positing the condition that if it were decided that Provincetown should be given the chance to finance a marina in the West End location, that the land be ceded to the town only on the condition that the town voters act to create a marina within a specified time frame, and if the town should fail to do so, "the entire 57 acres in question would automatically be included in the Cape Cod National Seashore." [20]

Until the day of the hearing on the marina, January 25, 1962, our efforts had been strenuous in the hope that the marina land-taking proposition would be avoided, but pressures at the hearing on behalf of House Bill #2686 were enormous. [21] One hundred fifty Provincetown residents attended, among whom were some of the most vociferous pro-marina voices. Representative Perry stood his ground, pointing out the contiguity of the land belonging to friends of Bessette who was already under Grand Jury indictment, but the sentiment in favor of the marina would not be swayed by this knowledge or by any other consideration than the emotional one of the fishermen having to ride out storms, unprotected, in Provincetown Harbor. There was no particular concern as to how the marina was obtained as long as there was one.

After weeks of letter writing that promoted the argument against the West End Marina,the position of the Emergency Committee for the Preservation of the Province Lands had to be altered at the last moment, due to the advice of the Governor's appointee to the Cape Cod Seashore Advisory Commission Josiah Child. He represented favoring the bill, with the addition of the provision that John DeWitt had outlined to Olson. We were all persuaded, at that point in time, to endorse this strategy, which Child felt was the only possible solution to the impasse. Rightly or wrongly, we did so, hoping for the return of the land to the Cape Cod National Seashore, which, indeed, did eventually occur. The action turned out to be the correct one, but it was fraught with risks, and defending it the week after the hearing to the redoubtable Representative Perry was the hardest job I tackled in the entire three-year encounter over the Province Lands controversy.[22]

Like a nightmare from which one never seems to awaken, the saga did not end with the passage of the bill to create the marina, for the specter of Van Ness Bates again loomed at the marina hearing and beyond. At the hearing on January 25th, Bates suggested that a mere paltry fifty-seven acres was not enough, and, on February 1, 1962, he launched yet another bill in the Massachusetts Legislature, #1934, his last official attempt on the Province Lands.[23] It seemed he was a multi-headed hydra, a veritable Medusa of a figure whose various schemes had to be cut off once and for all by some Perseus of a fellow. Ross set himself to the task, and, on February 3, 1962, he wrote a letter to the Chairman of the Joint Committee on Constitutional Law in the Massachusetts General Court suggesting that Bates's present plan was nothing but the old plan rehashed for further obfuscation. Artist Fritz Bultman wrote to Ross at the time expressing the heartfelt appreciation of the artist community at large: "The way you have constantly worked over the past years towards the Park is really just wonderful, and we feel most fortunate in having you there in Provincetown and never letting down a minute. We realize that, without your assistance, the New Beach Hilton and assorted golf courses, hamburg stands, etc., would be well on the way."[24]

A brief ray of sunlight came for Ross Moffett on April 27th, 1962, when Ronald Lee, the Regional Director of the Park, sent him a purchase order for an archaeological base map and site inventory to be prepared for the National Park Service. This made Ross Moffett the first official archaeologist for the Cape Cod National Seashore, an honor and a position he richly merited in every respect. The correspondence between the Regional Archaeologist John Cotter and Frank Barnes, Regional Historian, then developed on several important matters, and Ross was at work, almost at once, tracking down suggestions as to sites and compiling the data for the site survey map and inventory.

As to the Province Lands transfer, that light was also beginning to glimmer on the horizon, and, after what seemed an eternity, the Governor's bill was signed into law on July 26, 1962. Its significance was critical; with the signing of this bill, the Cape Cod National Seashore became an administrable entity, thus cutting off attempts at possible development violations at an early date, saving the government an indeterminate amount of money that might have been expended in litigation involving the acquisition of property that had accrued in value over time.

Man Hunting Arrowheads by Ross Moffett, 1932; lithograph, 9½" x 14"

Two years after this historic conclusion of the effort to create the Cape Cod National Seashore Park, Ross mused whimsically on the whole initiative and its outcome in the final chapter of his irreplaceable history of artists and events in the life of the first thirty-three years of the Provincetown Art Association, which he titled *Art In Narrow Streets*. Speaking of a prophetess in the midst of one of the Art Association's annual meetings, he allowed himself the only emotional phrasing of the whole endeavor as a kind of oracular vision:

> She called herself Cassandra; her real name we never knew. No longer young, her straight hair falling over her ascetic face, she appeared a wild and striking figure as she walked the dunes and woodlands of the Province Lands, an area whose guardian spirit she claimed she knew. She carried on conversations with a slate-colored junco, a creature she averred to be more intelligent and companionable than a sea gull. Like every prophetess, she often proffered gratuitous information about the future, and for this the Art Association sometimes afforded her a stage, although it may be doubted that she paid dues and thus had a right to predict on Association property. One of Cassandra's inspirations for foretelling came upon her at an annual meeting at this time. Unfortunately, no one recorded her exact words, but as nearly as one can remember, they were, in effect, a warning and an appeal, principally to artists but to others also, to watch for and to resist what she envisioned as a future attempt by ambitious interests to acquire and to exploit 1475 acres of the Province Lands, with the consequent leveling and destruction of the setting of natural beauty that had long been the most attractive possession of Provincetown. Cassandra thought this attempted ravishment of the public domain would come to a head in about the year 1960, and she admonished her hearers to oppose the proposition by word of mouth, by mimeograph, in the press,

Race Point by Josephine Del Deo, 1955; mixed thread woven tapestry, 15" x 30"

> on the floor of Town Meeting and, as she expressed it, "before Great Jove and committees of the Continental Congress." In her varied speech, she referred to Priam and to other notables of the Trojan world, and, since she foresaw the eventual discomfiture of the avid spirits against whom she felt so strongly opposed, she ended with the cry: "Beauty shall live; Great Hector is not dead."[25]

Ross Moffett now laid down his pen as sword, and his loyal troops could retire to a moment of well-earned rest. Looking back on that struggle and the unfinished business of the marina, which we still faced in the summer of 1962, the feeling is one of exhaustion even at the distance of many years, but the prophecy of Cassandra and the response to her plea had been fulfilled.

CHAPTER III

One Last Day before the Summer

1962–1966

SOON AFTER THE establishment of the Cape Cod National Seashore Park, on August 7, 1961, and the safe transfer of the entirety of the Province Lands from the state of Massachusetts to the federal government on July 26, 1962, those of us who had served on the Emergency Committee for the Preservation of the Province Lands felt we could finally rest from an endeavor that had required a watch nearly twenty-four hours a day, for Ross Moffett and myself especially, for nearly three years. The functional realities of the recently passed legislation gradually began to dawn upon the Cape Cod community at large, even upon those who had not welcomed its presence, and to confirm the fact that the Park had come to stay.

As we have seen, the priceless heritage of the Province Lands has never been compromised by the Massachusetts Legislature since the date of its having been deeded to the Commonwealth in 1654, although attempts to do so have been made from time to time. The state owned 3,000-plus acres of the Province Lands stretched across the back county, from its eastern boundary, which abutted private tracts extending to the Truro town line, to the furthermost tip of Cape Cod at Long Point. This constituted an enormous natural reserve of virgin woods, dunes, and lowlands which had been traditionally supervised by the state of Massachusetts. At the time of the Park's proposal, the Province Lands were under the longtime care and management of state rangers. State supervising ranger Henry Helmer had been satisfying the needs of preservation and security for many years. He was to be the last of those rangers, living out his time in solitary but contented surveillance of territory he roamed on horseback and which he loved and treated as his personal domain. As well as official ranger, he was also an artist and an excellent wood carver, and he occupied a forest abode in the Province Lands, which he had built himself and from which he ventured daily to establish his hegemony over duck and deer.

Henry Helmer's territory was immense, but he commanded it with a knowledge of the diurnal flow of life from the Great Beech forest in his back yard to the spectacular shoreline stretching between Provincetown and Truro. The Cape Cod National Seashore's establishment in 1961 and the final incorporation of the Province Lands within its domain in 1962 removed the necessity of his position, but it could never replace the intimate synergy of all the environmental aspects of such an expanse that the single rider on a single horse had maintained so efficiently and effortlessly and whose credo of management had been: "Do not disturb."

It was apparent to many, however, that such singular supervision would have eventually failed to forestall the building of a hotel chain at Herring Cove or a helicopter port superimposed on the remains of the old Civil War installations at Long Point or the general development that would surely have spread from harbor to sea with the result that, in the end, no one would have chosen to live or visit a community whose density exceeded the fundamentals of available potable water, reasonable living space, the means of disposing of both sewage and garbage and of providing adequate fire and police protection. With great consternation, one observes that these facts have become a pressing reality, to a growing degree, in Provincetown already, but the present density is as nothing compared to what it might have been without the protection of the Province Lands and of the rest of the adjacent acreage within the Cape Cod National Seashore, especially that of the Pilgrim Spring State Park in Truro. As it now stands, the Province Lands have become a firewall against the rage of unrestrained overbuilding at the very tip of Cape Cod.

In regard, therefore, to the changing of the watch, we were only too glad to see Superintendent Robert Gibbs as the first official superintendent of the National Seashore. He was a man of unobtrusive nature, not one to muscle the local norms in the "out back" and in all those areas where custom had long ago established access to elements of the natural environment and where a heavily disproportionate schedule of directives would have set the tone for a negative interaction between the Park, as a new neighbor, and the local communities. Gibbs took his duties as park superintendent calmly and in stride. He was steady and affable, and managed to guide the private interests within the Park through the various facts of the new situation with a loosely held rein of supervision, especially concerning regulations which the Park had, of necessity, to institute. As overseer, Henry Helmer, and his horse, had been replaced by Park Service personnel enforcing stricter rules. No more could dune riders, including ourselves, choose an arbitrary route across the challenging roll of the dunes fraught with thrilling drops and unexpected vistas.

In establishing hitherto unfamiliar bureaucratic policy, Superintendent Gibbs took an accommodating attitude. Meeting with the local Highland Fish and Game Club, for instance, he quickly fitted into their agenda as if he had been a member all his life. At the time of the Park's initiation in 1961, the Highland Fish and Game Club was a significant entity in the Provincetown community. Its three-hundred plus members included a full spectrum of types and many memorable characters, as well as regular guests. Such membership typified the local population and especially that portion of the natives who loved to fish, to hunt, and to partake of the offerings of a rich, natural habitat that had never been invaded by the collective commercial activities of man. They had always been available to such wanderers as the hunter in fall stalking his annual deer, setting duck blinds, making a sally into the underbrush to chase out a rabbit, or just pursuing path, track, and scents of game or pelagic varieties of fish in ways traditional to Paleolithic man, which have never altered much except by small degrees. The beloved "out back" meant life to these men and their sons and grandsons. They organized to protect hunting and fishing preserves with regular meetings, instructional sessions for teaching the young how to handle a gun, prepare wild game, and, under the supervision of conservationist John Alexander, learn the correct placement of nesting boxes everywhere in low-lying marsh and along Pilgrim Lake's sedgy edges, particularly. The Club monitored abuses and indulged small excesses according to a code of honor hardly ever broken and always with that kind of competitive camaraderie that had, at its best, instinctively understood that wildlife must be nourished and protected in order to offer up, within well-defined limits, a reasonable bounty.

In those days, there was, in fact, much bounty. Deer were plentiful as well as the deer ticks that went with them. Occasionally, during hunting season, a deer would be found on Commercial Street, chased from the surrounding dunes, who might wind up swimming across to Long Point to escape his pursuers. The early season for the bow and arrow always found a few "purists" treed in some advantageous spot, and there they would stay until their prey came within their sights or darkness removed their sight altogether. These men knew their woods like their own back yard, and they were not alone in that ancient environmental savvy. Many in the town had inherited the skills of securing the benefits of the land and sea in multiple ways that were soundly life-giving. Their sixth sense about nature was a phenomenal science which took into account the patterns of interdependency of all the environmental elements of the area. It was to such a traditional state of affairs, progressively tempered by evolving civilization, that the Cape Cod National Seashore was required to incorporate yet another dimension of conduct within the established "way of life."

The hunter-fisherman is still here and will always be here, although now diminished in numbers relative to the residential population. No one could have foreseen, however, to what extent the original legislation establishing the Cape Cod National Seashore would eventually protect and defend the individual rights of the independent hunter-gatherer man, but Superintendent Gibbs was clear about this from the very beginning. In this respect, many still maintain that Gibbs was probably the most understanding and the most easily accessible of all the superintendents the Park Service appointed during the first decades of its operation. As policy dictates in the National Park Service, however, he was assigned to the National Seashore for a stipulated stint of time, which was evidently defined as just long enough to establish good order and to begin to solve initial problems. Since this was the first park of its kind in the country, those problems regarding private property status and general, overall management issues were numerous. In retrospect, the impression of the policy he left us, at first, of a "live and let live" nature was a welcome paradigm.

Halfway house where surfmen from adjoining stations meet and exchange checks, J.W. Dalton, *The Life Savers of Cape Cod*, Barta Press, Boston, Massachusetts, 1902

We have only to review the traditional uses of the Great Outer Beach during the nineteenth and early twentieth century to understand the process of man in nature, as it proceeded in those times, and to follow that process to the present day in order to rewind the timepiece in a new calendar reference. Established fishing and hunting activities were continually in play as they had been variously practiced long before the recorded history of Cape Cod.

Herman A. Jennings in his valuable compendium entitled *Provincetown or Odds and Ends from the Tip End*, [1] speaks of the Provincetown-Truro colony and of the land reserved for "fishing purposes and for the squatter fishermen." This would have referred to the Province Lands, especially, that had been purchased by Governor Bradford from Samson the Indian in 1654 for the Plymouth Colony and later turned over to the Massachusetts Bay Colony in 1692.[2] The idea of the "squatter fishermen" implies some form of protection from the weather during seasonal fishing and, following the *modus operandi*, we can trace its course easily along the "back side" from one generation to the next with verifiable historical references, both written and pictorial.

One of the most important of these is an account made by Captain Nathaniel Atwood, one of Provincetown's most famous whaling captains, who left us a rounded description of fishing activity on Cape Cod from 1816 through the mid-century in his testimony before the U.S. Fisheries Commission in 1866 and in various lectures at the Lowell Institute at that same time.[3] He describes, with specificity, the life he led as a young boy. Atwood was born in Provincetown on September 13, 1807, on Long Point, and, by the time he was nine years old, in 1816, he was already fishing with his father for sea-herring. His account of seasonal fishing at Race Point, when he was ten, describes the cod fishing shore fishery technique that many practiced in those days:

> The next spring, I went with one other boy with my father in a boat cod-fishing. We went to Race Point and used, as the sailors say, to carry our "grub" with us. Before Saturday night, we had come in and got a recruit. We used a lap-strake boat a little smaller than a whaleboat. The whaleboat rows with five oars, and these had four oars, and we used to call them five-handed boats. There were six-strake boats and seven-strake boats. They were 18 feet keel and I should think about 5 feet beam with four thwarts. We sometimes used a small sail, which we made of 9 yards of topgallant duck. The mast was almost 12 feet long.
>
> We landed at the Race and hauled the boats up. We had little fishing huts there. My father built his hut there, which was 6 feet by 8 feet. He was 6 feet tall, and had a berth across the end and could touch his head at one end and his feet the other. The hut had a wooden chimney. We took such provisions as we could. Some fared better than others. We were pretty poor. I came from poverty and obscurity. I suppose we were there about two months fishing for codfish. During the season, a man and a boy, a youngster like me, would probably average about 25 quintals to a boat. That is fair average for the two months that we stopped there.[4]

Captain Atwood grew up to have a long and remarkably successful career as a captain in the whaling industry, but he also established himself as an amateur ichthyologist with whom both the federal government and noted scientists, such as Louis Agassiz,[5] consulted for his remarkable knowledge of the pelagic fish and fishing patterns of the North Atlantic region.

In a corollary activity that has always been protected on the back shore, especially in the environs of the Province Lands, we have an account of seasonal hunting, dating from the turn of the twentieth century. In a photographic archive from the former Provincetown Heritage Museum, which is now the Provincetown Public Library, there is a series of

The Wreck of The Jessica Howland by Salvatore Del Deo
1979; oil on canvas, 20" x 24"

ten photographs showing "Hunting on the Back Shore." They depict a hunting shack built by Al Neesan's great grandfather Louis W. De Pass, supposedly with wreckage from the Steamer "Portland" in the vicinity of Race Point Light. The photographs were taken in 1901 and 1902, and De Pass is shown standing in front of the shack holding the barrel of a rifle in his left hand and a string of birds in his right. In one of the photographs, a description is given that recounts the length of the journey from Provincetown to the shacks: "On the way from Provincetown to Race Point, 5 miles over the dunes." [6] Further down the Cape, or as the natives say "up" the Cape, in South Orleans on the Nauset outer beach and at North Chatham, a long tradition of duck hunting and dune cottage residency was maintained until the ocean gradually eliminated a large part of the entire community of cottages or "camps," as they were called, over the last twenty years.[7]

If we move from accounts of these traditional activities on the back shore to the long history of salvage and of life saving, the journey in time is also linked to maritime commerce and, subsequently, to rescue and life saving along the coast of Cape Cod from Peaked Hill Bars to Monomoy, what has been referred to by historians as the "graveyard of the Atlantic." The earliest efforts to save the crews of vessels brought to their sudden and terrible wreck along this stretch of the Atlantic began in 1786 with the Massachusetts Humane Society, which, aided with various appropriations from the federal government on an intermittent basis to assist the Society, carried on its rescue work for nearly one hundred years. The Humane Society was officially coalesced into what became the U.S. Life Saving Service in 1872. From that time, life saving stations were established at regular intervals with standing crews and full rescue equipment in place at all times. This provided succor for stranded vessels and their desperate crews and passengers. In 1915, the Life Saving Service, combined with the Revenue Cutter Service, became the United States Coast Guard.[8]

The early photographs and details of the Life Saving Service, in J. W. Dalton's valuable book, *The Life Savers of Cape Cod*, fully document the stations along the outer beach from Long Point in Provincetown to Monomoy in Chatham, also describe the halfway houses used by the station crews. From these, they could briefly recover from bitter weather on their daily patrols and were able to signal in one way or another, first by flare and later by telephone, to their various home stations, alerting them to the location of an ensuing or on-going disaster.[9]

These shelters, originally built by the Humane Society for stranded seamen, were stocked with the bare essentials of survival, such as matches, water, straw or hay, etc. They were of the same construction, more or less, as the fishing hut of the Atwood family and the hunting cabin of Louis De Pass.

From the squatter fishermen's huts along the "back side" to the cabins for seasonal

Above: Fishermen/hunter's shack, Provincetown-Truro Back Shore (exact location unknown)

Left: Halfway house, located between the Peaked Hill Bars and the High Head Coast Guard Stations, early 1930s. *Collection of David Mayo*

hunting to the halfway houses of the Life Saving Service and to the outbuildings associated with the several Coast Guard stations to the dune shacks of today, the derivative form follows function. The connecting element in each layer of habitation was based on the same or a similar principle: use implemented by a modest form of architecture, (with the exception of the substantial Coast Guard stations) for the accommodation of a way of life defined by the benefits and the hazards of the Great Outer Beach. This connecting link, between human activities pertaining to the great Atlantic and the great dunes at its doorstep and the way in which the Outer Beach had been an interface providing a means to garner nature's treasure and, at the same time, protection from its worst devastations, has, essentially, never been broken. This process may be exampled to the present time. As recently as Oct. 3, 1962, for instance, dune dweller Peg Watson wrote the following note to her friend Annabelle Jones, a fellow dune resident:

> Dear Annabelle,
> Enclosed explains itself. Interviewed Gibbs in transit and gave him propaganda on the people we rescue from time to time-including "Eugenie" episode when Esther Hill called Coast Guard, Al Fearing caught the men in the breeches buoy and Jones shack was the only shelter for thirteen wet Greeks.[10]

Watson's brief description of rescue on the back beach, in her cryptic, but humorous manner, recounts a classic episode on the "interface" of ocean and dune updated to the twentieth century with clarifying succinctness. Peg Watson, in this terse account, describes the Jones shack as a refuge and, once again, a kind of halfway house for battered sailors. This very small dune shack, coincidentally, conforms by location to a traditional halfway house, as it is roughly halfway between the former Peaked Hill and the High Head Coast Guard Stations, reaffirming man's consistent presence in the environmental equation. *The Cape Cod National Seashore inherited both a vast, unspoiled domain of a coastline fixed in geological time and also a modest expression of man's place in that domain over many centuries of minimal and manageable habitation.*

When considering, therefore, the historic background of the structures in use, over time, on the Great Outer Beach, it is pertinent to discuss the status of the dune shacks prior to the establishment of the Cape Cod National Seashore Park. In order to follow the community of habitation there with some specificity, it is most helpful to peruse the several diagrammatic maps created by Hazel Hawthorne Werner for her friend and fellow dune shack resident Andrew Fuller, which are reproduced in the Appendix (pp.) and that of Ray Martin Wells, also made for Andrew Fuller and Grace Bessay in March 1971. These hand-drawn sketches record, as accurately as possible, the positions and dates of the shacks and, in some cases, the persons who built the shacks and the lineage of their owners within the central area of the Peaked Hill Bars Historic District, particularly, between the years c.1920 and 1960. During this period, some structures were moved, some were altered, and a few disappeared altogether. These references are probably the most authentic record that can now be retrieved of the existing dune shacks within the area that later became designated as the central district of the "Dune Shacks of Peaked Hill Bars Historic District."[11] Added to these invaluable graphic recollections are several direct quotes and oral references from an oral history, and telephone conversations with several Coast Guardsmen who were still alive and who added their memories to the history of the dune cottages that I wrote in 1986 (see Appendix: Part I) and which make it possible to ascertain a chronology that can be relied upon, more or less, to the present day.

In addition to the dune shacks in the vicinity of Peaked Hill, which eventually became included in the proposal for a registered district of dune shacks, a similar grouping of dune shacks, farther to the east, were identified as part of the entire grouping of cottages on the Great Outer Beach at the time of the Park's inception. These easternmost shacks, having been situated within the precinct of Truro and within the Commonwealth of Massachusetts' Pilgrim Spring State Park, had now to face an uneven route of transfer between the commonwealth and the federal government, each authority having a special position of overview that had to be combined under the auspices of the National Seashore Park. The issues involved in this process developed, with some complications, as the passage of the bill to create the Cape Cod National Seashore seemed certain.

It was at this point in time that Grace Bessay and her friend Andrew Fuller, both of whom owned cottages in the easternmost area, became deeply involved in the formation of an organization called the Great Beach Cottage Owner's Association, all the members of which owned shacks on the Great Outer Beach, either in Truro or Provincetown. In a letter to Annabelle Jones dated September 11, 1963, Bessay makes the case for the cottage owners. She begins by firmly suggesting that the Commonwealth's National Resources Commissioner Charles Foster "should align himself with the National Park policy and extend the same right and privileges to all owners of structures and land."

Bessay goes on to say that "every effort should be directed towards aiding the inhabitants of the Park, many of whom have given great support both to the Park and to the public and private conservation movement. The victory for the Federal park was achieved in large measure by promising protection and fair treatment to all of the many inhabitants of the Park area." She might have emphasized the fact, which was implicit in her statement, that all of the shack dwellers in the Provincetown-Truro complex had weighed in heavily on behalf of the creation of the Park. Their testimonies and/or letters were eloquent in expressing their profound commitment to the concept of the Park's establishment. In the absence of any specific determination regarding the dune shacks, therefore, almost all of the back shore inhabitants were uneasy and many became alarmed at the possibility that they would lose their rights of ownership and habitation in this complicated process before any federal determination could be made. The difficult quandary of the status of the cottages continued to be exacerbated by a policy that appeared to be determined by a kind of continual rolling of the dice. The original statement of policy of the proposed Cape Cod National Seashore, which was prepared, at the request of Senators Saltonstall and John Kennedy, by Ronald Lee, Regional Director of Region Five in December 1960, for the exposition of stated Park goals during the hearing process, contained many general and a number of specific assurances, one of which needs to be briefly underscored here:

> In certain areas, the preservation of historic structures and the evidence of earlier ways of living as associated with the colonial and seafaring eras of Cape Cod would be a prime objective.[12]

This four-page overview mentioned historic values many times in various contexts and this appeared to be one of the Park's initial concerns and a prime figuration of the overall master plan. Without taking the statements in Lee's report out of the presentation, which emphasized a coordinated approach to recreation, preservation, and interpretive elements, there is still a fundamental guarantee, which the Park's legislation eventually provided when it was enacted: to protect all those whose residential structures that had been in existence before September 1959, provided that local zoning and Park directives concerning the protection of the environment were observed.

According to Lee, such protection would be especially pertinent to "historic structures." It seemed to those of us on the Great Outer Beach, however, that this presumed grandfathered protection was going to be adjusted and tailored in order gradually to eliminate the shacks and restore the land to a wilderness state by removing, one at a time, all habitations for whatever reason could be made to apply in each case. After the Cape Cod National Seashore had become official, one of the first dramatic demonstrations of such a policy was the burning of the Wood End Coast Guard Station in Provincetown in 1961, an act totally contrary to the preservation "of earlier ways of living as associated with Colonial and seafaring areas of Cape Cod."

The very real threat of elimination bespoke betrayal, therefore, to all of the back shore residents. As a consequence, the Great Beach Cottage Owners Association identified Massachusetts Commissioner of Natural Resources Charles H. Foster as the most immediate threat to the Truro cottage owner at this time, as Grace Bessay had expressed in her letter to Annabelle Jones. The cottages in jeopardy were those in the Pilgrim Spring State Park area, which had been created in 1955 by the Commonwealth of Massachusetts. Commissioner Foster had openly expressed antagonism toward these structures in a letter to Massachusetts Representative Allan Jones on August 29, 1962.

> In my judgement, the buildings are not suitable for year-round habitation, lacking sanitary facilities and are so unsightly that they should be removed in advance of any public use of the property.[13]

Foster's statement and his generally dismissive attitude led to a long exchange between the cottage owners, their legal counsel Robert L. Meade, and state representative Allan Jones, who excoriated Foster for his statements and general attitude, reminding him that no action should be taken to eliminate or, in any way, jeopardize the cottage owners within the Pilgrim Spring State Park. Representative Jones further reminded Commissioner Foster that he had been present at the creation of the Pilgrim Spring State Park and that any attempt at the taking of buildings or giving notice of their removal was illegal and improper according to the enabling legislation.[14] Representative Jones then addressed a letter to Massachusetts Attorney General Edward J. McCormack, asking for an opinion about the legal status of the Truro shacks at that present time and the proper treatment of the owners' rights under Chapter 523. McCormack then wrote to Chairman Foster advising him that he had no jurisdiction over the cottages in the State Park and that he should proceed to transfer the land to the federal government without reference to the structures.

Since the first conflict over the dune shacks in 1962, a fair and reasonable resolution of the issues still begs the question. Prior to the declaration of eligibility for National Register status, which the Registrar made in May 1989, every dune cottage, with hardly any exception, had to face the possibility of eventual or imminent elimination, and at least two were actually eliminated by the Seashore.[15]

This was not anticipated by traditional residents, nor has it proved workable as a management solution by the federal government, because the conflicting entrapments thus created have entangled the Department of the Interior's overseeing authority within their own definitions of principles of general purpose and of specific preservation. Even though the dune shacks were nominally protected by the establishment of their eligibility for registration as National Registered Landmarks after May 12, 1989, they still suffered, in certain cases, from "demolition by neglect." *Resident dune shack inhabitants continued to face eviction based on a previously mandated timeline variously negotiated with the intent of emptying out the legacy of habitation and installing a revolving population to fit the bureaucratic definition of "public use." The "public," so defined, cannot possibly provide the historical continuum and the grammar of a "way of life" learned by long usage, thereby compromising an essential element of the Cape Cod National Seashore that was initially declared as a priority.*

It is no longer possible to re-create the diurnal patterns of the Coast Guard Stations along the Great Outer Beach or to install their boat crews. There is still, however, a continuing vestige of viable habitation in a few of the outbuildings once connected to those stations, in one way or another, and in similar structures closely associated and dating from the same period and derived from the same or similar impetus of use as has existed on the Great Outer Beach interface long before the National Seashore Park appeared on the horizon. *I feel it is incumbent upon the federal government to guarantee that such a way of life in these dune shacks survives as part of our national cultural heritage.*

At the close of 1962 and early 1963, however, the most significant component of our national social and cultural history was not the successful establishment of the Cape Cod National Seashore, but the growing Civil Rights movement in America, which accumulated to angry proportions in the early months of 1963, culminating in the Birmingham protest of May 6, 1963, during which eight hundred were arrested for a lack of a parade permit. A huge rally in Washington, DC, on August 28, attended by more than 200,000 demonstrators, added a much larger expression of purpose, which never stopped growing until the untimely death of Martin Luther King, Jr., forever locked in the impact of social change. Most of the nation were moved to unusual energy in relation to the forces involved in this issue, including Sal and myself. In September 1961, for instance, Sal organized a Freedom Riders exhibition on behalf of the Congress of Racial Equality (CORE) in the Front Street Gallery, together with fellow painter and friend Tony Vevers and gallery associate Joe Miller. For the next several years, we had ample opportunity to take up the cause that absorbed the country as a whole.

Shortly after the Birmingham protest and three weeks before the Washington, DC, demonstration, Provincetown hosted a peace walk on Hiroshima Day on August 6, 1963, to address the pressing issue of preventing any future nuclear holocaust. On that day, I led the march to the bas relief opposite our town hall, which commemorates the signing of the Mayflower Compact, and introduced the major speaker of the event, Dr. Robert J. Lifton, to our assembled gathering of approximately three hundred persons. Others who spoke on that occasion were Amy Swerdlow and Dr. Edmund Braun, who organized the signing of the Ban the Bomb Treaty petition presented to President Kennedy. I closed my introductory remarks with the reading of a poem I had composed for the occasion:

New Pilgrims from Old

Those ghosts assembled at the tide's last marking
How lonely they, on that long strand, appear.
Some fear restrains their natural advancing,
As if they dared not breathe the desolation of the air.
Poised upon history, slowly they proceed,
Step by step into this unknown place,
Their sighted bearings by low mist obscured
And each exploring trail by shifting sands erased.
Now we are settled, Pilgrims no more,
Yet there is something of the old stir in us still,
A facing down of devastation far more vast
Than that first landfall after weeks at sea.
Across the oceanic hatred of men's minds,
Awaits the heart's uncharted shore
For those brave pilgrims who embark
Upon a trackless waste of apathy
To make new love, not land, the great discovery.

Kennedy, of course, later signed the Nuclear Nonproliferation Treaty. It was then, and remains today, one of the most significant pieces of legislation in Post World War history, but, within minutes, it seemed, President Kennedy was assassinated on November 22, 1963, and the shock rocked America and the rest of the world for months afterward. The exact moment and time of Kennedy's death most Americans, then living, recall with complete clarity. I staggered with the news and wrote out my grief in a long journal entry the same day. It included this observation:

> The larger crime here apparent is that of the encouragement and existence of an aura of violence in this country which is rising and regenerative on two counts, preparedness for war and resistance to civil rights. As citizens, we are in great danger, more so than we realized, and it will require extreme diligence and miraculous leadership from some yet unknown source to avoid the disasters ahead.

Life went on, regardless of the nation's mourning, which, in a certain sense, has never completely ceased to the present day. Kennedy's death loomed larger on the horizon with each passing year, for the direction of many national endeavors moved quickly to subsequent disaster, first in Vietnam, then to the shocking deaths of Martin Luther King Jr. and Robert Kennedy, and finally, to the demoralizing morass of the Watergate scandal. We were young, however, and able to hope for the future and enjoy the gathering of the Thanksgiving harvest, which we shared with Frenchie that year in our house. She wrote to us afterward in a typewritten note:

> It was so good of you to have me at your wonderful home. Thank you for thinking of me and inviting me on this day. It was good to feel like a bird in the treetops and also to walk through the fallen leaves to the goat. The children are such dear people and I still think that your home should have many more of them. Not only just two children should be in all this.
>
> I am glad that papa is there too.
> God bless you and your loved ones and your trees and your new basement.
>
> Love and thanks,
> *Frenchie*

Romolo and Giovanna on the beach at the shack, fall, 1965.
Photo by Alice Palmer

Frenchie's shack continued to be our magic refuge, particularly in the early days of fall. It was our annual festivity, and all of us, especially the children, made a great event out of commandeering the comestibles, the bedding, and the games to journey to that wild and beautiful shore that was so imbued with adventure, and to engage, once more, in the great challenge of living completely in

Frenchie's Shack Interior October 4, 1964. *Photo by Arthur Cohen*

Frenchie, Sal, and Giovanna at the shack on my birthday, October 4, 1964. *Photo by Arthur Cohen*

nature. Everything went with us for two weeks, our Labrador retriever Orfeo included, of course.

As the days moved on through 1964 and 1965, there were many gatherings and celebrations at the shack with family and friends, which annually included a party on my birthday, October 4. Even so, the ongoing dilemma that was developing concerning the status of the shacks was always in the background. The ominous specter of a gathering cloud of insecurity was constantly on my mind, and it became increasingly difficult to set aside that sense of a sudden knock on the fragile door of Frenchie's shack, in metaphor, at least. It was never completely absent, even through the distant and lulling sound of the surf.

Once again, the necessary reiteration of the legal and ongoing property rights of the dune residents had to be forcefully stated. The attorney for the Great Beach Cottage Owners Association Robert L. Meade wrote a letter to Superintendent Robert Gibbs on November 23, 1964, in which he presented a full list of property owners whom he represented, giving the description of the property, location, and plan dates. Within a week, he also addressed a letter to Jefts G. Beede regarding claims of ownership by his clients on portions of Beede's land within the Park, putting him on notice that "any steps taken in derogation of their claims of ownership will be strenuously resisted, etc." In the last days of August 1965, Cochairman of the GBCOA Andrew Fuller sent a three-page statement to the Secretary of the Interior Stewart Udall, which thoroughly outlined the case for the home owners on the Great Outer Beach, suggesting that their rights should not become "mere legal fiction." He also asseverated that, if the National Park Service broke faith with the home owners of Cape Cod, it would affect conservation efforts elsewhere. Finally, his long presentation requested that the cottage owners on the Great Outer Beach be given certificates of suspension from condemnation without delay. [17] No reply came from Secretary Udall's office, but from Superintendent Gibbs, the standard polite but repeated declension was sent. It stated that "the dwelling and the land must be in the same ownership," completely sidestepping the issue of the ongoing process of the cottage owners to establish their claim of squatter's rights on the Beede land, which was scheduled to come under eminent domain. The controversy over Beede's claim and the claims of the cottage owners would remain in limbo for the next two years.

Frenchie, however, continued her way of life with typical aplomb and a disregard for fate. In late August 1965, she ordered the bulldozing of a mountain of sand from the entrance to her shack and, once more, for the last time, Warren "Pinky" Silva, always accommodating, appeared to do her bidding, good genie that he was. From my journal:

> Today, I drove Frenchie to the dunes, our errand was to bulldoze our beloved shack and clear it of the impending tidal wave of sand. This we did with a great deal of trepidation (on my part). Now it is clear for some years and Frenchie is ecstatic.

A following entry ensues closely on the above:

> Another trip to the dunes saw Frenchie her old self again rebuilding the porch area of the shack, literally, with bare hands, tucking the sand in with fingers and pulling off boards without a hammer. We worked on the floor together like "dune rats" as she says.

Frenchie's Old Shack by Salvatore Del Deo 1964; oil on canvas, 16" x 26"

On August 25, 1965, I was at the shack with the children on one of the last perfect days of summer:

> Romolo, Gigi, and I spent the night at the shack after Marie, Tom, Sal, Fran, and Dot took us out. The whole day was completely idyllic. The children were such a joy, entering into the beauty of the situation, walking along the beach to say "goodnight" to the sun and rolling down the hill of sand with great glee. I told

Jo at the shack, 1965.
Photo by Salvatore Del Deo

them stories of my childhood under the stars and tucked them into a bunk in the little room together. The light lit and turned down, the distant surf seemed to be walking through my sleep. In the morning, we spotted a school of tuna, and the children were delighted to see them so close...Instant mashed potato pancakes for breakfast made an instant hit. They ate them, loaded with jam. Now I long to spend more days here. Started and nearly finished:

One Last Day Before the Summer

The sunning sand slips with the insistent wind,
Sliding to sanctuary in the quiet grass.
Roots, satiate with such sweet heat, incite to purpose
The tasseled triumph of their summer days.
Here where I lie, both hands to sea, the other parts
of me extended toward heaven,
Rose hips' crowding green low-screens
the single sum of my identity
The bee, close-droning, circles down upon
One rose straying to September.
He alone, pirating the promise of her cup,
Has lightly gathered in the season's treasure.

CHAPTER IV

Troubled Times

1966–1971

THE DEDICATION OF the Cape Cod National Seashore did not occur until 1966, when, on May 30, the combined domain of the Province Lands and the Pilgrim Spring State Park were officially turned over to the Federal Government from the Commonwealth of Massachusetts by Governor John Volpe. In presenting the deeds of the Commonwealth to the Director of the National Park Service, George B. Hartzog, Jr., Volpe cited the late President Kennedy's delight and renewal in walking the shores of Cape Cod. "It will forever be a memorial to him," he said. In receiving the deeds, Director Hartzog called the area preserved "the finest jewel of the nation's natural and cultural heritage." "Here," he said, "we may see the process that shaped our earth. The whole range of our history is spread forth in the National Park system." Senator Edward Kennedy returned to the famous words of Thoreau when he took the podium: "But the shore will never be more attractive than it is now. A man may stand here and put all the world behind him." Senator Leverett Saltonstall, co-sponsor of the bill to create the Seashore, noted that the late president was "particularly pleased to sign it into law," and observed that, with all the achievements of space exploration and the search of the ocean's depths, man "still needs the gift of wonder at what he sees."[1]

As the ceremony advanced formally through the official speakers, Representative Hastings-Keith, who had assisted the late president and Senator Saltonstall in drafting the legislation, pointed out that many who came to Washington for the hearings on the legislation were opposed to it. At this point, Ross and I turned to each other with wry smiles, recalling the fears of many Cape Codders who had regarded the establishment, with some dismay, as taking away the essential charm and independence of the communities through an inundation of tourist visitation. Keith then paused to introduce the first superintendent of the Seashore Robert F. Gibbs to whom he gave high praise for the caliber and character of his leadership saying: "All of the Cape benefitted from his guiding hand."

Shortly thereafter, Lemuel Garrison, Regional Director of the Park Service, acting as Master of Ceremonies, introduced other officials and guests on the platform, including Lieutenant Governor Elliot Richardson, Massachusetts Natural Resources Director Charles H.W.Foster, and Public Works Director Francis W. Sargent, who would later become governor of Massachusetts. When, at last, he introduced Superintendent Gibbs,

Senator Edward Kennedy speaking at the dedication of the Cape Cod National Seashore Park, May 30, 1966. *Photo by Paul Koch*

Secretary of Interior Stewart Udall giving the keynote address at the dedication of the Cape Cod National Seashore Park, May 30, 1966. *Photo by Paul Koch*

the audience broke into spontaneous applause, not only for the job that Gibbs had done to coalesce and unite the disparate elements of the new park within his domain and to lead it forward with an effort of fairness and equanimity, but in heartfelt sympathy for the loss of his nineteen-year-old son who had died a week prior to the dedication of the Park.

The poetry of the day, however, was left to Secretary of the Interior Stewart Udall:

> Now, at a later hour, we turn to this landscape to support and renew other values. We who have chopped and mined and built and machined our way to wealth and power, now grope out from our cities, puzzled, yearning, almost wistful, for something we cannot forget. Beyond the noise and the asphalt and ugly architecture, we yearn for the long waves and the beach grass; we see white wings on the morning air, and in the afternoon, the shadows cast by the doorways of history.

As I listened, I could not help recalling Ross's letter about the "yearning for the sight of a wild swan."

Udall went on to quote President Johnson: "A modern highway may wipe out the equivalent of a fifty-acre park with every mile. And people move out from the city to get closer to nature only to find that nature has moved farther from them." Secretary Udall finished with a return to the late President Kennedy's remarks:

> It was part of his conservation policy that a father should be able to show his children—all children—the wonders of nature he himself had known. The marshes, the seascape, the sea itself should remain inviolate for all time, for all men," he said. Then he ended with the firm admonition that: "This is our only world; if we care, it is our duty to love it.[2]

Ross, Sal, and I sat in the full sunshine of a bright and promising afternoon and remarked between ourselves about the plaudits that were being lavished on the various dignitaries on the podium, even upon some who had been latecomers to the cause and a very few who had had nothing to do with the creation of the Park whatsoever or who had failed to make a decision when it mattered. This recurring phenomenon in political life did not occupy our minds for long, however, as we basked in the knowledge of what had been accomplished and in the certainty that we would not be the last to share this exceptional place with Cassandra's slate-colored junco and the ever-blooming dune rose.

As the season advanced to summer, we partook, once again, with a sense of relief and a palpable expansion of our spirits, of the renewal of life at the shack.

From my journal:

June 9, 1966:

Sal took Frenchie out to the dunes this morning, and I went to pick her up. The water was cerulean blue, exquisite, bright, and clear. It was the first time I had ever seen terns' eggs. They lay in little piles of two and three scattered all over the beach—lovely, speckled eggs. We posted the nests as best we could with sticks to prevent sand buggies from running over them. The dune dwellers make it their spring duty, like a good Catholic saying his daily rosary—out they go to look for the eggs and mount the driftwood ramparts against careless fate.

July 27, 1966:

We had a true water testing today at the shack as we finally, after many years, got the old union off the pipe and put in a new pump. The joy in Frenchie's face was so astonishingly happy that I shall never forget it. She did everything but stand on her head. Indeed, we were all so pleased that we drank gallons of clear water, which we took turns pumping to be sure there was no sand left. Frenchie had just about given up on her well. Now, we can all rest assured that water will continue forever. What a beautiful thing water is. I can't think of anything more worthy of celebration.

Saturday, September 17, 1966:

We readied ourselves early to partake of the heady elixir of the dunes. Now we rushed to get to our little palace. The children were excited this time, probing us with questions and packing their playthings. Now, at last, the marvelous privilege and the joy of being there is part of them too. We stayed and drank in the sun which warmed us all to the cool bones of us who had languished behind hot but sunless stove and door, no more restaurant. Sal is recovering by doing nothing, although I can't relax as he does since I have inherited the disease of the ant, constant industry, but I managed in my own way to relax. The open sea before us has begun our fall "cure."

October 2, 1966:

On the dunes again today for my birthday. How privileged I am. The queen of queens in my palace overlooking the largest gem in the world and, at the same time, basking in the sun of my family's love and regard. There with me, too, were my dear friends, Joan and Tony Pereira, Phyllis and Izzy Sklar, and Arthur Cohen, and, of course, Victor De Carlo. Each one sharing in the joy of my special day. Sal had cooked a typically superb sauce for the rigatoni. Then, with little trouble, we broiled our steaks outdoors on the grill. Pictures were taken as always. The Dutch-cleanser-girl routine: Tony taking pictures of Arthur taking pictures of us. We placed a long piece of driftwood on the edge of the dune overlooking the sea, and it was finer than the Hotel Statler. Beach stones held everything down that needed holding, but nothing held down our spirits. The day was consumed all too quickly, and we squeezed ourselves into the buggy with regret.

The dunes have been especially precious this year. We have been out numerous times, but always it hasn't been enough to quench the great thirst for the sea and the solitude and peace of that holy place. Somehow, the worries and concerns of life that increasingly entangle one are never truly untangled anywhere else. Only there in the most marvelous of all human abodes can the mind wash itself clean. May such a spot endure forever.

Now that the Park was dedicated with proper speeches and celebration, one could sense that the intense heat of unrelenting controversy and the unsettling days and nights that had been required to bring such a thing to pass were behind us and the functional elements of a new historic entity were beginning to fall into place. At the turn of the page, however, there was an ever increasing darkness that threatened to eclipse this momentary sunshine of success. My journal is layered with entries concerning the war in Vietnam, and we were receiving letters from our friends, also greatly preoccupied with the war. Arthur Cohen wrote to us about the New York City protest demonstration. His letter was a striking portrait of the extent of the disquiet, which went on for what seemed an eternity, until its sorrows were superficially spent and the consequences officially buried, but not the ghosts of the conflict which continued to renew themselves and to emerge in our society for decades. In 1966, however, the war was steadily escalating, driving the young to paroxysms of protest everywhere. My diary entries became darker the following year

February 26, 1967:

We have started to mine small waterways in N. Vietnam and to shell heavily from warships in Tonkin Bay. This is unprecedented escalation of the war and can only lead to new disaster.

June 5 ll, 1967:

The Arab-Israeli War has come and gone leaving nothing but broken bodies and hopes in its wake. The peace is uneasy, and the long-awaited dreams of some kind of negotiations between Jews and Arabs is farther away than ever.

Then, for a brief moment on August 2, 1967, a ray of bright sunshine broke through the series of dark events with the appearance of Pete Seeger in a concert sponsored by the Provincetown Music Festival. It was momentous in a number of ways, for Pete symbolized, on the international stage, the protest against the war in Vietnam. My journal describes his visit in part:

Pete Seeger's visit was a success in every way. Knowing he was coming, we exerted ourselves to get hold of Loring Russell and his brother Anthony and Frank Aresta to play with him at the town hall. They were most cooperative and, I think, rather pleased to be asked. We arranged to entertain Pete and his family at dinner at the restaurant. The entire guest list included nine people: Pete's family plus Mr. & Mrs. Granach and the Hawthornes (Joe and Hazel). During the dinner, Pete got to talking about Mr. Brito's Portuguese bread and composed a song on the spot, which he sang at the concert. He is a gaunt man—looks a little threadbare at close range, but is very commanding and gentle. One can readily see that his wife Toshi engineers everything for him. The life of an entertainer, even one as full of integrity as Pete's, is the twisted life of unreality. His real life is with his banjo on the stage with a full audience; that was quite clear as he brought down the house with thunderous applause. A thousand people crowded the hall. After the concert, we bid Pete and his family farewell, and they gave us an album which Pete autographed.

In the late summer of 1967, the U.S. House of Representatives appropriated $400,000 to begin construction of a Harbor of Refuge for Provincetown. This made definite the location of the Harbor of Refuge in the central area of the town wharf and definitely eliminated the possibility that the area behind the West End Breakwater would ever be violated. The chairman of the Harbor of Refuge Committee, our good friend, the Rev. Ernest Vanderburgh of St. Mary of the Harbor, announced the action and assured the community that the project would be instituted after Senate passage of the bill. This announcement gave Ross Moffett and the rest of us the final closure of our fight to save the entirety of the Province Lands, for now we were certain that the West End marshes and clam flats would never be intruded upon and that, in a few years' time, the land that had been placed in some jeopardy would go back to its proper place as a part of the Province Lands to be preserved in perpetuity.[3] There was a general sigh of relief all around. The fishermen had their much-needed marina at last, the town had been given back its clam flats, and the Park would officially receive the entirety of the Province Lands, all in a breathless reprieve.

Also in the summer of 1967, Sal would become hugely involved in the effort by the Provincetown Art Association to establish a new and forward-looking program in the arts, which became known as The Fine Arts Work Center. He had just been appointed as first vice president to take the place of the retiring Ross Moffett. Ross, who had given that organization vital life support all those years, had determined to step down from his twenty-eight years as an officer of some sort at the Art Association. In taking his place, Sal brought the same kind of dedicated commitment to the position and introduced a number of new endeavors, in addition to the initiation of the Work Center. One of these was the institution of a children's program for the school children in grades one to six in the Lower Cape community, designed to give them an early opportunity to be introduced to art. These classes, which he had established in 1965, became hugely popular and were continued for fifteen weeks each winter from 1965 to 1971. In this same period, Sal and I worked diligently and continually to rally support for the proposed Fine Arts Work Center, which would establish a kind of master program to identify and assist serious artists in their early career years and to give them the advantage of working space and the even more valuable gift of time to develop, free of financial pressures. The story of the Fine Arts Work Center grew to unforeseen and immense proportions in the following years, but in those early days of 1967, when the first program of the Work

Center was initiated, Sal gave unstintingly of himself to help bring it into being. Again, the Reverend Ernest Vanderbugh was enlisted in this worthy cause and became its appointed Director of Development in September, 1967.[4]

As a consequence of all this activity, which proceeded on a daily basis without respite, the October days of 1967 arrived to sooth the heated pace of summer and offer us the annual solace of successive days at the shack:

October 22, 1967:
The family had dinner on the dunes today. It was sunny and warm. We enjoyed the splendid peace, I took a walk (the rest played ball), slept and read. I finished "George Holnes and the Telephone," a poem I had been working on a year...

October 28, 1967:
On Tuesday, we all went out on the dunes together for a longer sojourn, and how marvelous it always is again out there. I spent several hours making beds and getting supper, unpacking and doing all the necessaries, while Romolo tried the kite that Arthur had made for him. What a beautiful kite; it was like a huge moth! The individuality of everything Arthur does is such a joy. After supper, Sal and Romi played games while I finished making the beds. Between candle and lamps, there was enough illumination for all our little cozy world and more. The plastic over the windows rattled and the mice worked on the walls, but the other noises of soft surf and shifting sand were enveloping sounds to soothe the senses.

Sal painting a large canvas on the beach, October 1967

The next morning, the children went to school. Sal took them in at an early hour. The sun came up as it does nowhere else on earth. I gave Orfeo a run, poor blind animal, and he loved it. I worked the better part of the day finishing the play which I have just calmly relegated to the ash heap. The sun was warm, and I am very satisfied just to be working. Sal painted away at a large canvas (4' x 6') outside on the dunes overlooking the beach.

As the afternoon wore on, the children, plus Arthur and Victor, arrived from town. What a silly, wonderful time we had together! Arthur managed to get the kite in the air much to the amusement of all, and Victor, in his comical way, pitched ball fast and furiously. After a good hitting session, it came time for the hors d'oeuvres. We opened a bottle of Chablis outdoors and a can of sardines and a box of milk crackers. To this, Arthur added peanut butter and cheese to make it a total gourmet's nightmare. As Orfeo would sit down in the middle of everything, we had great trouble getting organized. Victor spilled the sardine oil in Arthur's wine; Arthur spilled the cheese on the sand, which Orfeo promptly polished off, and, in general, it appeared that it was Orfeo who was having the cocktail party and not us.

Sal painting on the dunes with Orfeo keeping watch, summer, 1967

By dusk, we were ready to head for a party at the Gregory's. The party was tumultuous and happy. Adelaide had baked two pies and a ham and had concocted a potato salad and other goodies. She takes the lid off and wheels freely through everything. John was tipsy and feeling no pain as he navigated precariously, but Adelaide ignored his behavior completely. After dinner, she pounded out some good, old "singables," and everyone joined in the fun. Victor did a fast-stepping routine, Tony played the harmonica. Everybody sang, and Arthur pounded his knee with glee. At 11:00 p.m., we headed back to the dunes for the night, taking Mewsy with us. We settled in comfortably at the shack after an uneasy ride out. Next day, I kept the children out of school and with us at the dunes. "Who knows what the weather would be" was my logic. Never trade a beautiful day at hand for one to come. So, there we were; the children played and gave us a puppet show outdoors. Sal painted. I wrote. We took long walks, played ball and, finally, sat outside to roast the hamburgers over a charcoal fire. We came home in the dark, the sound of the surf remaining with us all the way. [5]

The situation pertaining to the status of the dune shacks began to be critical in the summer of 1967, sparked by an unlooked-for and ominous event in the late spring of that year. The shack of artist Tony Vevers and his family in the Pilgrim Spring area of the Seashore was discovered to have been burned to the ground. The outrage of the Vevers family and of the Great Beach Cottage Owners Association was put into clear terms in a letter by the attorney for the GBCOA Robert L. Meade, on July 14, 1967, to ranger Richard Strange, who had been identified as the person who had burned the shack:

> I want, by this letter, to put you on notice of something that I am sure you, as a responsible government official already know, namely, that the Great Beach Cottage Owners Association will not tolerate any acts on the part of the Park Service or acts caused by them that derogate from the ownership rights of the members, and due to the unfortunate Vevers situation, I would expect that you would indicate in writing that hence forth, at any rate, the rights of such owners will be fully respected.

A written assurance from Richard Strange never materialized, so the GBCOA members quickly addressed the Seashore Advisory Commission requesting a meeting with them to discuss the matter which was arranged for August 4, 1967. Present at that meeting were Hazel Hawthorne Werner, Dr. Nathaniel Champlin, and Margaret (Peg) Watson. They presented a formal Statement to the Commission which contained the following:

> We have reason to believe that the building was burned down after an evaluation of the building itself and/or the use of which the building was put. Accordingly, we believe that there are criteria, reasons or bases for the act, and that these are not available, either to Mr. Vevers or to the GBCOA.

Indeed, the whole episode was never properly explained. Even though the Seashore Advisory Commission expressed sympathy, officials of the Park Service who attended the meeting were evasive and defensive, according to the members of the GBCOA present.

The circumstances surrounding the burning of the Vevers cottage were fully elucidated by Tony Vevers himself in a letter to attorney Samuel Angoff, who succeeded attorney Robert Meade in representing the membership of the GBCOA in 1969. They bear reviewing, briefly, for the shocking truth was that all aspects of respect and observance of the law, which should have been applied in this case, were violated by the Cape Cod National Seashore.

> Every winter the building was broken into, used or vandalized. From June 1964 to September 1966, the cottage was used by us, Geise and Douglas. In 1966, Doug bought a jeep. It was in June 1967, going out in Doug's jeep, we discovered the shack had been burned down... I used to write my address, phone number, etc., on a shingle next to the door handle for the Park's reference in case someone needed to get hold of me. [6]

The result of this official confrontation with the Seashore in regard to the burning of the Vevers cottage without any apparent attempt to contact Vevers or to notify him that such an action was contemplated and why, put every member of the GBCOA on red alert. Not only were the "troubled times" of the 1960s having a direct impact on the vulnerability of the shacks from random vandalism, but now, it appeared that the most deadly fear of all—that of burning—was not just a possibility due to careless intrusion from vagrants, but the dune cottages were also in jeopardy from acts of the Cape Cod National Seashore personnel, those who were designated as protectors of the territory and of the habitations and residents located within its domain. It was at this point, in November 1967, that attorney Robert L. Meade requested of Assistant Attorney O. S. Sughrue, Jr., of the Department of the Interior Land Acquisition Office, that the Secretary's authority to acquire property by condemnation be suspended for his clients. George H. Thompson, Land Acquisition Officer, sent Meade the requested forms, which were entitled: "Application for Certificate of Suspension of Condemnation of Improved Property."

The full measure of evasion, regarding the protection of the shacks, now began in earnest. A month later, in December 1967, the condemnation case of E. Bennett Beede et al appeared on the docket of the Park's acquisition proceedings. U.S. Attorney Paul F. Markham requested that Thompson act upon the request for Certificates of Suspension of Condemnation of Improved Property at once, so that the condemnation of the large Beede tract could proceed.[7] The government then deposited $117,900 into the Registry of Court in anticipation of the Beede settlement on December 20, 1967. Subsequently, on April 22, 1968, attorney Robert L. Meade filed "answers" for his clients as defendants in the case, and, by the end of the year, filed a motion to enlarge the time in which "discovery" was to be completed to May 5, 1969. Even though there were varied responses and conditions to be considered in each case, no such attention to variations of settlement were given, except to issue either a "straight" condemnation action" or an "action to quiet title." Stipulations were provided later, under which the conditions varied, but the legal basis for condemnation had been universal. It had become a "one case fits all" approach, so that the entire group could be swept into a containment framework and dispatched. On June 3, 1969, attorney Robert L. Meade retired as counsel for the Great Beach Cottage Owners Association, and, on August 22,1969, attorney Samuel E. Angoff took his place.[8]

It is quite reasonable to say that, with the loss of attorney Robert L. Meade, the continuity of commitment to the interests of the GBCOA was vastly diminished. At the head of the Association, however, was the formidable Andrew Fuller who, together with the capable co-chairman Nicholas Wells, filled, with remarkable prescience and consistent dedication, the efficient counsel in legal matters that Meade had provided. Fuller's inspired leadership and his able mind, which dissected every situation with clarity, determination, and foresight, gave cohesion and strength to the organization. It was Fuller who phrased the positions adopted by the Association with directness, purpose, and continuing resolve. His principles were never vague and his forward momentum was unhesitating. In a true sense, the survival of the dune cottages at Peaked Hill Bars rested in his hands during the years between 1962 and his last active participation in the fall of 1977. He died in 1981. Andrew Fuller astutely interpreted many Department of the Interior maneuvers, and his constant correspondence, not only with the legal representation of the GBCOA, but with its entire membership, was prompt and minutely attentive to the issues at hand. The Archives of the Great Beach Cottage Owners Association provide a lasting tribute to his leadership.

On November 13, 1967, my journal noted:

> Our fourteenth wedding anniversary today. We prepared, in a quiet way, to celebrate the occasion as a family, no friends or fanfare. The children went to school as usual. Frenchie called early and asked if we wouldn't go to the dunes with her for a last trip to take care of barricading the shack for winter. We agreed, naturally. We took Arthur, as Sal wanted to secure some large timbers for the uprights on his new deck at the restaurant. There we all were, heading out on a beautiful morning, much like the day we were married, to our back shore. Frenchie was wearing a traditional fantasy of clothing: a pair of winter galoshes, corduroy pants that looked like they would fit Jackie Gleason, pinned at the middle and with the fly unzipped. Her dog "Noonie" went along too. After wrestling with sand and a few old doors, Sal and Arthur took off to the beach to scavenge for timbers. Frenchie and I were left to our own devices. We manfully boarded over the bedroom windows with fish crates, nailed tight the front shutters and heaved doors in place until the boys came back for lunch. I had taken the previous night's fried chicken, and it naturally tasted like the best chicken we had ever eaten. With many a "heave-ho," the boys finally wrenched the pump loose from her mooring, and she came home with us to be stored safely for winter. It's always a sad business coming in on that last trip from the dunes. It was such a fine day, however, that we were somewhat assuaged.

Frenchie in her fantasy of clothing, November 13, 1967. *Photo by Arthur Cohen*

Frenchie, Jo, Sal and "Noonie" boarding up the shack, November 13, 1967. *Photos by Arthur Cohen*

Arthur sat on the back, putting his full weight on the timbers so they wouldn't roll off the deep end. It was a mighty heavy load, but we made it.

In the final months of 1967, the deadly war in Vietnam had its counterpart on the home front on a diurnal basis. We were learning too late that the aggressor pays twice, once with the actual dead and a second time with the living dead. Years after the events initiating the Vietnam War, it could hardly have been foreseen how much and how long the youth of America would pay the awful price of a preemptive and fruitless conflict in Vietnam. The underworld of the drug culture, which flourished in the 1960s, most especially as part of the anti-war protest, took hold and took root and became a toxic by-product of the era. Long after "agent orange" had destroyed the rice fields of Vietnam and poisoned its people, the drugs America had begun to incorporate into its life style, affecting the behavior of the young generation of the 1960s and beyond, would continue to plague and vitiate our society. The "troubled times" of the year 1967 were as nothing, however, compared to the deadly year that followed—1968.

As the year drew to a close, the drumbeat of the Vietnam War kept up its rhythmic undertone to all domestic events. Each day brought troubling news and underlined, in bold newsprint, the horrors and the insanity of the war. It was a seemingly hopeless cause, that of peace, but thousands still prayed. Senator Eugene McCarthy's bid for the presidency infused hope into the mix of despair, and for a brief moment, before the double assassinations of Martin Luther King, Jr., and Senator Robert Kennedy covered the nation in darkness, there was a light at the end of the tunnel.

On March 31, 1968, President Lyndon Johnson exited the stage and not long after Johnson's announcement that he would retire from the presidential race, the April 2 primary in Wisconsin revealed that the new kid on the block, Senator Eugene McCarthy, was on his way to rolling up a significant presence among the electorate. His numbers at the polls, fifty-seven percent as opposed to Johnson's thirty-five percent, seemed to indicate the seriousness of his candidacy. The country was galvanized by his quiet, intelligent leadership in opposition to the Vietnam War. On April 3, Hanoi took up

Washington's offer for peace talks. Then, on April 4, Martin Luther King, Jr., was assassinated. These events followed each other with lightning speed and left the nation gasping for breath. So much was at stake, so few were the venues for reprieve, and so deadly was the whole game. We had been catapulted into the second act of a three-act tragedy, the third act yet to come. The face of the nation was awash with tears, for the leadership which had defined the decade of the advancement of civil rights had been struck down. Forces to replace him were several, but none so committed to non-violence in the long term and none with the quality of hope that King emanated. Martin Luther King's death dramatically emphasized that the more insoluble and open-ended war was at home, perhaps, and not in Vietnam.

McCarthy continued at a measured pace—not a spectacular surge, but a steady accumulation of support. As the California primary approached on June 4, the meteoric rise of Robert Kennedy in the presidential race seemed certain to affect McCarthy's chances for the nomination, largely because of the great pull among black Americans, for one thing, and, of course, because of the very palpable ghost image of former President John Kennedy presenting his younger brother to carry on in his place. As the results of the voting began to fill in the percentages—forty-seven percent for Kennedy and forty-two percent for McCarthy, the momentum was obvious. Americans fully expected to wake up and welcome Robert Kennedy as the winner in California. The next morning, however, the chaos in the ballroom of the Ambassador Hotel in Los Angeles greeted the nation instead. Kennedy had been killed by Sirhan Sirhan, a Palestinian with Jordanian citizenship, and the country was once again in shock and mourning.

Not much in this assassination fitted the pattern we had previously witnessed in the assassinations of John F. Kennedy and Martin Luther King. In Robert Kennedy's death, one might see something in retrospect that we failed to note at the time. Hugh Downs phrased it then in larger terms: "There is a virulent anti-humanist element at work in our country."[9] Speculating on that fact now, with the benefit of hindsight regarding the war in Iraq and the cataclysmic experience of 9/11, we might easily confirm Downs's international perspective. The momentum for McCarthy continued, however. Now, more than ever, it became apparent that he represented the only real hope for the country at this crucial and terrible crossroad. Artists everywhere contributed their art to auctions for McCarthy and, in Provincetown, particularly, there was a great groundswell of this type of activity. At our restaurant, Sal's Place, for instance, we sponsored an auction which was well attended. My journal during these several days reads:

July 4, 1968:

Provincetown was treated to another visit and a concert by Pete Seeger. On this occasion, Pete brought his sloop *Clear Water* with him, and she was magnificent: a vessel that measures seventy-five feet overall length and twenty-five feet or so across her beam. She has a stick one hundred and six feet tall and that is a mast to behold. Pete was letting everyone aboard as she lay tied up at the end of the "T" at the pier. The sloop is a monumental piece of craftsmanship. The gaff rig of the sail is a replica of that on the old Hudson River sloops that used to transport goods up and down the Hudson. She steers by tiller just like the old boats and is rigged with dead-eyes instead of pulleys. Just the hoops alone on the mast are enough to impress. Pete was there, a little vague and seemingly dreaming as he always appears. His mind is never taken up with the mundane but with something illusory in a dream beyond him. He talks over the heads of the "present;" however,

Senator Eugene McCarthy and Sal talking politics at Sal's Place, July 5, 1968 (artist Victor De Carlo in lower right corner). *Photo by Francis Iacono*

on the stage, his personality is far more immediate and vital. He isn't meant to cope with individuals, only with audiences. Everyone here hopes his project is a real success and that the Hudson does indeed become clear again."

July 5, 1968:
Pete's concert was a fantastic success. The house was packed. His singers were very impressive, and no one minded the fact that Pete sang very little due to laryngitis. I had my mother and Jim in tow, and we sat in the balcony. At the very end of the concert, Freddy Hemley tapped me on the shoulder and said that McCarthy was in the restaurant. I nearly stood straight up, as if shot. I grabbed Tommy and the children and dashed out. The kids eventually stayed, but Tommy joined me and we ran (almost) all the way back. We missed him by about seven minutes. It was an historic miss, believe me, and one I deeply regret, everyone else had a chance to see him and shake hands and talk with him.

While America was struggling to right itself after Robert Kennedy's assassination, it was presented with the option to elect a president more securely focused against the Vietnam War on one side and one more fully committed to it on the other. Eugene McCarthy's candidacy and his convention delegates were losing ground to George McGovern, who had been selected to replace Robert Kennedy by his former delegates, and Hubert Humphrey's clique in Chicago finally destroyed the entire Democratic convention, the violence and tenor of the event sullying the sense of a civilized election process to the present day. When the results were sorted out, Richard Nixon stepped across the divide of the Democratic Party's disarray and united the country behind him. The war in Vietnam would stagger through another four years.

As in the case of the dark penumbra of events steadily moving toward unresolved policies and problems on the national scene, the dune cottages at Peaked Hill Bars entered the year bracing for a storm of controversy over their status. The first sign of trouble was a communication from ranger Richard Strange to Nicholas Wells, seeking information regarding his cottage. Wells responded with legal background information on the cottage owned by him and his wife, Ray Wells, but the information was sent through the GBCOA attorney Robert L. Meade. Andrew Fuller wrote immediately to attorney Meade on February 6, 1968: "As long as the Park remains at arm's length in this controversy, we see no reason to give them any information." Grace Bessay wrote to Meade in the same vein, i.e., that the Park Service should first give the cottage owners suspension from condemnation before requesting their history, etc. With great promptitude, Fuller rebuffed the request for information directed to him, of course, and advised members of the GBCOA to do the same, fearing that any information given the Seashore would be used against their case to establish legal status.[10]

For a full year thereafter, very little is in the archive to suggest that there had been any significant information on the shacks provided to the Park Service. In February 1969, however, the Park began to request that the individual cottage owners sign special use permits dated from January 1, 1969, to December 31, 1971. This prompted Co-chairman Fuller to issue one of his inimitable warnings entitled "After the Calm the Storm," urging the membership of the GBCOA not to sign such special use permits. In one of the last communications from their attorney Robert L. Meade on May 24, 1969, the members of the Association were also warned that: "In the present form of the permit, I would not advise any owner to sign." Meade's always-informed advice would soon be denied the organization he had faithfully served for seven years, as his resignation was pending, due to a conflict of interest in relation to a new position as a legal assistant in the preparation of consumer legislation for the federal government. His resignation would presage a serious breach in the standing dyke against overwhelming pressure from the National Park Service to eliminate the cottages at Peaked Hill Bars.

By July 1969, Co-chairman Andrew Fuller had issued a lengthy bulletin to the membership listing eighteen reasons why they should not sign the special use permits. Fuller knew that this moment in the progression of the evolving history of the dune cottages was crucial to their survival, and the review of his reasoned approach in the pursuit of a successful conclusion to the overall salvation of the habitation of the dune dwellers at Peaked Hill Bars reads as logically today as it did then. Had the membership stayed firmly together in the pursuit of the issues, many would not have lost rights to their cottages and, finally, might have made the case that Grace Bessay made twenty years later, after twenty-four years of litigation. The appetite for that kind of persistence, however, began to dwindle noticeably after the retirement of attorney Meade, and there seemed little that Fuller could do to shore up resolve on the part of some individual dune dwellers. At a meeting of the GBCOA on July 12, 1969, Grace Bessay was appointed treasurer to replace Sunny Tasha, who had resigned from the Association the previous year. A month after this meeting, Theodore and Eunice Braaten also resigned from the Association, and the handwriting on the wall began to appear as a palimpsest of earlier struggle and despair. Many members, however, did respond positively to Fuller's plea and refused to sign the special use permits with forthright resistance, as in the letter of October 7, 1969, to the Department of the Interior from Jean Cohen Burns and Donald Burns, which stated their position of resistance without equivocation.

In the meantime, the Park had continued to press the dune dwellers to cooperate in the matter of providing information for special permits. On September 16, 1969, the Seashore's new Superintendent Leslie P. Arnberger wrote to the new counsel for the GBCOA, Sanuel Angoff, requesting compliance from his clients and referring to the complications presented by condemnation action against E. Bennett Beede. Angoff's reply to Arnberger on October 8, 1969, again brought the matter of the dwellings destroyed by fire, as referenced in Meade's letter to ranger Richard Strange on July 14, 1967, specifically, concerning the cottage of Tony Vevers and "two other dwellings destroyed by fire in the same year." This latter mention of "two other dwellings" was added by Angoff, and referred to cottages in Truro in the vicinity of High Head, later identified as the easternmost group of cottages in the "Dune Shacks of Peaked Hill Bars Historic District..." [11]

Superintendent Arnberger's candid reply, on October 20, 1969, to the protest of Angoff, contained no reference at all to the matter concerning the burning of the shacks, but did explicitly state the long-range plan of the Cape Cod National Seashore in reference to the dwellings on the Great Outer Beach: "A decision was reached to issue Special Use Permits to cover the continued use and occupancy of the structures on government land during the lifetime of the present occupants. etc." The final conclusion of Arnberger's exegesis on this matter ended with the very definitive statement that the Park was trying to determine "as to how best to secure their eventual removal."[12]

This, of course, was not the protection of "improved property" implied by the Cape Cod National Seashore's original legislative purpose, which fact had been endlessly invoked by the attorneys for the GBCOA and by the dune dwellers themselves and would be cited by subsequent legal examination. Firstly, the assumption that all the cottages were on government land was incorrect, as litigation and factual evidence could and did prove. Secondly, the matter of an "improved property" definition in relation to these dwellings on the outer beach was inapplicable. They uniformly existed without the amenities of civilization for provable and logical reasons and because of this fact, among other relative qualities, eventually qualified these unique dwellings for registration on the National Register of Historic Places. This determination of eligibility, which the Park Service fought energetically to obstruct, engaging in deception and outright denial of the facts, would be established twenty years later. For the moment, however, the government was free-wheeling through the annoying dilemma of a feisty group of individual claims to status on their pristine outer beach, always with the final result in mind of a clear view of the Atlantic Ocean minus the vestige of any human habitation. In spite of the adamant position of the Park, so clearly enunciated in Arnberger's letter of October 20, attorney Angoff patiently reiterated recurring discrepancies in the Park's interpretation of the legislation and pointed out that: "The matter of the previous destruction of dwellings has not been resolved. This is a serious matter and cannot be ignored." Not only had the burning of the Vevers cottage not been acknowledged officially, but the right to rebuild the dwelling had also been completely ignored. This was a structure which had a titled and recorded deed, which more than qualified it to be rebuilt.[12]

Sometime in the 1960s, a much-touted philosophy of land use within the Department of the Interior had come into vogue. This was known as the Leopold Report, which posited the idea of wilderness and land preservation based on a theory of land restoration to a kind of condition that would have evolved had Columbus not discovered America. Such a theory was somewhat tantamount to positing that one should consider the pure evolution of the indigenous Indian tribes as they would have evolved had not Cortes introduced the horse and the gun. One critic described such a theory as "metaphysical mush."[13] Then there was another theory that "natural regulations" would restore a wilderness balance, which assumed that parks visited by millions can actually be left alone. The truth is that no park can be isolated from the effect of civilization and when "left alone," therefore, they do not revert to pre-Columbian status. Our larger parks such as Yellowstone need huge acreage to maintain any kind of a pristine ecosystem and, even then, such systems often are impacted by factors outside as well as inside their boundaries. What decisions remain for the pseudoscientific theories to acknowledge is what President Johnson so wisely expressed, as quoted by Secretary of the Interior Stewart Udall on the day of the dedication of the Seashore: "People move out from the city to get closer to nature only to find that 'nature' has moved farther from them." We bring every ill of our society with us, no matter what we do or where we move. *The overarching philosophy must always focus on how little can we impact our environment and how sensibly can we live in it together with the rest of the flora and fauna of the planet.* Our earth is hugely polluted and impacted and no single piece of soil or infinitely small specimen is free of that impaction, but we must prevail, on a daily basis, in preserving what we can and in a way that teaches us *how to exist in nature and not apart from it as a constant philosophy of sustainable habitation on earth.*

November 17, 1969:
As the late fall days approached, Sal and I headed for Frenchie's shack to enjoy just a little more of the summer weather still prevailing and to bring in the pump. When we got out of the jeep, a young boy was standing at Frenchie's with a puppy. He was sort of grubby looking and, since one can easily become enraged at the population of young vandals which are continually despoiling the shacks, we quite naturally greeted him rather sharply. To his disclaimer that he was the person who had ripped off a side shutter to get water, we were not completely sympathetic, but as the questioning wore on, we managed to adjust our first harsh impression. He rather helpfully offered to give us a hand boarding everything further along toward winter readying and we soon learned his name was Shayne. His little pup kept biting our heels with teeth as sharp as needles, and we began to rather like them both. I warned him, after he admitted to occupying Sunny's shack that he might easily be arrested if he didn't have some proof of occupancy from Sunny for the rangers. He said he had had intentions of going to see her, but never got around to it. After inspecting his occupancy of Sunny's, which bore out his claim of care, we offered to take him into town and introduce him to Sunny. He agreed to come and brought his little puppy.

As we drove into town collecting wood and taking our time, a thread of his history unwound gradually. Having run away from home at twelve, he had experienced alienation from a mother and father who, at that time, had divorced. He joined a carnival, then wound up in reform school and subsequently visited all the tender citadels where boys who come from such tortured circumstances find themselves. He admitted to wanting only a piece of land he could call his own and seemed sincerely to love the dunes. His recent history was so fragmented, it was hard to make sense of it, but between a motorcycle accident, hepatitis, and the prospect of the draft in thirty days, he was not exactly a candidate for the future. We left him at Sunny's, feeling we had done a rather good deed for the day and wondering at the ravages of life.

November 18, 1969:
Since the weather was still remarkably mild, we ventured out to the shack with a basket of roast beef sandwiches. No sooner had we made obeisance to the sea and sand, than Shayne appeared. He was quite disturbed and informed us that his little puppy had been killed the day before, just after we left him. Evidently, the dog had gotten underneath a car at the wharf and the driver didn't see him. The visible evidence of sorrow was not the only thing that wrung our hearts. He abruptly got up after sitting with us in the shack for a while, blurting out, "He's the only thing I had." Neither Sal nor I found working easy after this, but we did manage to do something. Sal painted on the beach, and I walked a long way toward Charlie's shack. I kept turning over in my mind the parallel between this boy and Brian. Brian's death seemed a symbol of this type of tough, Irish kid—a stranger to outward tenderness, but very tender inside. They were of the same breed, although Brian had had superior intellectual capacities. As we worked quietly, Shayne dove into the November sea. Again, I thought of Brian and that physical confrontation which he always felt he had to make with the elements. At nineteen, one does nothing but prove oneself, or try to. Brian tried to prove himself once too often. I began to worry,somewhat, about Shayne, for Sal and I had both seemed to see something very good in him.

Walking the beach made me aware of the purity of these young boys, or men, really. So many thousands like them played out their destiny. I put together my thoughts in "Children of God." It was really a poem for Brian that I had long been unable to write. Now I saw Brian over again in Shayne and saw them both as the pure lambs being sacrificed so readily by an unfeeling world and an impartial fate. I was nonplused by the experience, but yet could not help but wonder what force or mystic power had dictated our coming and our contact with this child of nineteen. Checking at Sunny's before leaving, we found the hill where he had buried his dog. The epitaph was nailed to a topmast from some stranded vessel. It read: "Here lies my dog Otie. Please let him rest in peace."

Six months later on Mother's Day, the attempt to shelter one's soul at the shack temporarily brought us back to bile and not balm. The ongoing war in the dunes was not over.

May 10, 1970:
The weather remained beyond belief today. The thermometer rose to ninety degrees and everything hung limp, still, and sultry except that the smoky weather still had freshness, not like the August sultriness. With an impetus born of great desire to get to the dunes, we packed everything up early. I sautéed some chicken and Gigi wrapped up her cake as a surprise and we headed out. The sand was dry, very loose. It took three tries to get up the sand pit hill. We finally had to put the tires down to eight pounds. There were many people climbing up over the first dunes. It always reminds me of an ant hill crawling with insects. That is pretty close, after all, warm weather brings them out. "We knew what to expect when we arrived at the shack. Nothing is sacred out there now. The community of kids with packs on their backs moves like a swarm of locusts across the country. They keep coming in increasing numbers. Here, it is especially difficult to ignore them. They break

Dune roses near Frenchie's Shack, 1970

into every place, leave their droppings, and move on. What they destroy in their path is patience, tolerance, privacy, and any sense of rational order. They are dismayed, disengaged from society—both the good and the bad aspects of it. They are capable of understanding the ills, protesting, but then they retire to a vantage point of complete negation and indifference.

As we arrived, we noticed first that the birdhouse was down. My heart sank as I felt sure it had finally gone, but no, there it was leaning against the shack. The shack was open, naturally, and filthy. As soon as I began throwing gear out, four kids appeared wearing the traditional costume of just about nothing. Sal and I let them have it with a verbal onslaught. They understand very little of what you say, but it releases frustration.

Presently, two girls showed up in that old underwear sacking that epitomizes "real" style. As they persisted in saying that the place was pretty clean, we told them to get the hell out in no expanded terms. It was a sickening experience as it always is. Somehow, the spirit is broken out there now, the respect for a way of life, a concept, an ideal, a love for the place has been violated to such an extent that everything has become affected by it. Many old-timers say they won't go back anymore. Sitting on the edge of Frenchie's dune world, overlooking the sea, one wonders sometimes what is left for those of us who came here twenty, thirty, forty years ago or more. The world is inside and when the outlook so changes, one looks out at the sea, not with exhilaration, but with weariness. The outer landscape is unchanged, but the inner landscape is blighted and raped. If the artist can find no peace of mind, no solitude, his world is destroyed. He has to have this in order to create. At least, we do.

We restored order presently, and ate our excellent lunch outside. Giovanna's cake was a marvel of edibility. The kids were happy. We played ball and then

Romolo and I took a long walk on the beach. The water was ice cold. He and I skipped stones, but I nearly threw my elbow out trying to match a skill I once had. As the afternoon breeze cooled, we closed the place again, always an exercise in futility.

The day was lovely, after all, and Giovanna phrased her simple joy in a description she wrote for her school paper: "As soon as you come to the first stretch of dunes, you just look all around because there is so much sand and space that you can't believe it. The towering hills of sand look so stationary and immovable, but by tomorrow the wind could change their shape. The sand below your feet is warm from the sun's rays, and you have a strange feeling, as if you were out on the desert. The wind whistles past you and kicks up a wave of sand. Beyond, you can see the dune grass or beach grass bowing in the sand. The sun casts a shiny glance upon it and turns it to a greenish gold. Just over the top of the next hill, little, red rose hips can be seen in their protective bush. They thrive well on the dunes, and a delicious jam can be made from them. You now see that there is real life on these dunes. The hills are not so barren, but are more beautiful than you thought. They are like parapets enclosing the bounty which lies inside their walls." At thirteen, Giovanna's referencers were joyous and lasting.

CHAPTER V

Eugene O'Neill Doesn't Live Here Anymore

1971–1978

IN THE LATE fall, when the nights were clear and a modest new moon did not overwhelm the sky with a full effulgence, the stars displayed numerous identities to those who already knew them intimately. I, however, was not one of those privileged savants. I would elbow the screen door ajar and, throwing out supper dishwater, glance up with awe at the luminary arrangements, pausing to admire the few constellations I could identify with any consistency: the Pleiades, Orion's Belt and Cassiopeia's Chair. I would then run inside to pick up my circular chart, adjust it for month and time and proceed to hold it over my head to decide what new star from this universe I might possibly identify. This method of learning astronomy with a flashlight I do not recommend; it inevitably leads to immense frustration. After many years, I have added little or nothing to Cassiopeia's Chair, and I am left with the sad conclusion that my mother knew more about the constellations than I ever would, having actually studied astronomy at Wellesley College, and that I was doomed to celestial ignorance. When I was younger, it didn't matter that I could appreciate the stars in a planetarium incomparable at the edge of the sea on a night filled with a plethora of stars that were, doubtless, already extinct. That I could not access their immortal existence by mortal nomenclature was a recurring annoyance. Cassiopeia's Chair, therefore, remained one of the few comfortable fixtures in my night sky of visual orthodoxy, even though I learned later that Cassiopeia was not a very nice character.

In spite of this, Cassiopeia's Chair is the name I have given to the chair I use to contemplate the Atlantic Ocean and other immensities. It is as fundamental a chair as the constellation for which it was named, with one straight plank for the back, which also comprises the back legs, one for the seat and one for the two front legs—three planks in all, nailed together. It was given to us by our good friend Richard Meads, who somehow retrieved it from the conflagration of the Provincetown Playhouse on the Wharf when he and other brave Provincetown firemen were trying to save that landmark property when it burned to the ground in 1977. I often sit in this chair, therefore, somewhat uncomfortably, to conjure up Eugene O'Neill, wondering where he is now and how much he knew about astronomy. I suspect he knew a great deal, for mythology is what he so successfully left us as inspiration and advice. Eugene O'Neill does not live in his residence at the old Peaked Hill Life Saving Station on the back shore anymore, his residency there being rather short, but hugely productive. The old Lifesaving Station was a real home to him and his family from 1919–1924. It is where he wrote some notable works that have perpetuated starlight in the night sky, so that we may experience his creations among the other constellations of past and present time and appreciate the light they have loaned us, even if the source no longer exists.[1]

Attached to the comet trail of O'Neill's years in Provincetown are many legends that we still trace in the universe of the theater. Historical references to most of them are widely extant in a number of places and need not e hold over one's head to access. One of these legends, however, not usually singled out, is important to mention in the context of this memoir and to briefly elaborate upon. Jasper Deeter was an actor-director who was associated with the Provincetown Players in the 1920s. He became one of the most respected and best-known directors in the world of the American repertory theater. His life trajectory across the sky conjoined with that of O'Neill's and with the Provincetown Players. He joined the Provincetown Playhouse in New York City where he acted in O'Neill's *Emperor Jones* in 1920 and where he also directed and acted in Susan Glaspell's play *Inheritors*. This play by Glaspell became, for Deeter, his lifelong lodestar. From 1923, when he founded the Hedgerow Repertory Theater Company in Moylan, Rose Valley, Pennsylvania—reputed to be the best repertory theater in America for many years—until 1954, Deeter produced *Inheritors* every season.[2] Susan Glaspell, of course, was one of the founders of the Provincetown Players in 1915 in Provincetown, together with her husband George Cram Cook and others. This inspired company drew O'Neill from dark oblivion to brilliant achievement, the stardust of that achievement falling upon the shoulders of many who were associated with him in that early period.

In Deeter's case, he carried the luminosity of the Provincetown Players with him to the Hedgerow Theater, where many subsequent stage stars apprenticed, performed, and profited from Deeter's remarkable energy and insight. Jasper Deeter unabashedly attributed the genesis of his inspiration to playwright Susan Glaspell. In a letter he wrote to her, dated December 7, 1936, he said: "Your vision taught me how to look, your insight taught me how to perceive, your words enabled me to speak, and your play gave me a life to live."[3]

The immense influence of the Hedgerow Repertory Theater Company, to which I belonged briefly in the late 1940s, left its mark, in turn, upon me. Many years later, I have occasionally felt the penetrating inspiration at odd times of creation and through countless moments of reflection, not only upon the stars in the night sky, but on what the experience of Hedgerow provided me in full circumference. Jasper Deeter died in 1972 at seventy-eight, having taught a small but vital company how to act, how to think, and how to interpret the real thing—life itself. He succeeded beyond any theatrical personage I have been privileged to know or observe. His method was raw guts, informed insight, empathy with the soul-force of the characters in the drama, and inspired acumen as to what the dramatist had in mind. He brought that empathy and inspiration to every performance at Hedgerow. His audiences shivered to his gut-wrenching interpretation of Shaw's *St. Joan,* to his startling involvement of the audience in the production of Dreiser's *American Tragedy,* to the last scene of Chekov's *Cherry Orchard,* which remains with me to this day, because of his direction: "silence, silence, silence, endless silence and then, the distant sound of an axe."

What I failed to be aware of in Moylan, I very belatedly learned in Provincetown: through my term as an understudy at Hedgerow. I too was part of the Provincetown Players' tradition, and my early association in Provincetown, from 1951 until 1960, with our beloved friend, the poet Harry Kemp, was a continuation and an augmentation of that relationship. Serendipitously, I had followed the trail of the comet to Provincetown without knowing it, and the trail led me to Cassiopeia's Chair and to the location of that burning star still shedding its light abroad a quarter of a mile away at the location of the old Peaked Hill Life Saving Station.

In 1938, a group of actors in Boston who were interested inheritors of the tradition of the Provincetown Players established the New England Repertory Company. One of the group was Edwin Pettit, who had been part of the Hedgerow Theater in Moylan. The other founders were Catharine Huntington and Virginia Thoms. These dedicated souls moved their company to the wharf in Provincetown in 1940, then owned by the painter Heinrich Pfeiffer; they called their theater The Provincetown Playhouse on the Wharf.[4] When I was fortunate enough to encounter the charismatic Catharine Huntington and the strikingly beautiful Virginia Thoms Le Peer in the early fifties, the company was in full swing, giving O'Neill's plays, among others, and carrying on the tradition of the original Provincetown Players.

As I remember her, Catharine Huntington was the most determined inheritor of the O'Neill legacy in the company. She had that natural empathy and constancy of almost ephemeral devotion to the theater, which eliminated all obstacles by grace and by strength of character, but was belied by her diminutive stature and refined comportment. Around her, the company maintained a presence of huge importance to American theater long after O'Neill's first plays struck dumb the nucleus of George Cram Cook's sodality in 1916.

Catharine Huntington in her favorite place, the deck of the Provincetown Playhouse on the Wharf (date uncertain—probably c.1966)

Fifty years later, in 1966, the Playhouse put on a commemorative O'Neill Festival of ten of his plays. One of these was *Ah Wilderness,* in which Catharine played Essie to the utter delight of the audience privileged to see that production. Catharine was a familiar star in the firmament here until her eventual retirement from the Playhouse on the Wharf in 1972, when Adele and Lester Heller purchased the theater. Catharine died at the age of 100 in 1987. Her companions of remarkable stage presence and ability, Virginia Thoms Le Peer and the director and actor Edward Pettit, have also retired the stage of life, but not to oblivion. In giving an encomium to Catharine at her death, Pettit excelled in a verbal tribute which included the following: "Upon hearing of the death of William Morris, Bernard Shaw said, 'You can lose a man like that by your own death but not by his.' Those of us who are blessed in the knowing of Catherine can only feel so about our beloved friend."[5]

The old Peaked Hill Bars Life Saving Station, built in 1872, sliding into the sea, January 10, 1931. The second Peaked Hill Station, built between 1913–1914 and established as the U.S. Coast Guard Station in 1915 and seen in the distance, is the current site of Frenchie's shack. *Photo from* Provincetown Advocate

Although it is most probable that we shall never see such a company again as the Provincetown Playhouse on the Wharf, there are emanations of the old esprit de corps in place in Provincetown still, which, seemingly, may never completely disappear. Over the years, these variations of the old tradition of the Provincetown Players have re-emerged from time to time, taking on a variety of talent and productions, and sometimes merging with a summer company from outside; they eventually subside, only to be brought back to life by another enthusiast of the theater. They do not always represent a professional combination of actors, scripts, sets, or directors, but "theater" goes on here, and it lives by an association with an idea and a tradition which, however fragile at times, refuses to give up the ghost (in this case, O'Neill's).

If it appears that this brief notation of theater activity within the context of the dune shacks of Peaked Hill is an anomaly, it must be observed that from the old Peaked Hill Life Saving Station, which served as home to Eugene O'Neill for a brief moment, to the nearby abode of poet Harry Kemp, who was intimately associated with the Provincetown Players and O'Neill, to the habitation built by Frenchie on the site of the second Peaked Hill Station, approximately a quarter of a mile away from the first, there is a connecting path of light, both between these various habitations and locations, both in the sense of a physical presence and a spiritual affinity. Is it fair to say, then, that Eugene O'Neill doesn't live here anymore? The answer is "yes" and "no." He has declined, by the unalterable decree of nature, to be among us, but his ghost lingers here with some substance and has been doing so in Provincetown for almost a century.

In the years 1970, 1971, and 1972, the war on the dunes persisted intermittently and unabated. On Labor Day, 1970, Josephine Ford's cottage was burned to the ground. In a touching card to Andrew Fuller on February 22, 1971, she expressed her grief and anger:

> Dear Andrew,
> Quite a confusing bulletin—feel quite helpless as to exactly what I must do—still very ill re: our place (just can't believe it)—my only refuge—keep hoping it's only a nightmare. Al Fearing, Esther and Gerald Hill, Jeanne (Frenchie) Chanel and yourself could sign affidavits proving my adverse ownership. Somehow, God willing, pray we can rebuild. Who was the person or persons (demons) who could have done such a desecration? The years until we finally acquired it, took so many sacrifices. Please help me so that all those years will not be a heart-rending waste.[6]

The cottage of Josephine Ford was very close to Frenchie's shack, and it was in total amazement that we came upon this tragic destruction of the abode of one of our near neighbors.

The bulletin that Josephine Ford referred to in her card to Fuller was an in-depth notice from him to the members of the GBCOA regarding a very important communique from the Assistant U.S. Attorney for the District of Massachusetts, James Gabriel. Dated

Pen and ink drawing of Josephine Ford's shack by Salvatore Del Deo, 1954

February 20, 1971, it explained that Gabriel intended to press for a trial of the case of E. Bennett Beede in March and that "all persons who own cottages and land in this area by adverse possession, as well as those assisting them as witnesses, keep me informed of their whereabouts, etc." Fuller's bulletin gave a very complete exegesis of the circumstances that the dune dwellers would face regarding the proof that would be necessary in order to establish adverse possession. The period of usage of land, according to Gabriel, must be over twenty years and must start before December 1947, as condemnation took place in December 1967 in the Beede case, etc.[7] Of all the documentation that Co-Chairman Fuller provided the members of the GBCOA during the lifetime of the organization, this was probably one of the most crucial.

All through the months of March and April 1971, there was a great flurry of activity among those cottage owners and residents who could claim to be legitimate squatters on the land of E. Bennett Beede. Witnessed documents were provided among the shack owners, assisting one another in the process of verifying dates of established residency, and a great deal of correspondence went back and forth between themselves and their co-chairman Fuller, who was in constant communication with the GBCOA lawyer Samuel Angoff. On March 17, 1971, Fuller issued another bulletin to the membership to alert them to the dangerous circumstances which had been woven around Attorney Gabriel's push to resolve adverse possession:

> To: Members who are defendants in the "Beede case":
> You will shortly receive from your attorney, Mr. Samuel Angoff photocopies of letters and other data sent to him by Mr. James Gabriel, Assistant U.S. Attorney, relating to an offer of stipulation.
>
> This stipulation, in effect, is the same old permit which was previously offered by the National Park Service, but in a different guise.
>
> Innocent as it may appear, it is a most dangerous document, as it would have the following effects.

The thirteen effects he described included: "no right to rebuild; no right to repair or enlarge or improve; no right or provision for use of land for wells; and the list is extensive and completely cuts off any rights of ownership." The admonition continues in additional underline: "Please note that Mr. Gabriel is attempting to subvert the law by redefining 'improved property' to mean only a dwelling which complies fully with local building, sanitary, and safety regulations. There is absolutely no such provision in the Cape Cod National Seashore Act.[8]

It was at this time that Hazel Hawthorne Werner created the valuable map of cottages that were within the Beede Tract between the years 1920 and 1960. She sent it to Andrew Fuller as background and proof of the rights of members in the Association who professed adverse possession on the Beede land.[9] At the end of March, co-chairman Fuller sent another "shot across the bow" to the GBCOA membership: "Do Not Sign Under Any Circumstances" and suggested that each member reply to the stipulations directly through attorney Angoff, which most of them did, some very forcefully rejecting the stipulations.

I think it is fair to state, at this point, that in the decade between the inception of the Cape Cod National Seashore and the initiation of the end game regarding the cottages on the Great Outer Beach, which was playing out in 1971, attempts were being made to finalize the last moves, if possible. The Park had long made its trajectory clear, indirectly and directly, as in the case made by Superintendent Arnberger: the dune shacks were to be removed from the Seashore at the first possible opportunity and the lifetime stipulations, granting only temporary rights of occupancy by the residents, would be eliminated as soon as they ran their course—no survivors. The process by which this was to be accomplished needed to be as free of encumbrances as possible, both political and litigious. There had been consistent inattention, however, to the details of any objective process of jurisprudence which did not fit the formula the Park had predetermined. This would be proven over and over again in the course of time. Endless management plans and successful dodges of legitimate claims were never seriously addressed except through the Park Service's convenient "legal fictions," as Andrew Fuller referred to the stratagems invoked by studies, statements, and evasions. These things need to be emphasized here, especially in relation to the history of the GBCOA. The organization began to run out of money to provide legal representation and the will to stick together in order to maintain a united front. Finally, it lost the invaluable leadership of Andrew Fuller, which, though never admitting defeat, could not last forever.

In the midst of this critical attempt to save the various cottages entangled by the Beede case, Frenchie enjoyed a rousing tribute to her love of animals, from the town of Provincetown, which gave her a fete on March 18, 1971, to raise money for an animal rescue shelter. Known as the "bird lady" by many youngsters, she never failed the earnest plea for help for a stricken creature from any visitor to Frenchie's Corner. Just as she had sung and chanted in her inimitable style in Paris as a free spirit, so she once again captivated her audience to plead her cause.

Although the GBCOA was left without an attorney to represent them after the resignation of attorney Samuel E. Angoff on June 17, 1971, the members went on faithfully and diligently to represent themselves and the issues of the Great Beach Cottage Owners Association. Addressing the worsening conditions concerning the abuse of the dunes by excessive foot traffic and vehicular violations, Jan Gelb Margo, the Association's chairman of the environmental committee, wrote to Superintendent Arnberger on August 16th:

> The members of our Great Beach Cottage Owner's Association, most of whom have summered at the Great Beach for decades, have watched with horror the constantly worsening destruction of the dunes and dune grass during the past few years... We love these dunes and have hoped that the National Seashore would make their preservation possible, but steps must be taken to do this soon, or damage will be extensive, if not irreparable. We believe it would be unfortunate, if not downright cynical, to wait until "studies" are made of what is already so obvious.

Frenchie joined Jan in this appeal for the protection of the dunes, but she took it much further in emotional depth and intensity. She addressed a letter to Rose Kennedy, mother of President Kennedy, stating the case for protecting the dunes with such an intelligent and heartfelt plea that nothing more needed to be said or could be said with any greater clarity. Frenchie's letter attempted to close the gap between use and abuse and to alert those in command what they would have to do to keep safe the dunes, the dune shacks, the terns, the plovers, and all the world of the back shore and its way of life. She had rallied to the need; she was leading the charge: "The dunes cannot live through another year without being mortally wounded." Because her words cannot be paraphrased without betraying her metaphor, I include her letter here in its entirety:

Provincetown Advocate, August 19, 1971: (copy of letter to Rose Kennedy)
It is hard and I feel inadequate to compose a letter good enough for a great lady like you.

I am asking you for help for my town and its surrounding beauty. Through your intervention, and by the memory of your son John, our beloved President, I will be able to achieve the help and the attention I am looking for.

Your son John gave the permit to make a National Park of our dunes. It was a well-intentioned deed, but the officials are having a hard time coping with it.

I understand that National Parks are, first of all, established to protect the beauty of the area so future generations will be able to enjoy it, and to protect the wild life that abound in it and the vegetation and the great beauty of the area.

For thousands of years of years, nature took care of this. Creation looked on it and said, "This is good."

Now man is destroying it, destroying the nesting grounds of the great tern, destroying the natural beauty and protection of the vegetation so necessary for the existence of the dunes and for the protection of my town. If the big dunes are leveled, the winds will blow the sand over the town and so also destroy our living.

I have read and understand that the officials are now, after 10 years, asking scientists to do a study of and for the protection of the dunes. It is commendable and well-intended. But, no matter how great a scientist might be, it is up to nature to recover from the wounds that threaten the heart. For thousands of years there was no scientist needed to study nature. In my estimation it is the people and their careless destruction of nature that need to be studied.

Frenchie posing beside her shack on the dunes (undated)

The greed for money has made manufacturers turnout more and speedier vehicles that level the land.

Progress and speedy over-sand vehicles are fine, but not in a small area like our dunes.

The dune taxis are careful and stay in the track and so do the few people that have inhabited the dunes for generations. But thousands of others do not walk or drive with cars over the sands to look at the beauty of nature. They make the dunes a speedway or a hideaway for drinking parties or whatever the law might think is good not to permit. We few dunes people clean the face of our dunes up after they have had their fill of them. They all leave without having seen God and his creation.

For a generation a few of us lived up there, including the great playwright

Eugene O'Neill and the great poet of the dunes Harry Kemp. We lived there under privation, yes, but with adoration of the beauty that we were privileged to behold. We need more people to care for the dunes, including scientists. The tremendous job the rangers have is too big.

With the few people that love and understand the dunes and love my town and the good people of my town, we are waging, I fervently hope with your help, Great Lady, a war against the destruction of what creation has built. We turn to you to help us to contact the people we should talk to. The scientific study might take too long. The dunes cannot live through another year without being mortally wounded.

I am sad, but I show the world a smiling face all the time. That is only to keep from crying. They tell me I care too much. How much is too much?

I am reaching high by writing to you and hoping for an answer, but as Browning wrote: "Ah, but a man's reach should exceed his grasp, or what's a heaven for?"

Jeanne "Frenchie" Chanel, Provincetown

The war on the national front seemed to drag on in tempo with the conflict on the dunes without resolution, and then, on January 23, 1973, my journal reads as follows:

> On January 23, 1973, President Nixon announced that the cease-fire in Vietnam would take place on Saturday, January 27 at 7:00 p.m. Somehow, the world was disbelieving. After the Christmas bombing, most of us were still numb. This peace has come as an anti-climax, but no less welcome, so tonight, January 27, the peace in Vietnam we have all been protesting to achieve has arrived, and we are the peacemakers, not Nixon and his political henchmen, nor Kissinger, nor any diplomat, but we, the American people, those of us who knew and protested and prayed and kept the watch.
>
> We lit candles and all the kerosene lamps, and I put up streamers and we said a silent, standing prayer at the table—just the three of us, as Sal was at the Beachcombers Club. We watched a kind of newscast about the pull-out of troops, signing the treaty, etc., and felt quietly good. It is a new feeling to go to bed and know that Americans are not killing men, women, and children in a far country that means very little to us really and whose problems are not going to be molded by our concepts of "fitness." We have been terribly wrong, have misjudged very badly, both our military effectiveness and why our military might was being used at all. Thanks to those of us who cared enough to say so, the course of history has finally reversed itself.

So ended my entry in my journal for January 27, 1973, and so ended, officially, the war in Vietnam. The fallout from this military maelstrom, however, played out endlessly in America itself for decades longer.

Although the war in Vietnam was now a matter of history, the end of the war on the dunes in Provincetown and Truro was far from resolution. In the final discussions with attorney Samuel E. Angoff during the spring of 1971, members of the GBCOA had desperately tried to ward off condemnation proceedings, which had been introduced by Assistant U.S.Attorney James Gabriel. Many of the dwellings were located on the large tract of land owned by E. Bennett Beede and so were swept up in the proceedings as of December 1,1967. A number of cottages in Truro were also included in condemnation procedure, even though their structures had never been officially passed to the federal government by the Commonwealth of Massachusetts; only the land had been transferred.[10]

In the case of the Beede tract, it appeared that all of the dwellings that had been bundled in the Beede condemnation could claim "squatter's rights" by definition of a twenty-year established residency since 1947, which was required by Gabriel's instructions as being paramount for establishing freedom from condemnation. No concerted action was taken, to the best of my knowledge, to follow through on these adverse possessory rights. In several discussions with attorney Angoff in March and April, 1971, however, Grace Bessay did attempt to introduce a solution. This would have satisfied conditions in both Truro and Provincetown by separating the condemnation of the land from the buildings and pursuing the issues separately. In both cases, the dwellings would have been protected.[11] Of course, this was far too involved and problematic for the Park Service and even for attorney Angoff, who was three months away from retiring completely from the representation of the GBCOA. Even if the cottages could have established "squatter's rights," it is not certain that they would have ever been able to successfully disprove the definition of "improved property" that the Park adamantly insisted on applying to these cottages. That definition permanently stood in the way of the salvation of the cottages from the first days of controversy to the present time, even though their designation as eligible for Registered Landmark status in 1989 freed them from this stricture by their eligibility.

In a letter to Andrew Fuller dated October 19, 1973, Congressman Robert F. Drinan, from the 4th District in Massachusetts, set forth the elements of the pertinent discussion of "improved property" to Grace Bessay and Andrew Fuller:

> It appears that the National Park Service has added their own requirements to the meaning of "improved property" which do not appear in, or seem to be justified by the Cape Cod National Seashore Act. Indeed, if the facts presented by Ms Bessay in the condemnation proceedings are as you say they are, then the land acquisition might fail on the grounds, that is, on the ground that the National Park Service has misinterpreted the law, and on the ground that the National Park Service has inaccurately assessed the facts.[12]

Representative Drinan also referred to the fact that the National Park Service appears to want a "litigated result." The litigation process, which Rep. Drinan refers to in this letter, continued for more than two decades longer, as it turned out, and the question of the definition of "improved property" continued to condemn the dune shacks to the state of limbo in which they find themselves as I write this history. Grace Bessay's long, tortuous defense of her right to a way of life in her dwelling on the dunes is discussed in chapter eight entitled "Bessay and Goliath."

Above: The new shack rising from the old

Left: Building the new shack: Romolo Del Deo, Tom De Carlo, and Sal

In 1976, Frenchie tried to accommodate to the conditions imposed upon her, as did almost every other dune resident within the Beede tract who were now losing their permanent status as rightful homeowners through the condemnation process against Beede. She decided, however, with some misgivings, but with a determination very characteristic of her fortitude, to rebuild her shack. This was, of course allowable under the legislation establishing the Park, provided that the rebuilding did not exceed the footprint of the original structure begun before September 1, 1959; Frenchie's shack had been built between 1945 and 1946.[13]

Sal put his shoulder to the task at her request, and the first timbers, which overlaid the tarpaper, driftwood tenacity of Frenchie's original inspiration, rose against the skyline. It was a bitter-sweet process. I was torn by the pull of sentiment for the old place and by the memories of its happy life. It seemed to me that so much of my life was being subsumed with the burial, literally, of all that had housed our life and love for more than twenty years. The reality could not be avoided, however. There was no way to assume the burden of digging the shack out by hand each spring or after each major storm, and the deterioration of the sagging siding would require the rebuilding anyway. Finally, it was just "time," as Pete Seeger so often told us in his "turn, turn, turn" singing of the realities of life and death.

In the spring of 1977, the final days of controversy between the government's acquisition office, under Thomas B. Coleman, Chief Acquisition Officer, and the cottage owners, there were some politely heated exchanges. The several dune dwellers who defied the government's right to acquire their cottages by condemnation did not hesitate to express their position. Among these, were the following:

Andrew Fuller to Thomas B. Coleman:

"My cottage referred to (etc.) constitutes 'improved property' as defined under Section 4 (d), of the Public Law 87-126 (etc.) and is exempt from condemnation. No permission for your appraiser is given." April 21, 1977

David and Connie Armstrong to Thomas B. Coleman:

"The Park Service considers all of the denizens of the domain with benign and protective regard. The fact that deer, foxes, rabbits, turtles, weasels, field mice and other creatures great and small, as well as sea gulls and a vast variety of wild fowl, find this seemingly harsh environment to be nurturing to them is of great interest and is, in fact, a major reason for the existence of our National Seashore. *But the Seashore has a human history as well as a natural history and we few who have patiently and persistently maintained our humble dwellings by the sea against the destructive forces of the environment and have found this environment to be nurturing to us, and to our children and grandchildren, are entitled to consideration." April 22, 1977*

Nicholas and Ray Wells to Superintendent Lawrence Hadley:

"Re: Your file L-1425-NAR (L). CACO: Within the meaning of Public Law 87-126, to wit, The Cape Cod National Seashore Act, our cottage is improved property and we consequently are not subject to the government's condemnation process...Any rights which the government asserts by means of a conveyance from the Commonwealth of Massachusetts is subject to any information in the title which they undertook to convey or to conflicting rights and claims of title and therefore is subject to our own title claims with respect to the cottage and the land alluded to." May 28, 1977 [14]

None of these protestations and border forays created the desired result for the dune dwellers, of course. In June, Charlie Schmid, in his anger and frustration, wrote to Andrew Fuller about the continual harassment of the government and expressed strong sentiment that "We should do whatever we can collectively."[15] Facing endless cul de sac attempts to save the way of life of the dunes, however, the collective will had been drained away by attrition. The notable exceptions, perhaps, were Grace Bessay and Andrew Fuller, who carried on their battle for rights of habitation within their dwellings through every discouragement and retreat, only to start out again toward their goal. Andrew Fuller was tiring, however, and his last memos to the membership of the GBCOA were handwritten, although nonetheless clear and unflinchingly determined in the expression of both purpose and principle.[16]

By September 1977, the shack was nearing completion. On September 12, my journal reads:

A Monday on the dunes: Bright September has blessed us with a glorious sunny day as our day of rest. After delivering museum receipts and filing the Historic District article for the October town meeting warrant, Sal picked me up at town hall and we began to prepare for a trip to the shack. Both Tommy and Sibylle [17] came along and Romolo with his recent girlfriend Adrian Margolies, Boris's niece. Piling into the back of the truck, we managed to get started by 2:00 p.m. Sal and Tommy brought a lunch and I my trusty camera.

The sea was relatively calm and the deep Prussian blue that is such a compelling experience, going beyond color to emotion. Everyone seemed relaxed and happy.

Even with a cast and the difficulty in walking in the sand, it was pleasant to be once more at the shack, which is coming along splendidly. The roof is on—French doors in and windows also. The shingling has yet to be done and getting it secured for the winter, but really, the bulk of the hard work is over. Sal went out many times this summer in order to finish the major construction When we arrived, Romolo gave me his arm to get up the hill and so we topped the rise. I saw that the birdhouse was down after all the years, and I was upset about that.

I lay in the sand and fought off the horse flies which are inevitable inhabitants of the dunes in the fall, but I eventually dropped off to sleep under a golden sun. Tommy fixed a splendid lunch of rolls and cold cuts and Joe Servis's garden tomatoes in his usual organized manner. Suddenly appeared above us a kite sailing jauntily along. We all groaned—intrusion, but, of course, the intruder was none other than Arthur Cohen, the man himself. Arthur is mirth and magic rolled into one. We enjoyed the remainder of the sun and then folded our tent and prepared to depart.

As we traveled at a great clip near the shore, we remarked on the confetti of shore birds dipping and scattering along the water's edge. Suddenly, the water broke in dozens of splashes, and we knew that a school of fish was just off shore, within arm's reach. Then began one of the funniest and zaniest episodes of our many dune days. Sal jumped out of the truck. Tommy followed him with Romolo not far behind. With uncanny instinct, Romolo picked up a clump of seaweed and found lodged therein a lure for bass. Sal hollered back to him to tie the lure to Arthur's kite string, which they did in jig time. As soon as the line and lure were ready, Sal took the rig and whirled it around over his head like a lasso and, "plunk," it landed in the water not too far off shore, whereupon Tommy ran with the line, as in a trawling technique, all along the beach. After two or three of these sallies into the deep, damned if they didn't land a beautiful bluefish, about eight pounds. By this time, fishermen were appearing from everywhere and hauling the blues out of the water as fast as they could cast.

Meanwhile, Adrian, who had jumped out of the truck with the boys, grabbing a shovel as she went, plunged headlong into the water swinging at the fish with her shovel. She came up dripping but happy, and thereafter shed everything down to her bathing suit and gamboled in the water for half an hour. Sibylle was in stitches, laughing at the whole procedure with great glee. It was a day to remember and to recall with a golden corolla ringed forever around the memory of such innocent happiness.

A month later, during the first week of October, we went to the shack for another several days of recuperation from the busy summer schedule. I also needed to rest in preparation for the special town meeting scheduled for mid-October in which a local historic district for Provincetown would be considered.

The preparation for this proposal had taken four years to research and develop, from 1973–1977, and would eventually include approximately 1,300 properties, if passed. Each one of these properties had to be identified by exact location, architecturally described, historically annotated, and photographed. Our committee[18] had identified a significant selection from the whole area to be included. To this was added approximately 360 properties the Commonwealth had identified through the Massachusetts Historical Commission several years before, making the representation already catalogued over

500 properties. The Historic District Study Committee, of which I was chairman at that time, had carefully structured the zoning by-law that would accompany the district and had revised it eight times in keeping with sentiment expressed at several public hearings. Its overall intention was to keep the human scale of the architecture and to stay clear of too many finicky details. Restrictions as to general architectural integrity were several, but the idea was to allow new building to proceed unregulated except through restrictions of regular zoning. Our main concern was always to preserve the valued and historic aspects of the town. In spite of this rather extraordinary effort and attention to the very nature of this unorthodox community, which Pete Seeger once described as a "shaggy little town," the historic district went down to defeat by a significant margin. In 2003, thirty years after the initiation of the idea, however, the Provincetown Historic District became a reality.[19]

October 6, 7, 8, 1977—The Dunes:

What a beautiful shack greeted me as we arrived here on Thursday in the late afternoon! I couldn't believe my eyes. Sal's labors of the summer had produced a miracle. Frenchie had seen to it that the walls were finished with windows in appropriate places and that a porch had been added which cantilevered out just enough to sit on at a small table overlooking Portugal and Spain. Right now, the little deck is standing on one leg like a lone heron, but eventually, it will have two legs. The French doors, which look out over the sea, are no less than sublime. They are the final touch, the artist's dream come true, for, at every moment, they allow the natural world to be observed through the unobtrusive eye of civilization. Frenchie, in her own inimitable fashion, has created another shack of her very own, different than her cozy dungeon, but just as unique.

As I write here with Romolo beside me reading *The Agony and the Ecstasy*, I am totally at peace and grateful for that remarkable aura which surrounds Frenchie's shack and which I experience in no other place on earth. Sal and Tommy have just gone in to take care of the animals and get the cards so that the ongoing game of scopa can continue uninterrupted. Outside, the dying embers of the campfire remind me of our gourmet repast just completed. Tommy, in the late, grey afternoon, landed a whopper of a bass. It must have weighed all of twenty pounds and was a beauty. Tommy was ecstatic, and I took a couple of shots of him coming up the beach to prove it. Romolo, present and accounted for, built a fire to roast the supper, and there we were with our broiled bass, tomatoes, and fire-roasted potatoes and onions under the stars. How can one even describe the luxury? We felt remorse for the masses, but not much.

Today, the second full day of residency in my heavenly home, I completed another vignette for the *Compass Grass Anthology*. It now consists of about fifteen sketches and should be about twenty-five at completion. I have much that requires my commentary, not all of which will go into these short vignettes. A lot will probably contribute to the novel, *Footprints on the Sea*. I wrote "The Passing of the New York Store" yesterday and recopied "The Divorce" and "Town Meeting." I finished "Tamarisk" yesterday as well, a piece for Mrs. Caliga and Mrs, DeWitt (that I had never quite completed).[20] The energy I have here is exciting. I am thrilled to be working at "my life" again. It is so restful to be writing my inner life for a change. I have one more full day before a return to my historic district and town meeting, the museum, etc., but I try to put them in their place. Sal is patient

Romolo Reading in the Shack, pen and ink drawing by Salvatore Del Deo, 1977

and bears the burden of going back and forth twice a day. His devotion enables me to remain these few days unmolested by any schedule. We both know what that means.

In November 1977, the activity within the family was intense. Sal had been scheduled for a one-man exhibition at the 47 Bond Street Gallery in New York on November 20th, his first in the city. The preparation for this was totally consuming for a number of weeks, but in tandem with such a momentous event was another, equally singular and absorbing of our energies. We had planned for many months to spend the winter of 1978 in Italy and to experience a kind of palimpsest of our honeymoon in Forio d'Ischia, twenty-five years before in 1953. At the same time, we wanted to introduce the children to their Italian heritage. With both events to plan and to initiate within weeks of each other, no space was left for any errors in scheduling. Promptly, therefore, on November 18, we left for New York with a full truckload of art; the exhibition on November 20 provided impetus and inspiration for Sal's painting career for a considerable period thereafter.

A month later, Sal, Giovanna, and I collected ourselves in the Boston airport for our flight to Italy. Romolo had already left for a quick European tour before joining us in Rome. The days and weeks that followed, both in Italy and France, impressed themselves upon my writing life for years to come. After the Christmas holidays with Sal's family of cousins in Forio, we parted company with Romolo, who wished to spend time in Pietrasanta to study stone carving for several months, prior to entering Harvard in the fall of 1978. We then accompanied Giovanna to Aix-en-Provence for her winter studies in French at the Vanderbilt University overseas program, which would be accredited to her studies at Williams College.

While spending time in Aix, I completed a short novella about our sojourn in Ischia at Christmas, for which Giovanna later added illustrations. Sal, meanwhile, took full advantage of the opportunity to explore every aspect of Cezanne's favorite motifs, especially Mont St. Victoire. It was, for us, a once-in-a-lifetime experience and some of that sentiment flows through the narration of *Amandava-Amandava, A Christmas Journey to the Island of Ischia*, which is an intimate and reflective personal account of that period in time in which Italy had begun to normalize life after the war and to regain equilibrium and to reestablish old customs with a new dimension. Such a way of life, which I reflected upon then, is, thirty years later, no longer quite the same, but it is still the paradigm of an Italian point of view which alters very little from generation to generation and is tied, inexorably, to the love of the land and to a set of philosophical values that, hopefully, will not change beyond the brief "change" absorbed by each generation of Italians in the manner of their legacy from the Phoenicians and Greek occupations to the present day. In a moment of rare good fortune for me, William Cavness, that raconteur par excellence, who once regularly presented the world's classics and other selected readings to a devoted audience of his program on WGBH radio, read *Amandava-Amandava* on WGBH during the Christmas season of 1980.

Jo at Frenchie's shack, October 1978

The intensity of my interest in the Italian culture has inspired a significant amount of my writing overall. The travel vignettes I later composed and published related to the unforgettable trip with my family in 1978 and to an extensive tour of southern Italy in 1985 with Sal, which surfaced in published form in a collection entitled *Passaggi—Passages* in both English and, later, in a dual-language translation, for which Giovanna again provided the illustrations.[21] Most pertinent to this text, however, is a play I wrote as a result of the 1978 sojourn in Forio d'Ischia entitled *Il Sole di Chi E?* or *The Sun, Whose Is It?*, which I found myself initiating in the fall of 1978 on the dunes in Frenchie's shack.

This play, as may be imagined by its title, is not just an Italian-inspired episode spliced into the cable of my conscience, but yet another outgrowth of a certain lifelong preoccupation. The basis for my direction in writing, for my interest in the environment and for the way I have lived my life and chosen my goals for personal fulfillment are clearly apparent in *The Sun, Whose Is It?*, but beyond that, this play reflects one of the philosophical principles and environmental concerns of a number of my predecessors at Peaked Hill, of whose legacy I too have now become a part. I am a resident of a community of dune shack inhabitants, both past and present, whose creative energies and varied interests represent a metaphysical sense of place over time. A vital reiteration of the human spirit is alive and well in the historic domain of the Peaked Hill Bars and will be as long as the dune shacks are protected from the hazards of an unintentional or deliberate misinterpretation of the significance of the way of life in these "temples by the sea."

CHAPTER VI

The Temples

1978-1984

THE ANCIENT GREEKS did not have to live in so swift a flow of events as that to which we are subjected in the second millennium. As a result, they established themselves securely with a projected authority that defies "time's fell hand," her temples still standing on certain shores and her memory defiant, if increasingly fragile.[1] We may, therefore, have the privilege of examining the evidence and drawing our own conclusions. On the sweep of a green sward flowing to the sea, the Greek temples of Agrigento in Sicily, for instance, stand in the Valley of the Temples, as if placed there by an artist's discerning hand and remain without too great an intrusion by the clamoring presence of admiring eyes and reverent visitation. We are privileged to observe the skill and beauty of a fortunate civilization, represented by structures now empty of their original protagonists but still inspirational to following generations.

Dune Poet by Salvatore Del Deo, 1978; oil on canvas, 16" x 12"

These magnificent Greek temples impressed me mightily in 1978 when I first saw them, and I drew from their message the poem I later composed for my own temples, the dune shacks on the back shore of Provincetown and Truro at Peaked Hill. Placed as they are, at the edge of the sea upon a sweep of dune grass, the dune shacks are almost entirely free of undue intrusion. They confront seasonal weather patterns with an enduring presence of their own, which may or may not claim equal status with the Greek temples' successful confrontation with the elements over many centuries. They will, I believe, survive the attrition to their physical form with a continuing adaptation of their vernacular architecture in which to perpetuate the inspiring presence of their "gods." If the constancy of this spiritual habitation does not waver, surely they will continue to provide a place for future generations to invoke the most precious of all man's possessions, which is the eternal fire of life within.

The temples of Agrigento, of Paestum, and other remarkable sites where the Greek symbol still stands as testament to man's reach to the stars, remind us of their great statesmen, their orators, poets, heroes, philosophers, architects, artists, and playwrights and their informed citizenry. These are what come to mind when regarding the architectural articulation of their culture, not just the temples as physical entities, but what they represented. Historic preservation is a civilizing bond from one generation to the next, not only of specific material achievements, but of the record of man's presence in the universe and of the process which shapes it.

The Temples

(After Agrigento)

How great a solitary strength there is in place unoccupied.
Suggested gods and goddesses reside in these, my temples—
Shacks shut tight against all presence, seasons and myself.
They dwell a distance that is moonlit dune or dream away,
Not now, forever stand between the sand and stars.
These are my temples by the sea,
And I would praise their flawless, Greek simplicity,
Yet am afraid my words might make them art.

There is a price to pay, however, for the most pertinent salvation of man's cultural achievements, and this is largely one of perpetual diligence and informed perspective. Someone, or some city, state, nation, or group of particular proponents on behalf of beauty, wisdom, learning, and all the rest, which incorporates our high aspirations toward the continuance of the same, needs continually to be active, to be far-sighted in the midst of discouragement and of the shortsighted, self-serving elements of our society. There must be an understanding, in other words, of the past, an expectation of the social continuum to the future, and the assumption of responsibility for unifying both in the present. With this in mind, Sal and I have been committed, throughout our life in Provincetown, to the conservation of the environment in which we have chosen to spend our lives, and in which to create our art. We have moved in tandem with consistent dedication to the vision and understanding of a sense of place in this remarkable atmosphere, both physical and spiritual. Since Provincetown has incited an inspired participation in many others, in this respect, it could be said to be a Greek colony of its own.

Throughout the decade of the 1970s, Sal and I found ourselves involved in historic preservation initiatives to an extraordinary degree, activities that would follow through the next decade and beyond. In 1974, for instance, we were part of a very vocal sodality of citizens in an effort to preserve the 1860 Center Methodist Episcopal Church from a number of proposed commercial enterprises. In 1958, after an intense controversy within the church's membership, this magnificent building was purchased from its congregation by Walter Chrysler, Jr., who turned it into his private museum to house his extensive art collection. Since then, the fate of the building had never been completely secure. Eventually, after a number of years of operation, Chrysler decided to abandon the building here and move his collection to Norfolk, Virginia, thus taking with him some invaluable collections of local artifacts, such as Sandwich glass that had been secured on the promise of their permanent residency in the Provincetown location. An interim operation of the building as a Center for the Arts initiated, primarily, by Jules Brenner, jeweler, artisan, and protege of Ed Wiener, did not succeed. Other plans for its future involved some unsavory uses, plus its possible destruction to provide another parking lot for the town.

It became apparent, therefore, to those of us who were determined to save this magnificent structure, that an immediate action would have to be initiated to preserve it. Provincetown's three-mile shoreline was dominated by the Center Methodist Episcopal Church sitting atop an elevation somewhat above the low-lying architecture of Commercial Street and commanding the view, both from sea and land, as one approached the town. Without her majestic and protective presence, Provincetown would have been without its central focus, with the exception, of course, of its dominating historic landmark, the Provincetown Pilgrim Monument, announcing to the world the location of the Pilgrims' first landing in America. The prominent and magisterial presence of the 1860 church, however, provided an architectural center from which radiated the everyday civic heart of the community. No fisherman ever steamed in around Long Point without the comforting sight of the church dead ahead in his mental radar, and no citizen ever returned home down Route 6 without sighting her staunch figure, like a mother hen hovering over her brood, as the town emerged on the horizon. As foreclosure appeared imminent, spelling the probable physical destruction of the church, or, at the very least, of its symbolic presence, a group of us, together with The Provincetown Historical Association, headed by its energetic president Cyril Patrick, Jr., sponsored its designation as a National Historic Landmark. The Massachusetts Historical Commission acted promptly, and, by October 1975, its status as a National Registered Landmark had been declared.[2]

On November 12, 1975, after intense campaigning on the part of all of us dedicated to preserving the now-designated landmark,[3] I presented an article at a special town meeting to request that the town designate the church as the Provincetown Heritage Museum, an entity that would be dedicated to the heritage of the community, and, especially, to that of the Portuguese legacy, and to the fishing history of this important seaport. I spoke on behalf of the committee, which had been appointed by the Board of Selectmen to research such a proposal and which, upon passage of the article, would become the first Board of Trustees of the Museum.[4]

Somehow, the Heritage Museum managed to survive those first few years of operation with a very modest budget and no paid personnel except the janitors; everything else was volunteer, from the Board of Trustees to the volunteers who manned the desk from 9:00 to 5:00 daily, from May to October. Eventually, we earned our operating budget and had only to request the capital costs, which we held to a minimum. The initial cost of the building's interest on the purchase loan was entirely paid for by grants from the Massachusetts Historical Commission. These facts remain, for me, a point of pride and a lesson in the value of commitment, freely given, to secure the success of a worthy

Above: Captain Francis "Flyer" Santos and the *Rose Dorothea* under construction 1978

Left: The Provincetown Heritage Museum, opening day, July 4, 1976

endeavor. The building was immense, however, and in need of structural repairs that went beyond the daily functional problems. The attractions we had installed were inventive and modest, but our major goal for promoting visitor attendance was to build a half-scale model of our most famous fishing schooner, the "Rose Dorothea," a spoon-bow schooner that had won the Boston-Gloucester Fishermen's Race in 1907 and was the epitome of the fishing tradition in Provincetown. This model was constructed under the guiding supervision of master boat-builder Captain Francis "Flyer" Santos, who volunteered his labor over a period of eleven years from 1977 to 1988, with the assistance of a number of experts in sailing experience and/or as able craftsmen, almost all of whom were volunteers. The devotion of Captain Santos to the construction of the "Rose Dorothea" is now legendary,[5] and the model he built is a living legend. It can be accessed every day in what was once the sanctuary of the old Methodist Episcopal Church and now has become The Provincetown Public Library. Its spectacular presence draws admiration from all who see her. The Center Methodist Episcopal Church has survived sequential transitions from its original use expressing religious faith in 1860 and continuing through three successive transforming uses over a period of 150 years. It illustrates, I believe, what I have previously emphasized, that commitment moves history from the "fire within."

At about the same time as the Heritage Museum was successfully launched and the construction of the "Rose Dorothea" was getting underway, The Provincetown Playhouse on the Wharf was destroyed by arson in March 1977, as has been discussed in the previous chapter. The Playhouse, however, attempted to rise from its ashes with the concerted effort to rebuild it through a national competition sponsored by the National Endowment for the Arts' Department of Architecture in 1978. William Marlin, who was the architectural adviser for the project for the National Endowment, selected several well-known New England architectural firms for an on-site charette process of designing the new theater in Provincetown with the added feature of allowing the public to participate in the process by giving them an opportunity to view the architects at work. This took place in Provincetown between November 8 and 19, 1978.[6]

Among the distinguished jurors for the competition, which included I. M. Pei, Arthur Cotton Moore, Raquel Ramati and others, were Sal and myself, chosen because of our knowledge of the town's historical background. The highly interesting and challenging approach yielded an excellent design that was appropriate to the town's historic profile and incorporated all the desirable features prescribed in the guidelines for the competition, including an archival area for O'Neill's legacy. At the time, the whole effort received a great deal of national attention with none other than Helen Hayes officiating at the award ceremony in the Universalist-Unitarian Church and I. M. Pei announcing the winner of the design competition, who was architect William Warner of Rhode Island. Unfortunately, the playhouse was never constructed, thus bringing to an end the last performance of The Provincetown Playhouse on the Wharf.

When we returned from Italy in the spring of 1978, I again picked up the uncompleted task of preparing the former Historic District Study Committee inventory, which still required a significant number of listings, for presentation to the Massachusetts Historical Commission as a National Registered Historic District. This would differ from the previous local historic district proposal only in the matter of its lack of effective implementation of an accompanying local zoning by-law, but would be valuable, nevertheless, from the standpoint of selected historic preservation status throughout the community, depending on the eligibility of individual historic elements. The possibility of financial assistance from the Commonwealth, therefore, would be a real assistance if historic status could be determined in individual cases. After the enormous amount of work accomplished by our study committee, this seemed the only avenue open to us to

Inside the Provincetown Playhouse on the wharf, a famous landmark where whaling ships once provisioned and boats were built. A summer company under the same management since 1940 continues here. Provincetown's theater tradition began in 1916 when Eugene O'Neill's first play was performed in Provincetown.[7]

salvage what had already been done and bring something to fruition. I proceeded, together with my good friend and former committee member Claude Jensen, to detail the remaining properties, about 800 in all, with photographic identification and historical and architectural background. This work would require another year-and-a-half to complete.

The cure for all the fatigue of my combined community activities, not to mention those of our family life, was always available to me at Frenchie's shack. Sal and I stayed at the shack as time permitted, and most often, of course, in the fall when seasonal responsibilities were retired. In October 1978, therefore, I made a solo sojourn to the shack:

October 17, 1978:

Today is the beginning of a new way of life for me. I have felt it coming for several months, but today has proved something altogether special. There has been no sensational occurrence or even strong emotion, but I left the house for the dunes at 11:15, and from then on, the metamorphosis began. Sal, bless his heart, working so hard on the house, took time to drop me at Snail Road. I had not walked that route for years, but it is the shortest way and the most spectacular. Of course, it was always Harry's road. I carried a paper bag with a piece of bread and a slice of the pound cake Tim had made for me, plus my glasses. The wind was strong and right down the old NW chute straight at me, but it was invigorating and thrilling to get that old sock in the puss-wham!—when you come up over that high climb and see the sharp line of Prussian blue against the neutral sand. It never fails to produce aesthetic shock in me—a breathtaking rebirth of beauty.

So I took it easy—not walking rapidly and trying to breathe steadily, since I haven't felt exactly fit these days. Instinctively, however, I know that my accelerated heart beat and sleepless nights are mind-produced maladies, tied up with frustration, overwork, responsibilities, worry, etc. Moments of calm come often when I can switch my mental concerns and re-track my thoughts. So today, after a full week of putting the museum to sleep and taking care of a mountain of problems there, I decided that a change was needed. Perhaps I am too good at what is expected of me and too poor at doing what I expect of myself.

Walking to the shack, preoccupied with the flora at my feet, I was truly liberated. It came to me that, at my age, I was still well enough to enjoy comparative freedom. I had no longer the cares of early motherhood nor the debilities of old age, and I had an understanding spouse who did all he could to enable me to express my limited self in whatever way I chose. The tremendous distance to self realization is but the short distance of earnestly desiring to accomplish it, not later but immediately, and so I took a tack or two through poverty grass and lovely lichen, cranberry patches and rattling scrub oaks, and marveled at the firmness of certain sandy areas and the softness of others. The sky was melodramatic. Nothing equals its spectacle on these blustery days. As I picked one little sprig of bayberry, I prayed I might not even find a foot step near my shack. Then the birdhouse hove up against the charcoal sky and the leaden sea made darker by those white, curled breakers joining hands endlessly down the great bars of Peaked Hill. I opened the door easily; all was in place. Outside, my sweater still hung on the line-yanked about at the shoulders by the intolerant wind.My first duty was to light the fire which took a remarkable amount of time to come to life in that small stove. I then fell to work at once, spreading some peanut butter on a few less-than-crisp crackers. I filled out the dramatis personnae for *Il Sole di Chi E?* (*The Sun, Whose Is It?*) over a two-hour period. There will be thirteen characters in all. I was impressed with the number when I finished.

I later characterized each of them as a particular musical instrument combining in a composition of orchestral scoring. After almost an hour, my scrambled eggs began to congeal on the stove sufficiently for consumption. When I finished my small repast, I wisely took to the warmth of the blankets and read for another hour, *I Knock at the Door* by Sean O'Casey, falling asleep, finally, with the ancient Atlantic in my eye and ear.

October 27, 1978

The weather was mild and beautiful. Using the key to the Snail Road entrance, we managed the steep incline we had not navigated for years. The sensational "sand to sea" vista was the same intense impact I had remarked on the other day when I came across the dunes there alone. It almost hurts the senses, it is so sharp an experience—that blue line suddenly drawn across the entire horizon as far as the eye can see. So we hovered breathlessly there and dipped down between the old landmarks around Harry's and up to the birdhouse from the beach and "home!" With a bit of tugging, we freed the lock of sand and loaded our weekend supplies inside. Outside, the sun was timid but tempting. We had a beer, and I began immediately on the play. With some luck, I finished the scenery description and began the initial dialogue. As the stars came out, Sal and I had a delightful supper of our tinker mackerel and fried potatoes, and, after a walk under the bright and numerous constellations, I posed for ten sketches—brush and ink.

October 28, 1978:

Sal rose and prepared coffee. We took our time getting underway and after he drove to town to do the chores, I completed my exercises and started work for the day at 10:30, pulling my chair up to the door in the sunshine. A few hunters could be heard popping guns in the distance (it's pheasant season), and I instinctively shoved the chair back from the door an inch or two. At three o'clock, Sal began to shingle the sou'west end of the shack, and I went out to help him for an hour. I had just completed Scene I of the first act.

October 29, Sunday:

I had wanted to stay until Monday, but after a full day writing with great intensity, the evening began to close in a little chilly, and Sal suggested we return to town. There was much to do. In the fading light, I read him the full first act, and he was terribly impressed, enthusiastically so. For some reason, I had not expected his enthusiasm, but it was truly a moment of great happiness for me—to have so struck a cord of response in him of such depth and intensity. He thought it was the beginning of a powerful play. Something of that special moment will always stay with me—the finishing of one act of a concept and a total expression held inside for many months—its unwinding in the atmosphere that breathes life to me, and then the delivery to another who understands and loves the same things I do. In the fading light of a perfect day, I felt renewed and on my way to realization, if for no other reason than the initiation of a dream. Tomorrow it may all seem

> less noble, less intense and less worthy, but the day was truly sufficient unto itself. We drove back to civilization, having gathered courage to do so, each in his own way.

Romolo's matriculation at Harvard and the attendant circumstances of Parent's Weekend and other pleasant introductions to what would be his home for the next four years left us no time for any more creative work at the shack. Winter set in almost abruptly, and so, on December 3, a very late date for closing the shack, we went out to the back shore with Tommy to close Frenchie's domain.

> Sal, Tommy, and I piled into the jeep and headed for the sand pit. Tim (Everett) had come up briefly to tell us that he had taken his law boards at Northeastern and had applied to Harvard, Columbia, N.Y.U., Virginia, and Vermont schools. He'll probably make one or all. The sky looked so snow-filled, we hoped the weather would hold until our chores were completed. The dunes were spectacular in that winter coat of walnut brown shrubbery against a gun-metal sky, set off by an occasional small dot of dallying red rose hip, reluctant to welcome winter. Once at the shack, we had a fine lunch. I had brought with my homemade bread and cranberry crunch cake and then set about immediately to board up everything. First thing was to take the french doors off—then board up the back window—then the lower level had to be protected so sand wouldn't overwhelm the pump. Even the shit house had to be nailed shut. While the boys were banging away outside, I packed up everything inside. It was a reasonably easy job. We found that someone had broken in and stolen a length of pipe from the stove, but that was all they had touched. Tommy put all the rolled roofing inside the shack at my direction, (the stuff is so expensive these days), and, after carefully nailing everything, we finally locked up and called it a season. On the way home, Tom spotted some spouting whales which I couldn't see. It began to snow and the landscape was just plain heavy and restful.
>
> Back at the house, I found a note on the door from Tim. In the envelope was Edwin Dickinson's obituary. Now Dick is gone too, and all those golden days are truly only a memory. Nothing in death diminishes what this man was in life. As time goes by, the critics will, one by one, renew their interest as his true genius is appreciated. Dick is a unique painter—a one-of-a-kind man. He was the type of eccentric people take pleasure in remembering, yet his art will be remembered beyond and above his oddities and not just because of them.[8]

Copying this excerpt from my 1978 journal, I am instantly reminded of the days of "back shore" visitations that Edwin "Dick" Dickinson and Ross Moffett shared, in 1916 and 1917 particularly, and of Dick's hearty enjoyment of his contact with the Coast Guardsmen of the Peaked Hill Station. My 1979 interview with one of the station crew, Louis "Spucky" Silva, for instance, reveals Dick's characteristic obsession with the naval rituals. Silva amusedly recalled their energetic exchange of semaphore signals on Dick's numerous visits to the station. The close friendship of Edwin Dickinson and Ross Moffett, which I described, in my biography of Ross, and the kinship they enjoyed on their walks to the "back shore" bears repeating here:[9]

Frenchie's Shack Interior, pen and ink drawing by Salvatore Del Deo, 1979

But the sense of the freedom and wildness of the "back side" as it is affectionately called by natives, has disappeared with the necessity to share it with the rest of the world which cannot imagine or ever experience, for instance, those invigorating cups of coffee brewed by the Coast Guardsmen of the old Peaked Hill Life Saving Station, as it was designated until 1914, and later when the nomenclature was changed to the U.S. Coast Guard and a new building housed the crew at Peaked Hill. A few excerpts from Edwin Dickinson's 1916–1917 diaries give an intimate sketch of these shared moments.

> 1916, November 11 a.m.—boxed and sent 4x7—p.m. walking with Ross in dunes—met Luks there & eve home and at Boogars saw Lisboa celebration.
> 1917 January 21 a.m.& p.m.—Ross to dinner short walk. eve etching & Tibi and I reading "Pride and Prejudice" Snow on Point and far shore
> Feb. 18—late breakfast—work—p.m., Bill (Boogar) Ross and I walked on the dunes, eve in Mary S...[10]

Thus, the sodality of painters, playwrights, and poets may be recalled as tangible reality in physical space, not just as vague remembrance. At that time, the community of Peaked Hill Coast Guardsmen, as well as those of the other stations on the "back shore," shared a vital life with the streets and by-ways of their connecting communities, so that tying the landscape of both together was a daily experience so essential to their mutual survival.

In January 1979, I was still preparing the profile of the unique skyline of Provincetown's marvelously intact human-scale architecture, but it would be another year before the entire historic district could be presented as a National Register proposal to the Massachusetts Historical Commission. Weary as I was, the inventory had to proceed. Giovanna was in her last year at Williams College and was scheduled to graduate in June, having had access to some of the best art history professors in the country, including F. Lane Faisson and Richard Stoddard. Romolo would continue his first year at Harvard with enthusiasm, creating both a 300-pound plaster model of two entwined giraffes as well as a small poem that revealed the strong and early enunciation of nature in his choice of metaphor.

We are garbed in seaweed panoply
Horseshoe crabs, dead shell, helmet-
We are going out to sea
In wooden boats our father made
No sail,
No motor,
Intricate imagination
To take us to the battle
Deep.
—*Romolo Del Deo, January 8, 1979*

In the spring of 1979, Sal went to Florence, Italy, where he had been given a one-man show at the Galleria Davanzati in April. His landscapes proved captivating to the Italian audience, unaccustomed as they were to the sights of the sea and the backshore and the high cliffs at Highland Light. For another eight months, I continued my steady pace of preparing the Historic District for a National Register status, and in February 1980, Sal and I delivered the completed inventory to the Massachusetts Historical Commission, some 800 additional sheets. No preservation commitment had weighed so heavily upon me as this district proposal, and in June of that year, the antidote to such intensity was, as always, to be found at Frenchie's shack.

June 1, 1980:

Summer begins. Sal and I went to the dunes today, probably sharing a relatively free moment before the duties of a full season of obligations begins. The spring has been fatiguing and tiring, but today the sun was brilliant, and we took our macaroni and wrenches and the old Coleman stove and headed across the dunes. I had somehow forgotten that the dune roses were beginning to bloom, and the joy of seeing them again was great. So many white roses are scattered along the route. When we arrived, someone had broken the lock and evidently stayed the night. Little was amiss, but it is always unsettling to find the place abused. We began wearily to set everything right at once. Sal immediately attended to the birdhouse, putting it properly back on its post with great care, never disturbing the nesting material so snugly accumulated in the "four apartments." At once, it seemed, the swallows returned and dove and swooped a glee of finding their old digs miraculously materialized. Daddy warbled and chortled his gratitude on the driftwood Frenchie had nailed up against the post. Then, of course, we hauled out the pump and put it to soak. The place was full of benches, ladders, and sand. Sal took the plywood off the French doors and there was sea again in the frame of the porch, a picture annually renewed to perfection. The rug was hauled out, and I began to sweep out the winter's sand and the little bits of paper chewed by the mice. Everywhere, the mice had nibbled and especially had partaken of the soap.

Little by little, things came clean. The old shack came back, and we sat down to our repast with a glass of wine, but the heat was enervating, and after our lunch, it was a struggle against drowsiness to put pen to paper. I sat out in the rear of the shack gazing distractedly at the roses whose fragrance was powerful, even though many had not opened. I was determined to start a vigorous writing schedule, even with the pressures of summer, and with this in mind, I wrote a few pages, heat or no. It was not an inspired effort, but inspiration is a luxury one does not always enjoy.

The work I began on that perfect dune day was a novel about Provincetown, which I had long contemplated and which I later entitled *Footprints on the Sea*. It was a novel by definition but not by traditional format, as it was structured by an episodic series of events and portraits of people that linked together the two most congenial but disparate and enduring elements of Provincetown in the decade of the fifties: fishermen and artists. They had been joined since the painter Charles W. Hawthorne established his school of painting here in 1899, The Cape Cod School of Art. Though at first glance there appears to be a certain anomaly in closely linking the fishermen and the artists, one is easily made aware of the interaction between these two elements after even a cursory examination of Provincetown's history over the last one hundred years. In addition, the attraction of artists, internationally, to seaside locations is a well-established fact, the colorful elements of fishing life and seaside villages and the equally interesting physical landscapes all combine to inspire a painter endlessly. Sometimes, these repositories of inspiration expire as the world of art transforms itself, but the fishermen usually remain until the fish abandon them for other shores and with such migration or extinction, the colorful life of the fishermen also disappears and becomes memory.

Although Provincetown, one of the great but small fishing communities of America, on the shore of what has been reputed to be the second largest natural harbor in the world, is not likely to succumb to extinction any time soon, its active fishing life is now diminished and its artists' life somewhat changed from earlier days, but, nevertheless, they both still thrive. The two ways of life still intertwine, but not so much. *Footprints on the Sea* is, therefore, an invocation of the past, as I experienced it among my contemporaries, against the perennial vicissitudes of nature, which are always dramatic in this village by the sea.

Following this trip in June, a longer sojourn to Frenchie's shack in July continued the program of writing I had begun the month before. A year later, work on the novel was still ongoing and I remarked on its progress during a routine visitation to the shack:

July 7, 1981:
Today finds us again in our beloved shack. A strong, sou'west breeze has made putting in a new screen on the westerly window a bit of a "flap," but we managed. I had to sew a new piece on it, because the window is so large. This is the second consecutive Monday in the dunes. Yesterday, when we arrived in blazing heat, we immediately dove in the ocean. What a splendid refreshment! We later took a second dip. The water is probably 70 degrees. The Park Service still has the tern lines across the beach, and that suits us just fine. We love to see the terns fluttering and whirling and hear their sharp remonstrances against intrusion. A half-dozen swallows are patrolling Frenchie's birdhouse. It gives us such pleasure to see them nurturing yet another generation. Sal has managed two or three watercolors this time which are beautiful. The ability with which he handles the medium is remarkable. I finished a little section of "Footprints" yesterday, probably the last interlude addition This will be the third draft, a year's effort. I also finished a short story here in June—"Rappacini's Daughter (after Hawthorne)." I like it, but it needs much more work.

Back in town the following day on July 8, I chronicled a moment on the tidal flats at the West End breakwater looking for specimens for the salt water tanks at the museum:

July 8, 1981:
Started the day with two hours on the tidal flats at the breakwater. Tim Sawyer and I found the largest oyster shell I have ever seen out there. The brackish pools were slimy but beautiful in their murky way. Suddenly, as if from nowhere, a town youngster appeared. "What's up?....what ya lookin' for?" he said. The kids are out there as if they grew there. You don't see them approach, but they emerge as druids in the forest. I call them druids of the flats. Today, it was Richard Meads's youngest son, Jeremy, who confronted us: "What ya lookin' for?" They're curiously involved, as if it were their territory. They themselves are catching green crabs or eels or just anything, because they love the lure of the place. They'll probably never be completely aware of the very few of us who saved that world for them in 1962. While I live, however, it gives me great joy to remember, as I gaze across the protean world in the tidal flats, how remarkably fortunate were the efforts to preserve this treasure of an estuary providing such a "wealth of bounty everlasting."

August 4, 1981:
Last night in the heat and humidity, unable to sleep, even here in paradise, I pondered rather sadly on many things. Though still possessed of creative powers, there is something vitally missed with the children grown and gone. The old shack reverberates its joy from a by-gone time through the more comfortable accommodation of the new one: The tarpaper walls and smoky kerosene stove vibrated and smelled. The card games kept one awake. The mechanical toy lion had personality, and the

mystery and specialness of being there was so scintillating a thing, one could barely refrain from complete happiness. Now, we are quiet, composed and at peace to produce our art. The irony is always the same; amelioration does not exist, so that each frame of a man's life presents awesome, inhibiting factors to the creative process. An element of strength, power, inspiration, peace, etc., is always missing. Determination, alone, bridges the gap of imperfection.

August 20, 1981:
The weather was superb. We spent a gorgeous day on the dunes with Alice on Monday. The days are somehow more circumscribed in summer; however, this one was perfect. Our dune trips with Alice go back twenty-eight years, since our marriage.[11] She was always so pleased to share the back shore with us and to paint herself or to take numerous photographs of the dunes in their varied moods over many years. Toward sunset, we all went down to the beach together to see if she could get a shot of the horses coming along the strand for the evening ride. Sure enough, right on schedule they came galloping. Let's hope the shots are good.

Horses at sunset on the beach at Frenchie's August 20, 1981. *Photo by Alice Palmer* [11]

The remainder of the summer and fall passed quickly, and we soon found ourselves at that last golden moment, having brought our creative efforts to temporary fulfillment:

October 31, 1981:
This month has been most unusual in every respect. Of the twenty-seven days between my birthday and today, sixteen have been spent on the dunes. Some of the days were only partial in residence, but just to wake up out here to the glorious sky and sea and to hear no sound but the mighty, singing throat of the ocean is worth weeks in any other place. The completion of the novel had been set in my mind to occur on October 27th, the anniversary of my father's death,[12] but I had

to miss it by one day because of the storm which kept us in town. The exciting truth is that, from June 1, 1980, to October 28, 1981, I was able to write *Footprints on the Sea* under the most difficult schedule imaginable. Since the entries in my journal are usually written at night after a day's work, and often when I can hardly hold my head up from fatigue, they may seem, at times, to be illogical or ill-phrased. I have the compulsion, nevertheless, to describe a small part of my thoughts.

November 1, 1981:
Now the novel is completed, in its first draft at least. Some passages written sixteen years ago have been included, but not many. The idea has been in germination that long. By Christmas, I intend the first retyping to be done for continuous appraisal by my family. Until then, the reading of each individual chapter to Sal after a strenuous composition during the day, has been my only basis for perspective We had marvelous moments at the shack. Just at sunset, all summer long, as the horses came by with their daily seekers of sand and sea, Sal and I would sit on the porch, have a glass of wine, and I would commence the day's chapter. It was a jewel-like pause in the day. Generally, he was impressed with what I had done and always made constructive comments. My style became more discursive and adhering to plot structure as the work developed. I believe the opening chapters have creative verve and impel the work forward as things now stand, but the challenge has been to connect this energy to an overall design. The perspective I have achieved is given to very few, for my insights are rooted in experience over a considerable time frame, not floating on the surface of contemporary observation. My judgments, therefore as to character and action, are tempered by in-depth knowledge and, I hope, by empathy and understanding as well.

By 1982, serious illness had impacted several members of our family as well as myself. It became a daily battle to confront, the exigencies of life and death. Understandably, the lesser aims of pursuing philosophical constructs and the creative pursuits of art and letters had to be set aside for the main endeavor of just staying alive. In all respects, it was a very difficult year and one in which my journal records but minimal achievement of the spirit, except the essential one of focusing on improved health.

Coincidentally, this was the year that the back shore community lost one of its residents, Charlie Schmid. With his demise, his dune shack, in the midst of the great Atlantic flyway, also met its end, being summarily bulldozed by the National Seashore shortly after Charlie's death, so that the possibility of remembering his life among us with some kind of dignity was abrogated with the scattering of his personal effects on the sand without any consideration to allow even their modest burial.[13] It appeared to the dune shack community at large that this lack of respect and this insensitive destruction was meant as an example and warning, and it sent shock-waves through the heart and soul of the dune shack society. What we had imagined to be a reasoned approach to the lingering problems of our presence on the Great Outer Beach was exposed for what it was, a cover-up for unilateral and summary action and a predetermined intent to eliminate the dune shacks and their residents' footprint as each one died. No further claims would be considered, either physical or spiritual.

The result of this insensitive elimination of a long-standing presence among us, one that had gathered a considerable respect for the serious dedication to ornithological observations it represented, sent a clear message: we were now considered antagonists to the administration of the very entity we had encouraged and supported. We had believed that, somehow, the Department of the Interior understood that, among well-established areas of residency on Cape Cod, there were the residents that included the squatters on the back beach. We had believed that the Department would have reasonable, fair, and long-term consideration with regard to the dynamics of habitation, as opposed to the standard formulae of "wilderness" parks previously established and, more or less, comfortably administered, where the parameters of the parks did not particularly include a density of habitation. This, we had believed, would characterize the approach of The Cape Cod National Seashore's policy on Cape Cod, which is what I described as a "new challenge" for the Park Service: accommodating preexisting communities in a way that would allow reasonably regulated public use and traditionally established private use joined together in a partnership that would amicably honor the goals of preserving a unique and fragile natural environment on one of America's already populated eastern outposts, while, at the same time, preserving a cultural and historic residential legacy. We had begun with belief and were now confronted with the erosion of that belief, which went to the heart of our very existence. Needless to say, this was a pivotal moment of change after two decades of seeming functional accommodation. None of us would ever be completely at ease again in dealing with the Department of the Interior as represented by the Cape Cod National Seashore. It was from this point in time that all ensuing activities gradually came together to achieve the declaration of eligibility, by the Keeper of the National Register, of the dune shacks at Peaked Hill Bars to be included on the National Register of Historic Places.

As life propels us forward, it also tugs at us from the past, so that we are constantly reminded of the fact that we are inseparably part of the past, of the present, and also of the future. We are, in every sense, a determinant of the landscape of our days, of all whose lives are intertwined with ours, and even of those we will never know. One should be conscious of these verities and project them with a certain omniscience. In 1983, for instance, the lives of three souls near and dear to us came to an end: my mother, my husband's older brother, and lastly, on November 2, 1983, Frenchie. All died in that year, and we were hard-pressed to sustain the losses, but our life at the shack assisted us in our extremity.[14]

October 21, 1983:

Here we are in the almost intolerable heat of our Sears Roebuck stove in the dune shack. The wind has, for four straight days, blown NE at our French doors and jiggled the latch, breezed in under our feet and shivered those moments when we forgot to stoke our faithful stove. It has been a dramatic and exciting dune stay so far. I have managed four uninterrupted days in which I have finished, almost, that *Compass Grass Anthology* which has been so close to completion now for a number of years. Today, for instance, I wrote a final piece on Frenchie for the anthology. She is dying now—has not eaten for nearly twenty-five days and takes only water from the dunes. Sal took some water from the dunes yesterday for her. One has to feed it to her with a spoon. She is very weak and debilitated. Schatzi keeps on. She is in tough shape, but she doesn't give in—takes care of her mother faithfully and with loving tenderness. I have seldom seen such determined loyalty.

As I wrote today, a huge never-ending flock of swallows passed in flight. It was an exceptional sight, so many birds at one time passing the shack. I felt it was Frenchie's color-guard They must have known her condition and flown by in salute.

The days are balm to my spirit here; the wind and surf war; the nights are howling; the moon comes up like lemon alabaster and startles light upon the fuliginous sea.

November 6, 1983:

I've decided to print the *Compass Grass Anthology* myself and have received an estimate from Ed Rudd at Shank Painter Press. I spent half the afternoon recopying manuscript pages that needed extra cleaning up due to changes. It seems an endless task to prepare something for the press.

November 2, 1983:

Frenchie passed away this morning at 11:30 a.m. Schatzi called me to tell me at 2:00 p.m. I was grateful to her for letting us know at once. It was such a strange coincidence: I had prepared and combed the manuscript for last-minute corrections and had everything truly completed including title page, contents, etc. I had a 3:00 p.m. appointment with Gillian and Ed Rudd at Shank Painter to set up the production. It was as if Frenchie continues in my tribute to her, passing from the actuality to the legend without the loss of more than three hours. Schatzi is taking it rather hard but holds. She cannot hold back the tears, however. I will give her Frenchie's piece to review.

In my journal, a note from Frenchie is carefully preserved which appears to have been received on October 31. At least, that is the date indicated beside the letter, although it probably was written some time before. It speaks eloquently, as always, of her love for us and her faith in the future:

> My very dearest Josephine, Sal and dear, dear children and all the animals. No one, not even you, Jo, can imagine how very deep in my heart I feel happy for you all. You, mother, and you, dear Sal, father stay up in that cloud and do not even look down from it.
>
> With all my gypsy power I will hold that happiness for you forever. In case that happy cloud gets wet, remember, behind it there is sunshine always. It is strong; it will come through for you all the time. That I love all of you, this you know, Frenchie

The evidence of death does not come suddenly on the dunes. It is usually stark and leaves its mark, after a time, in the weeping dune grass where the wasted carcass of a seal shorn of flesh by a coyote is hidden or on the sorrowing canvas of the sandy beach with the dry and shriveled remains of a dead sea gull. These morsels are occasional moral reminders of our fate. They are not hugely evident, only startlingly discovered as colophon to a dune walk or a stray step from shack to shore. Frenchie died at her home in Provincetown, but her death truly transpired at the shack, for there she left us in spirit and there her spirit resides "forever" as her words so firmly assured us. I have no trouble in acknowledging her presence in the shack, along the shore, at the foot of a cluster of rose hips at the crest of the hill where the sand has been building a small citadel in back of her shack and where Schatzi scattered her remains after cremation.

Writing this memoir, I am always aware of Frenchie's presence in the air, at my side in the shack by my chair, in the call of the gull, for there she deliberately chose to live, and there her "gypsy power," as she phrased it, is as strong as ever. Who will question such a legacy? The ancestors of the Wampanoag tribe roamed across this lookout upon the Atlantic and left their remaining arrowheads and their shell heaps as testimony of their survival skills and who themselves were subsumed, at last. Their presence still has an effect upon our quick and our dead; we feel them here. Although no one can claim trespass on territory that will eventually lie under the ocean's unremarked ubiquity, we now may say something about the life that passed and re-passed on that "long day's journey into night" as O'Neill whispers to us from his still-visible sanctuary of sand at Peaked Hill. It is easier, therefore, to guess what our future will be here at the Peaked Hill Bars than to predict almost any other long-range trajectory of human habitation on the planet. The land will gradually be removed from under our feet, the markers of civilization will disappear, and the messages now extant that vision provides will be either forgotten, or worse, lost in translation, but the spiritual ethos that man may create while he stands here, temporarily unmolested by the threat of death and pulsating with the hope of life everlasting, will survive somewhere between the sand and stars.

CHAPTER VII

Defining a Way of Life

1984-1988

THE "FOREWORD," WHICH I wrote for the *Dune Cottages at Peaked Hill Bars—A Survey* in 1986, at the request of the then-superintendent of the National Seashore Herbert Olsen, refers to the way of life they represent and to the metaphor of their symbolic presence at Peaked Hill Bars, again as "temples." Therefore, I shall include it here, with slight alterations, as both colophon to the previous chapter and introduction to this one:

> The family of dune cottages clinging tenaciously along the "back shore" of Provincetown and Truro, between an area roughly described as extending from Race Point in the West to High Head in Truro in the East, is, without doubt, a classification of structures unique in American history, not alone because of their architectural simplicity and impressive recycling of found materials, but more especially because of their cultural genealogy. They are, metaphorically speaking, almost a multidimensional archaeological resource, having been structures used at different periods for varying purposes: the several buildings of the Coast Guard Stations at Peaked Hill, a boat house, small buildings similar to the half-way houses of the Life Saving Service, a fisherman's shack or a hunter's cabin, to poets' abodes, painters' studios, naturalists' lookouts, a home of essential spiritual retreat and rejuvenation from every walk of life. Layers of existence have occupied these structures or their derivatives, and each layer has added its personal emphasis and left us an historical reference.
>
> Taken together, these references would fill a large volume and are no subject for such a brief overview, but, if only quickly, I would like to indicate some of the elements, where I can, of their character and provenance as constituting a National Landmark legacy, with the hope that my references, and those of others who surely will be able to provide valuable contributive material to such an important study, may help to establish their right to forever cling to their tenuous watch on the Atlantic.
>
> As in the case of the Greek temples of ancient times, wherein the contemporary religion was transformed to the daily needs of the society, it is perhaps through the particular transformation which may occur in such modest "temples" that our

own culture may survive; these small, nameless abodes by their very simplicity serve to teach and to retain for our society the first lesson of nature, the law of survival for all the creatures of this earth.

Hundreds, perhaps thousands, have sought inspiration here, and many more will come to worship in these shelters of the human spirit. They, therefore, are a symbol and a presence, neither to be disassociated from the other. Those who have been moved to live and work here are a community of one urging the preservation and the continuation of their legacies and their lives for the benefit and the enrichment of the legacies yet to be established and the lives yet to be realized.

In the fall of 1984, the entries in my journal chronicle the golden moments in which we partook of the elixir of dune life in quick succession:

October 11, Thursday:
This turned out to be the loveliest day of all—quite warm and very little breeze again. Sal had to return to town to supervise many secondary but necessary events He was glad to do this, but I regretted his losing such a glorious day. As I lay in Romolo's lawn chair resting and reading, facing toward the sea, a sparrow fluttered on my chest and stayed there for a moment, totally unafraid. He looked up at me quite quizzically and then darted away. "Ah," I thought, "Frenchie's spirit is here with us." The sparrow was as bold as she was. I am not sure if it was a Savannah or a Seaside sparrow. It had a yellow splash on its wing, but was otherwise drab.

I had worked out the rest of the Fine Arts Work Center material in the morning. Each day, I was reading Ross's old *Art Digests*—1929–1938. They yield some interesting facts and a lot of pertinent trivia. Sal came back tired but satisfied, bearing groceries and good cheer. Our evening repast of peppers and homemade sauce I had concocted from our garden tomatoes over a good plate of spaghetti was all one could ask. Dice sleeps endlessly in her chair, but tonight, we took her out for a walk in bright moonlight beside the sea. I cannot remember a clearer, more brilliant evening. Nothing but our shadows intruded on the miles of beach in front of us. The air was warm and the moon full. We walked what seemed a long distance toward the former location of Charlie Schmid's shack and then back again. Occasionally, a fishing boat passed on the blue-black ocean, but the bass fishermen are absent this fall from the shore—no bass running. It's strange not to see their chariots parading past, long beams of light plowing the beach many yards ahead of them.

October 12:
I began to recopy "The Watercolor" manuscript this morning and worked two hours straight. It has good stage possibilities. The characters are easily type cast, and it moves along. The dialogue is odd, but to the mark of truth. As is my predilection, I prefer the naturalness of a Chekovian approach. In the late afternoon, we walked a good 1.2 miles to the previous cut-through and then back to the shack. The dunes are a marvel of rich color. Sal was able to stay here today, but the sky began to cloud. Even so, he is racking up some excellent dune studies.

October 13, Saturday:

Finished typing the comedy. The sea is picking up a bit and the sky still overcast; however, we had a truly delightful afternoon inside by our cozy wood stove. Talilla came over and posed for Sal. He did an excellent little study of her. She then insisted on doing a drawing of me which I thought was quite insightful for a 7-year-old.[1] We all had a lot of laughs and spaced the posing with an Oreo cookie or two, which she loves. It was late before Genevieve took her home, and we spent another cozy, warm evening listening to the lullaby of the sea. Tomorrow, because of hurricane "Josephine," we shall go in for the day.

October 16:

Sal, while we were walking along the pounding surf, remembered being here in the summer of 1960 when he was working for Hazel, Frenchie, and Boris as a back shore attendant, doing errands, etc. That, one day, as he was walking along the same pounding surf, he suddenly heard an unearthly sound of music coming over the dunes. It was the painter Byron Browne, who came out every day at sunset to play his bagpipes at the ocean's edge. He remarked on the beauty of that sound and the eerie quality of the experience. Sal added to that memory of Byron Browne, the further image of his coming up to the very edge of the sea and playing the pipes fairly on top of the incoming surf, so that the augmentation of both was dramatic. Byron was a large man with a shock of blond hair, and he always wore the kilts when playing the pipes. Of course, one can only speculate on what kind of lungs he must have had to play pipes at the same time as he was walking on sand.

And so we chatted a bit in between our endeavors, Sal out on the dunes painting and I here writing letters, reading. I put a chicken in our little top-of-the-stove oven, having prepared a reasonable dressing and stuffed the bird and lit the wood stove after pumping water for the day. It will take all afternoon for the bird to cook over the wood fire, but it should be excellent. We ran out of gas, and so, this is our only alternative. Sal cut a large pile of wood, and I did also.

Journey at Afternoon's End: By four p.m., we had determined to take our afternoon walk. We started out along the beach going west with the surf pounding along beside us with six-foot breakers thundering up the beach mercilessly. As far as one could see, the surf was breaking in long lines of white caps, successively and relentlessly racing shoreward. The air was very warm, however, and we walked along in comfort. The tide had just gone past its highest mark and was receding a bit, but the spume from the surf sent a haze, as of fog, down the coastline as far as the eye could see. Had we had the energy, we would have gone to Phil's shack (Phil Malicoat), but it was much too far, The sun periodically broke through and glanced the water to a bright blue and the ripping waves to a white, white note. The sky was shafted with the sun's rays in that afternoon extravagance of last spectacular showmanship of light changes. We draggled up the bank by Hazel's shack Euphoria and came through a dense field of dune grass. One has to be careful that it doesn't throw you, as you can easily catch your feet in its overlapping and matted base.

Down the steep embankment in back of Euphoria, we were dazzled by the silver sheen of each grass blade as the whole field caught the light skipping across its surface and making it seem as if the compass grass was either soaking wet with dew-shine or simply a new kind of silver hay. Descending steeply, we looked up at the high hill on which Euphoria is perched. Walking along in the hollow, it was a discoverer's delight—our bejeweled bayberry bushes hung with grey-white aromatic berries, very thick clusters of them this year, and snakes of poison ivy vines along the ground, red-backed and ready to strike terror to Sal's heart, and the colors so diverse and accented by the light tan sand, which treats every natural object as if deserving of the finest linen canvas on which God may paint his wonders, and wonders enough there were. Soon we spied a miniature forest of bright red maples which lacked only a small Lilliputian to emerge and establish its scale, and so too the deep thickets of pine, oak, maple, sumac, and verbena wildly entwined and protective of their hidden valley of growth in a landscape sparse as a Hokusai print. We skirted this stray forest and came eventually to the road which moves in back of Malicoat's shack and meets the cut-through just west of Boris's. Down we went into a cathedral arch of pine and oak, the pine two-toned in straw and green, some of the needles having been dipped in a dune chemistry of pine disease that turns their needles brown, but it only made the healthy branches richer in deep, green hues.

When we came to the road as it turned to the beach, there were Frank Milby and his wife picking cranberries. Art's beach taxi stopped and exchanged a few pleasantries and commented on the state of the shoreline.[2] The last leg of our our journey at eventide brought us abruptly up and over the hill in back of Harry's shack and, on our right, Fearing's shack and Fowler's cabin. The three seemed cozy friends there, perched on their settled territories. The sinking sun was yet high enough to bless each sacred domicile. We arrived home and smelled our chicken at a distance of the outhouse. The stars at 9:00 p.m. were so numerous that we couldn't find Orion, the Pleiades or Taurus, just Casseopeia's Chair.

New Moon at the Outhouse

I topped a dune and saw rash Phaeton's Fire
Extinguished by the sea.
A god's last frenzy following the sun,
While, at my back, night, not-now, and day,
yet-still, were held in delicate decision.
The opal sky, uncertain as to stars,
Which to reveal and which should fall,
Left twilight to define my shadow self.
In such half-light and state
I sat between the minutes, waiting the
lunar dark
To steal the crescent of the rising moon
And fasten it, surprised, upon the outhouse wall.

The following day, on the seventeenth, we set out once more for a brief walk at sunset to photograph the three shacks—Fearing, Fowler and Harry. After taking what I hope to be a spectacular shot of Harry's domicile from the rear looking toward the ocean, we walked up to pay Harry a visit, and, lo and behold, the door was open (not locked) as was Harry's way. Sunny hasn't changed his manner of

Sal at Harry's shack, fall 1984: "There were books as of old..."

conduct. The shack itself was absolutely beautiful. The sun shone across a bed covered with a rose-colored spread and pink pillows, so that the afternoon sun made the shack glow with the reflected warmth. There were the books as of old—a stove with crooked pipe and candles—all neatness and order untouched by intruding hand. The windows are unshuttered and unbarred the way Harry would wish his world to be. I took shots of the interior with Sal.

October 18, Thursday:

Today, as promised, was quite warm, and the ocean rhythms have settled to an andante roll, mezzo forte, as opposed to presto pourings, fortissimo. In the morning, I typed a long letter to Tim,whose birthday is the 28th,and a long addition to Romolo's letter. Sal stayed at the side of the shack looking out to sea and did a delicate, very sensitive seascape that I'm sure is his best study yet. The skyline was hardly discernible from the ocean's side. The afternoon saw us enjoying a gentle sun outdoors—I reading Stanley's essays on poets and Sal painting on top of our dune overlooking the world beyond and in back.[3] I eventually fell asleep after finishing Stanley's impressive critique of Robinson Jeffers et alia. With the dozing came a desire to finish up that idea for a poem I had last week when the moon stole up on the birdhouse unawares. I completed it in my head and awakened to put it down, Sal still painting.

In spite of the endless inspiration of the vast Atlantic, with its diverse moods and weather, and the corollary of the dune landscape that resonated with the effects of such variable and thrilling aspects, there were many days when the recording of such inspirations, through the painter's eye, presented no small risk to his health and to his canvas. So it was that in the fall of 1985, a permanent indoor studio space for Sal had to be addressed. We still had the right to build, over the exact footprint of the old bedroom we had so romantically occupied in 1953, a small space that could be visualized as a modest repository for his ongoing creative life without too much interruption from adverse weather.

We started, therefore, in late summer to construct the room after procuring permits from the town and permission from the Seashore. Providing essential assistance, with his usual debonaire but expert approach to carpentry, was our dear friend Richard Meads, who faced every challenge with the attitude that it was "just routine," even if "routine" involved fronting winds on the roof like a weathervane in distress. Richard and Sal went forward together with resolute accord, and I picked up the job of making coffee for the crew well into the cold days of late fall. On one such occasion, Richard, with a twinkle in his eye, complained about the brew, remarking that it tasted like an old Brillo pad. Deeply offended by such an accusation, I checked the pot, and, sure enough, I found a neglected Brillo pad at the bottom. Ever since, I never make coffee on the dunes but

Richard Meads braving the elements to build Sal's studio over our old bedroom

when I hear the ridicule of that hilarious moment, from which humiliation I have never quite recovered my culinary dune *élan*.

By the time the room was closed in, it was almost November, and the stored art, a shovel, a kerosene light, and other sundry supplies needed on the dunes were put away for the winter. Even though small in square footage, this extra space made a huge difference in our dune life, so that, even today, with the little room as an addendum to the main living area, we consider the shack a domicile with all the conveniences of home.

In our terminology, the shack has always been what the Park Service refuses to refer to as "improved property." The issues which would swirl around the definition of "improved property" in the near future, had not yet surfaced so persistently at that moment in time, however, and little did we imagine that the National Seashore's definition and that of the Department of the Interior would be the primary reason for essentially denying shack owners their right to their habitation on the dunes.

In late 1985, the National Seashore was approaching its twenty-fifth anniversary, which would occur in August 1986. The quality of life within the confines of the Park had been largely maintained as promised with certain exceptions that appeared to be ongoing. One of these, of course, was the status of the dune shacks on the Great Outer Beach, which, from the beginning, had caused controversy, contention, and vastly diverse arguments regarding their maintenance and survival. The dialogue with the Cape Cod National Seashore began to intensify after the destruction of the Schmid cottage in 1982.By 1985, serious and widespread concerns surfaced regarding the shacks, their preservation, importance, and just how to maintain them in a manner both satisfactory to the inhabitants of the shacks and to the Park Service.

Because the National Park Service was a highly organized bureaucracy with strictly controlled management agendas, it was occasionally subject, as in all such bureaucratic systems, to contradictory and inconsistent operational guidelines and perceptions, especially in relation to changing conditions that could not always be anticipated. The purposes of preservation, which had been spelled out in general and, in some cases, specific terms in the original legislation, needed interpretation from time to time and also a certain flexibility in respect to their implementation. The authorities connected with the administration of the Seashore, accordingly, had created a commission known as the Seashore Advisory Commission, which became an essential interface between the day-to-day operation of the Seashore and the life of the communities within its parameters. This commission fielded the issues so critical to the entities, both communal and individual, in relation to the Park and attempted to defuse any serious maladjustments that arose. From time to time, the Commission faced serious attempts to eliminate its existence and subsume its responsibilities, because, understandably, administering policies would have been easier without a relatively objective discussion and overview. Fortunately, on each occasion, the use and value of the Commission was reaffirmed and its status sustained by political advocacy from Congressional support and by local insistence on its maintenance.

One of the major adjustments confronting the Advisory Commission on the agenda of their December 13, 1985, meeting was the status of the dune cottages. At that hearing, a considerable number of people were heard, all of whom expressed the overriding concern for the preservation of the shacks. It was plain that an agenda to save the way of life of the dune dwellers had to be defined and that those of us who cared about the shacks needed an opportunity to be heard. Statements made at that hearing phrased the issues very well. Among those present and speaking were Dr. Barbara Mayo, Dr. Julie Schecter, representing the inchoate, at that time, Peaked Hill Trust, our local historian of infallible recall George Bryant, Gordon Peabody, Sal, and myself and others. Numerous officials attended, but only those who had requested permission to be heard were allowed to speak. Superintendent Herbert Olsen reiterated the intention of the Seashore to review all the shack histories in order to discover their importance from an historical perspective. This was done the following year and the results were published in 1987, which came to the conclusion that no shacks had historical significance.[4]

In the meantime, I had moved in the same direction as the Park officials, and had begun to prepare a capsulated history of the dune shacks in which I set down as much information as my research could confirm at the time. At his request, I gave a copy of this small study to Superintendent Olsen for the records of the National Seashore, as I have previously noted. Since that time, I have made revisions in the material as some new information has become available and so have updated this history as part of the Appendix, Part I.

Although the dune shacks within the Seashore had survived by certain stipulations and through various systems of life-support since the first definitive altercations regarding their status began in 1964, it was now apparent, after more than twenty years, that the government eventually, and probably soon, would gain a complete upper hand in deciding their fate, due to the natural process of decease, primarily, but also because of variable and inequitable trajectories that favored some and threatened others. The owners of these shacks, which were still extant at Peaked Hill and as far east as the Armstrong cottage in Truro, were, consequently, alarmed and alert to the eventual threat of elimination and to the loss of their legacy to future generations. This alarm spread throughout the dune shack community, and, in fairness, to all who were inhabitants, both long-standing and of lesser longevity. The concern was not only about their own bond with the dunes and that of the previous generation of dune dwellers, but the bond that would be and should be forged with the next generation.

It was in this frame of mind and in this threatening environment of loss and indeterminate existence, that a group of determined and dedicated people brought forth an idea that would attempt to address the overall use of the dune shacks for years to come. Central in this group was Dr. Barbara Mayo whose devotion to the natural world as a marine biologist and as a founder, together with her husband, Dr. Charles Mayo, Jr., and Dr. Graham Giese, of the Center for Coastal Studies in Provincetown, was well known. Barbara Mayo's commitment to the environment was not only professional, as a scientist, but also philosophical and personal. Joining her in this serious dedication were Dr. Julie Schecter and sculptor Joyce Johnson, long-time dune resident and founder of the Truro Center for the Arts, Castle Hill. With apologies to others who were spiritually and/or peripherally part of this initial galaxy of activity, one might say that these three energized an idea for dune shack management that they proposed and which they named The Peaked Hill Trust.

My contact with the concept of the Trust began in 1985 and has continued. In the early 1990s, we shared intense efforts, together with others, to craft a long-term lease arrangement for three cottages bereft of their owners through decease and allowed to deteriorate by the Park Service to a deplorable condition. In essence, this neglect by the National Seashore had amounted to "demolition by neglect," a circumstance completely forbidden by federal legislation. (see Chapter Nine)

Reviewing my correspondence concerning the aims and structure of The Peaked Hill Trust for this memoir has alerted me, once again, to the several dilemmas that such an organization presented to the dune dwellers. Their long residency on the dunes was not then, and is not now, totally and satisfactorily resolved to those of us whose habitation there is still threatened and whose way of life has been indirectly characterized by some as "elitist." We have been, and are, individually responsible for an ongoing trajectory of time, not infinite, but, nevertheless, beyond the bureaucratic interpretation. The bureaucracy regards a private person in a private place as somewhat less than friendly to the American public at large, as opposed to a non-profit entity that represents a selected group habitation on a lottery chosen, time-share basis. In spite of the fact that there were some 600 such private residences, more or less, within the Seashore when it was initiated, the overall hierarchy of the Park Service refused to come to terms with the fact that, essentially, the Cape Cod National Seashore is a different kind of Park, with well-established use and traditions that will refuse and resist the alteration of their sense of place and purpose. This area is needful, it is true, of environmental protection and protocol, but not at the expense of historical and cultural legacies that do not threaten the environment.

My correspondence with Dr. Schecter began in November 1985, as she presented the proposed format of the Peaked Hill Trust to the Seashore and to others of the community long associated with preservation and historical perspectives. Her message was direct, clearly stated, and seemingly logical. She did not assume, for instance, that the shacks would be allowed to stay indefinitely in the "then" status they enjoyed. Both she and her colleagues in the Trust went about forging a plan that they hoped would satisfy the concerns of the Seashore as protectors of the public use and the need for access to the shacks, minimizing the serious side effects of that use. She detailed the highly structured and definitive overall plan in the draft for the Trust dated November 11, 1985. In correspondence with me at the time, she requested my comments and support for the plan, which I, of course, provided with as much honesty as I could bring to the issue, but for which I also held personal reservations, even at that moment of peril for the shacks. Writing to me about her group's idea on November 11, 1985, Dr. Schecter stated very plainly that they didn't believe that the Seashore would back up enough to allow private ownership of the shacks to continue indefinitely, even though it was a workable solution. "I hope that you and the Historical Association will agree that the shacks are special enough to warrant saving, even if under difficult conditions."[5]

My reply to Julie's plea was to write a letter on behalf of the Provincetown Historical Association, the private nonprofit association that had funded the "Rose Dorothea" project in the Heritage Museum and which had continued actively to provide financial assistance to numerous museum projects. I stated the support of the Association for the approach and the intention outlined by the Peaked Hill Trust, which emphasized that: "The Peaked Hill Trust does not want to see the cottages kept only as museum pieces, as reminders of a time past. The value of the cottages is in their use. We propose continued use of the cottages, adopting use patterns of Hazel Hawthorne and the Audubon Society's Wellfleet Bay Sanctuary. The Trust was formed to counter the loss of the dune cottages." Nothing in this initial presentation of purpose went counter to the perception that I and the other dune dwellers shared.

The issue was then, and still remains, in our definition of the word "use," not that which the Trust envisioned but that which had been well established by the occupancy heretofore and which could continue to do so without sacrificing the "way of life" that the Trust, very sincerely, wished to protect. Eventually, the kind of use that the Peaked Hill Trust proposed would succumb, we felt, to bureaucratic structuring. Within the dune shacks' operational agenda, it would create a system that would, most probably, erode their legacy by substituting a standard format of rules, regulations, and attitude. The purpose would be to provide an easier overall surveillance of those seekers of solitude and contact with nature for a prescribed time frame, and a period of visitation that could be transferred to the next occupant so that the environment could be "experienced" by the many who desired to do so.

The problem is that such a time-sharing on a limited basis cannot substitute for the real thing. What happens when the pump breaks down, when a corner of the roofing is ripped off by winter winds, when the outhouse needs a solution to some unsavory problem? The Trust, of course, comes to the rescue and fixes the problems. This is a sorry gift of the pretension that one is in true contact with a dune shack life. It is as if America had saved the habitations of the various Indian tribes after having evicted their inhabitants so that some ardent enthusiast or interpreter could "experience" the diurnal rituals of the indigenous tribal entities that once "lived" there. By this analogous example, it is easy to see what the difference is between "visitation" and "habitation." It is a huge difference which no system, no matter how carefully constructed, can ever equalize.

The March 1987 report of the Division of Cultural Resources, NARO, found that no dune shack had any historical significance. It was a blunt conclusion based entirely on a judgment that took nothing into consideration but the vernacular architecture and made no effort whatsoever to link the enormous cultural history connected with the shacks to any previous or contemporary habitation, even to the astonishing negation of Eugene O'Neill's ownership and occupancy of the old Peaked Hill Life Saving Station between c.1919 and 1924. During the whole of 1987, the preparation for a major battle regarding the preservation of the dune shacks began to take definitive shape. On January 9, 1987, for instance, Dr. Schecter, Executive Director of the Peaked Hill Trust, sent out a plea for members and interested persons to address the Cape Cod National Seashore and to present their views of the experience of staying in the shacks and to concentrate energies in urging that such experience continue. Not only on the Lower Cape, but throughout Cape Cod, many were discussing the issue of keeping the shacks viable in some way for future generations.

Throughout this uneasy period of disruption and anguish concerning the fate of the shacks, there was always the consolation of actually being at the shack for a few days at a time all summer and fall. Schatzi shared the weeks with us on alternate visits according to both our schedules. We exchanged notes as to weather, maintenance, and the complete joys of being in such a place:

> *From Schatzi, 1987 (late summer)*
> Hi—Never did get here yesterday, but sure made it today—Finished the remains of the glazing compound, but 8 panes left to do—Ellen was about to throw away the unused candles and red and white paper plates, but thought you might use them. There's plenty of light left in the candles. The weather absolutely gorgeous with a fall "nip" in the breeze. Guess we'll take another walk on the beach and then back to "People"...Oh well, there's next week. I bet this house is very happy with its year-round boarders plus visits from the "4 rats."—Love, Schatzi

> *From us to Schatzi, July 16, 1988*
> Here we are back again, Schatzi. You're right. The water was marvelous. We had two great swims. How we enjoyed that welcome relief. Altogether, we had a wonderful weekend. I was inspired, of course to start on the biography again and did some very good, concentrated writing. This place is magic. (But we know that, don't we?) Sal did a package of spiritual watercolors and, in spite of heat (great), we just rolled along.

From the beginning of 1988, the discussion concerning the dune shacks had widened and intensified. The Seashore Advisory Commission met on March 18, 1988, a year after the NARO survey had been made public, and devoted a segment of its meeting to the issue of the dune cottages in Provincetown and Truro. Speaking on behalf of the preservation of the dune shacks at that meeting were George Bryant, Dr. Barbara Mayo, and Mr. Brown, among others. Mr. Brown spoke eloquently as follows:

> These cottages and the way of life that they represent, are a piece of Americana, and they represent a rugged, individualistic value, a lifestyle that has really passed from the scene.

Dr. Barbara Mayo followed:

> I certainly would welcome a reaffirmation of the endorsement of the Commission for the continued use and preservation of the dune cottages.

George Bryant urged the Commission to adopt the concept of retaining all the dune cottages. In the end, the Commission unanimously voted to seek some form of public and private responsibility for maintaining the shacks for the future. Sadly, Dr. Mayo, whose dedicated commitment in finding a solution for their preservation, died on May 24, 1988, just two months after the meeting. In a letter to the Peaked Hill Trust membership, Dr. Julie Schecter wrote the notice: "My first task is the hardest. Dr. Barbara Mayo, friend, guide, and colleague, died earlier this year on May 24th. Among her many contributions, Barbara was a founder of PHT and our first president. Our work is part of her legacy; without her advice and steady hand, we would not have known where to begin. Her obituaries requested that memorial gifts be sent to PHT, and we have started a fund in her name."[6]

That the dune shacks' status at Peaked Hill Bars could ever be determined through bureaucratic *leger de main* was now recognized by almost everyone to be a failed policy. The Park began to come to terms with the central issue of their preservation in keeping with the National Preservation Act of 1966, which had been updated in February 1988, establishing the clear mandate of the preservation of cultural, historic and architectural resources by the Federal Government.[7] It became obvious, in fact, that the only avenue to ensuring preservation was in the declaration of the eligibility of the dune shacks for inclusion on the National Register of Historic Places. Since someone had to formally request such a designation, Norman Mailer and I wrote to James Bradley, Chairman of the Massachusetts Historical Commission, on July 14, 1988, requesting that the dune shacks be placed on the National Register of Historic Places.[8] Our letter was followed by one from Paul Christo, Chairman of the Provincetown Board of Selectmen to James Bradley on July 15, 1988, which made an identical request and added the further request that the National Park Service immediately cease any action to destroy the dune shacks.

On August 26, 1988, therefore, a public hearing was held by the Massachusetts Historical Commission in the Provincetown Town Hall with an estimated attendance between 150 to 200, overall. According to the Commission's report of the meeting, one hundred thirty-eight people signed in at the hearing, giving them a right to speak if they wished. Thirty-one people spoke at the hearing, but many others gave written testimony. Persons who gave oral testimony were listed and briefly noted in the report. It was an outpouring of tremendous interest and passionate support for the dune cottages and for the "way of life" they represented.

Wells Cottage by Salvatore Del Deo 2001, oil on canvas 20" x 24"

In all of this testimony, two dune residents, in particular, simply and clearly expressed the core issue that was central to all of us who were, at that time, residents of the shacks. Ray Martan Wells and Carl Tasha each emphasized, forcefully, the rights of the dune residents to remain in their habitation and to pass on their "way of life" to their heirs or assigns.

Less than two weeks later, on September 6, 1988, a legal memorandum from staff attorney Maria Letunic of the Massachusetts Historical Commission to the Commission concerning "The Cape Cod National Seashore Analysis of Issues Surrounding the Dune Shacks" gave a precise and definitive analysis of the issues in regard to the designation of the dune shacks as eligible for National Register status. In her two-page letter, Letunic said:

> The extensive legislative history of the Act reveals substantial concern for legal protection which would be responsive to the interests of Cape Cod residents. Congress recognized that Cape Cod is not an unsettled "wilderness area," and stated in its analysis of the Act that "lower Cape Cod" cannot be considered solely as a geographical area with certain physical characteristics. The Lower Cape must also be viewed as a way of life—a culture—which, though conditioned by its environment finds its essence in the people who have lived and are living there. The Bill seeks to preserve the way of life which these people have established and maintained on the Cape.

Accordingly, Letunic went on to delineate the authority of the Massachusetts Historical Commission, concluding in her last paragraph:

> Consequently, the Massachusetts Historical Commission has statutory authority to determine the historical significance of the Provincetown and Truro Dune Shacks which form a part of the National Seashore. In the event that the properties in question be deemed eligible for inclusion in the National Register, the Massachusetts Historical Commission would have authority and standing to review any proposed action by the National Park Service which could have an impact on the historic value of the Dune Shacks.

Hopes were high that eligibility for National Registration of the dune shacks would be forthcoming, although, of course, there was no certainty as yet. On the last page of my statement to the Massachusetts Historical Commission, which I had presented at the August 26, 1988, meeting, I had summed up the case for National Registration status as follows:

> We realize that National Landmark status has to have definitive limits as to standards, and we respect that, but we also know that this commission recognizes that much more than ascertainable fundamentals of preservation that pertain to materials and chronology need to be used here as criteria. We believe that you believe that an entire heritage belonging to the best of American cultural traditions is at stake here, something that does not just vaguely fall within your purview, but is substantially within your jurisdiction. This cultural legacy is now in total jeopardy. It may disappear forever from the American landscape; it may well do so. If it remains, it will remain to remind us, and generations to come, that art is part of the nation's honor; that poets are indispensable statesmen and creativity, no matter who expresses it, carpenter or astronomer, is the heart of the nation's survival.
>
> Harry Kemp, the poet of the dunes, left us many examples of his vision inspired by the way of life in his dune shack. "Transit Gloria" is one, and I quote it here:

Transit Gloria

Our sun, with all its worlds, drops down the sky,
For, banked in shining heaps the great suns fly
Onward in fiery swarms like golden bees,
While, from all sides, the everlasting seas
Of night break on them as they thunder by, and
Ignorant generations live and die
Amid this storm of stars and feel at ease.[9]

Can we feel at ease with our conscience if we deny that this kind of vision has existed in the cottages at Peaked Hill and might exist again? In asking the Massachusetts Historical Commission to declare the entire group of eighteen cottages at the very edge of our continent as National Registered Landmarks, we request much more for the future than for ourselves. I have stated previously something which I feel is appropriate to repeat: This constellation of dune cottages constitutes a continuous enrichment of the American dream traditionally derived from the freedom to imagine and to advance new worlds. This freedom and this dream should not be lost.[10]

CHAPTER VIII

Bessay and Goliath

1988-1991

IN 1988, DUNE dweller Grace Bessay's long travail in defending her right to own and occupy her cottage located at Peaked Hill Bars, known as the "Grail," was apparently drawing to a close. On September 15, 1988, less than a month after the tumultuous Massachusetts Historical Commission hearing on August 26,1988, her case was heard before the United States District Court, District of Massachusetts, by Judge David Nelson.[1] Two major issues comprised the elements of her case: did Bessay have adverse-possessory rights to her cottage and did her property meet "improved property" status as defined in the act establishing the Cape Cod National Seashore? On the issue of adverse possessory rights to the land, the judge ruled in her favor; however, in the matter of "improved property" rights, he ruled against Bessay's claim.

Bessay's lawyer, Jeffrey Axelrod from the firm of McGregor, Shea & Doliner, P.C. of Boston, appealed Judge Nelson's decision on April 18, 1989, less than a month before the Keeper of the National Register of Historic Places declared all of the dune shacks at Peaked Hill Bars to be eligible for listing on the National Register. Although Axelrod did not have the final determination of the Registrar at the time of this appeal, he was able to cite the findings of the Massachusetts Historical Commission in their determination of eligibility status for registration.

In the opening statement of "significance" of the dune shacks, Beth L. Savage, Architectural Historian for the National Register had this to say:

> The dune shacks and the dune landscape surrounding them are eligible for the National Register as a historic district under criteria A and C because of their exceptionally significant associations with the historic development of American art, literature, and theater, and for their representation of a rare, fragile property type. Additionally, the Tasha Cottage and the district are significant for historic associations with the productive life of Harry Kemp under criterion B. The dune shacks and the dunes themselves represent a historic cultural landscape comprised of a distinctive, significant concentration of natural and cultural resources united by their shared historic use as a summer retreat for the Provincetown colony of artists, poets, actors, and others. The importance of the dune shacks is embedded in their collective association with the historical development of the arts, their

Spartan, utilitarian forms, and their unique relationship with the harsh dune environment.

Savage went on to say:

The dune shacks provided shelter while minimally intruding into the contemplative solitude of the environment that provided the impetus to an abundance of artistic and literary work. The shacks' unpretentious, predominantly one-room structure, their simple materials and craftsmanship, their mobility, and their lack of amenities such as electricity and running water enabled their inhabitants to experience a survivalist relationship with nature. Celebration of the Cape's natural environmental qualities is eloquently embodied in Thoreau's *Cape Cod* (1865) and in Henry Beston's *The Outermost House* (1929). This same attitude was perpetuated by the inhabitants of the dune shacks as attested to in the oral history contained in Josephine Del Deo's account of *The Dune Cottages at Peaked Hill Bars* and in the multitude of letters from a variety of literary figures such as Edmond Wilson, Norman Mailer, Jack Kerouac, Hazel Hawthorne Werner, artists, historians, numerous longtime residents, members of Congress, the Provincetown Board of Selectmen, and other interested parties advocating the preservation of the dune shacks.[3]

These findings corroborated "the fact Ms Bessay's cottage is part of the 'historic way of life' which John F. Kennedy acknowledged."[2] Thus, the great irony here was that Grace Bessay's appeal of April 18, 1989, was heard only three weeks before the actual declaration of eligibility of her shack, together with all the others existing in the Peaked Hill Bars Historic District, for placement on the National Register of Historic Places.

The May 12, 1989, declaration of eligibility for historic registration of the dune shacks, which contained within the reasons for eligibility that, "their lack of amenities such as electricity and running water enabled their inhabitants to experience a survivalist relationship with nature," *made mute the Park's insistence on the presence of the same amenities, the very lack of which provided one of the strong reasons contributing to the shacks' registration status.* It contradicted the continuing expectation on the part of the Cape Cod National Seashore that the shacks could individually and collectively be condemned on the basis of not possessing the civilizing attributes, which could not possibly apply to these dwellings, had never applied to any similar structures for varied seasonal use on the Great Outer Beach, and, furthermore, the presence of which would have made them entirely ineligible for registration on the National Register of Historic Places.

This contradiction should have immediately altered the Park's management of the dune shacks and engendered a philosophy of use to accommodate the status of their eligibility for historic preservation. It did not. The National Park Service continued to depend on its prior *modus operandi* and to ignore the squeeze play in which it had been inexorably placed. That it would continue to do so for the foreseeable future was a matter of huge surprise and dismay to those of us who had looked for protection under the Federal Preservation Act of 1988, not to mention the clear and purposeful intent of the legislation which had established the Cape Cod National Seashore in the first place and, finally, to the declaration of eligibility of the dune dwellings for National Registration.

The devil was in the procedural details by which the Cape Cod National Seashore had handled the issue of the dune shacks from the beginning. For instance, in the report from the Northeast Atlantic Regional Office (NARO) in 1987 regarding the historic importance of the dune shacks, the determination had been made that none of the shacks had any historic significance and were, therefore, not eligible for listing on the National Register. In my statement at the public hearing before the Massachusetts Historical Commission in Provincetown on August 26, 1988, I had carefully pointed out that there were unforgivable errors in the NARO use of the historical background and information available to them, not only in relation to my report of the history of the dune cottages, which had been prepared in 1986 at the request of Superintendent Herbert Olsen, but also in the substantial evidence in support of National Registration eligibility on the part of so many others at that hearing, which had been multi-faceted and impressive.

The Massachusetts Historical Commission, however, had taken steps to properly monitor the process of determination and had added their own very definite opinion on the eligibility of the dune shacks for registration with a media advisory on January 20, 1989, which stated:

> Secretary Connolly, Chairman of the Massachusetts Historical Commission said: "I do not accept the opinion of the Park Service that the Dune Shacks lack historic value. I am concerned that the NPS failed to recognize the cultural and historic significance of these properties. Our intent is to pursue this listing with the Keeper and to see to it that the shacks are listed in the National Register of Historic Places."

The advisory went on to add:

> The staff of the MHC also expressed their concern that the National Park Service has not recognized the cultural and historic significance of these properties. Without National Register eligibility, the National Park Service will be under no obligation to protect these 18 cottages. In similar cases, without this designated protection by the Keeper, properties have been demolished.[4]

Attached to this media advisory in my records was a news release from the Department of the Interior, National Park Service that cast the dune shack listing, should it occur, into murky water, with this comment as follows:

> "The issue of the preservation and continued use of the Dune Shacks will not be answered by listing on the National Register of Historic Places which affords no guarantee of protection" stated Herbert S. Gables, Jr., director of the NPS North Atlantic Region. "We intend, with full public involvement, to address the issues surrounding the potential retention of the Dune Shacks in the revision of the park's Statement of Management," he said.[5]

As had been the case ever since the establishment of the Cape Cod National Seashore in 1961, the Park Service saw no lasting benefit in preserving a way of life on the Great Outer Beach, which has lasted for more than two hundred years, and which had established, by many and varied uses of simple dwellings constructed to adapt to a meaningful relationship with nature, an uninterrupted and continuing interface with the natural environment.

These two totally contradictory statements from two official sources, both issued at approximately the same time, left us with no doubt as to who was anxious to preserve the shacks and who was indifferent to their protection. There have been several Statements of Management over the years since this media advisory and news release were written and numerous forays have been made in the territory of solving the long-term use of the dune shacks, but all have ended in the same impasse between the National Park Service and the dune shack inhabitants and other interested parties. None have solved the central issue of allowing a "way of life" to be carried on by those who were in residence when the Cape Cod National Seashore was created. As I finalize this manuscript, the Dune Shacks at Peaked Hill Bars Historic District have been declared eligible for registration on the National Register of Historic Places for twenty-two years, but they have yet to be officially placed on the Register, although promises keep being made and the latest one appears to be realized shortly, according to Park authorities. There is every reason to believe, therefore, that such stalling has been deliberate in the hope that more death and demolition by neglect, if not otherwise, would take care of the whole issue, and, eventually, the Park Service would enjoy what they had always sought—a clear view of the ocean without the debris of human habitation, with the exception, perhaps, of an interpretive outpost or two describing a past way of life that they had systematically destroyed.

In the meantime, Grace Bessay was an object looming very definitely on the horizon of a projected unencumbered natural habitat in 1989. Her course of action led through the courts and continued the fight that her friend Andrew Fuller had had to relinquish at his death in 1981. Andrew had eloquently and consistently championed the cause, not only on behalf of himself and Bessay, but on behalf of all the other dune shack inhabitants, beginning with those who belonged to the original group of the Great Beach Cottage Owners Association and of others. As it turned out, this case, begun in 1967, was the longest civil action ever to be pursued in a U.S. Federal District Court.[6]

At the same time that Grace's case went to appeal on April 18, 1989, another scenario was developing in the towns of both Truro and Wellfleet regarding overbuilding and, sometimes, illegal building, within the Cape Cod National Seashore. A series of articles were written in *The Cape Codder* newspaper by journalist and reporter Joyce Johnson from April to October 1989. These articles tracked cases in both Truro and Wellfleet in which owners of private property had expanded their residences by more than fifty percent, which was the figure the Park had suggested was the maximum expansion commensurate with reasonable expansion of need that could be accommodated without impacting the environment of the towns within the Seashore boundary. Since this suggested guideline was only a suggestion, however, several owners in Truro and Wellfleet had taken it upon themselves to ignore the guideline and to expand their residence well beyond the suggested fifty percent and, moreover, had done so with impunity,[7] because the National Seashore, literally, could not refer to a local zoning law in place in either of these towns which might have made a fifty percent expansion rate a zoning restriction,

With this dilemma aggressively staring the Park in the face and accumulating more transgressors as time went on, the Park had no option but to pull the owner's certificate of exemption. This meant that, when selling such a property in the future, a prospective buyer would not be protected with a certificate of exemption and, thus, there would be no guarantee of freedom from condemnation of the property. Clearly, this would be a huge deterrent to moving real estate within the Park, and was meant to be so in the original legislation.

The threat of adverse consequences from violations had no teeth, however. After the Park's nearly thirty years of existence, there were very limited funds left to acquire property and no handy source of extra capital for acquisitions was in sight. What little funds that were available had to be carefully apportioned and, because of this and the fact that the market value of properties within the Park had vastly increased over the years, the Seashore was very reluctant to issue condemnations of property, which entailed the possibility of having to come up with their purchase. Thus, the Park was a paper tiger and this status was a heavy burden for the local building inspectors, who correctly identified these activities of over-expansion as a violation of the "spirit" of the law that created the Seashore, which certainly was meant to curtail overdevelopment as much as possible.

Let us compare, therefore, the threats to the principles incorporated within the legislation which established the Cape Cod National Seashore at this juncture in time: On the one hand, there were some private property owners expanding their residential homes by, in one case, as much as four times the original size, and two or three times in others, and owners deliberately destroying historic elements in order to build entirely new structures while claiming they had retained "elements" of the old in order to satisfy the rules for saving historic buildings. All of this was carried on with a knowing cynicism, because the lack of established local law, in every case, allowed them to do it.

On the other hand, there was a single individual not asking for any expansion of her home nor caring about living without the amenities of what the Park referred to as civilizing improvements: these were impossible to implement in the primitive conditions of the Great Outer Beach and had never existed there, except in the case of the Coast Guard stations to a degree. Not one single violation of any local zoning laws or of the Cape Cod National Seashore's general environmental concerns was created, nor did it cost the Park Service one penny of outlay for maintenance or repair.

When Senator Leverett Saltonstall promised the people of Cape Cod that "your homes are safe within the Park," he meant exactly that. Now, however, the Park was rolling the dice: Which home was the Park, either indirectly or directly, choosing to protect—the self-interested violator of the "spirit of the law," because a lack of vision in its administration left the possibility of violations open to exploitation, or the dedicated defender of the "spirit of the law" who lacked the promised protection of the law and thus was made to be a violator by official interpretation?

In the legislative history of these two vastly different cases in 1989, the towns of the Lower Cape within the Seashore had shown a willingness to cooperate with the Park in firming up the zoning to include the protection necessary to control over-expansion, but the actual incorporation of such zoning measures took many devious turns and many long years to implement. The towns of the Lower Cape, however, had always firmly supported the dune shack residency without requesting or mandating any "improved property" particulars, knowing that such mandates were unrealistic, and, at the same time, acknowledging the value of the dune shacks to the "way of life" in their communities and the great tradition that they represented on many levels. Had the Park chosen to do the same, the fight of Grace Bessay and others would not have happened. The Park Service chose, instead, to initiate countless variations of their familiar end game—the Statement of Management—thus leaving open-ended the resolution of status of an indigenous group of homeowners and inhabitants on the Great Outer Beach who had willingly entrusted their fate to the Department of the Interior in 1961. In the process of seeking such a reasonable judgment, Grace Bessay sought fairness and justice, and never hesitated in expecting both from the federal government.

To this end, Grace Bessay brought the issue forward in a May 26, 1989, letter to then-Secretary of the Interior Manuel J. Lujan, Jr., in which she detailed the pertinent elements of her situation. In doing so, she established the same case for all the other dune cottage owners as well. Nothing that could be written now about the entire complexion of the dilemma would be any more to the point or provide a better basis for a reasoned overview for a changed policy than what Bessay stated then:

> Dear Mr. Lujan:
> I am the owner of a seasonal home, and the land on which it is situated, in the dunes in Provincetown. This house was built in the late 1920s or early 1930s and has been lived in seasonally since it was built.
>
> I remember an article published in a Cape Cod paper before the Cape Cod Natioinal Seashore Act was passed. The headline of this article quoted Senator Leverett Saltonstall:
>
> YOUR HOMES ARE SAFE WITHIN THE PARK
>
> It was because of assurance such as this by sponsors of the bill to create the Cape Cod National Seashore, and because of assurances by Conrad Wirth, then-Director of the National Park Service, that all existing homes would be exempt from condemnation, that the homeowners of the Cape allowed the Cape Cod National Seashore Act to be passed.
>
> Congressional Record - Senate, June 27, 1961, on S. 857 on page 11391, regarding Report No. 428, Senator Bible states: "This report delineates in detail, on page 10, the homes which are located within the proposed boundaries of the Cape Cod National Seashore. So long as the homes in private ownership are maintained in accordance with zoning provisions adopted by the affected towns that conform to standards established by the Secretary of the Interior, the Secretary's authority to condemn such private property will be suspended."
>
> All of the dwellings in the dunes in Provincetown are similar in facilities.
>
> The Malicoats were granted a homesite exemption on three acres in 1971. I am enclosing a copy of the instrument showing this homesite exemption in the dunes in Provincetown.
>
> The Malicoats were entitled to this homesite exemption and received it without litigation.
>
> These dwellings in Provincetown in the dunes are about a mile from electricity, and none of them have electricity either by overland or underground lines.
>
> The usual source of water in the dunes is by a hand pump in the low areas where it is available. I do have a hand pump in the low area on my property giving good drinking and washing water.
>
> My house is one of the seasonal homes in Provincetown and Truro which were designated by the Keeper of the National Register on May 12, 1989, as eligible for listing on the National Register of Historic Placers as an Historic District.
>
> I had spoken in September of 1962 to one of the sponsors of the bill to establish the Cape Cod National Seashore. I had then been concerned with cottages situated in Truro in what was the Pilgrim Spring State Park, in which the Commonwealth of Massachusetts owned the land and various individuals owned the cottages.
>
> I was told by him that it was intended by the sponsors of the bill and by the legislators who voted for it, that all existing dwellings should remain and be exempt from condemnation, including those in Truro in the Pilgrim Spring State Park.

These dwellings in Truro were similar in facilities to the dwellings in Provincetown.

I am trying to save my historic dwelling and land in Provincetown.

One of the prime reasons for establishing the Cape Cod National Seashore was to preserve the way of life on Lower Cape Cod.

This is just what I am doing-preserving the way of life on Lower Cape Cod.

The case by which the National Park Service is trying to take my cottage and land was begun in 1967, and has now become, as I understand, the oldest pending federal case in the whole United States.

The position of the National Park Service is that if I don't have electricity, running water in the house, modern septic system, cement foundation, and insulation, my dwelling – which has been lived in for over fifty years – is not a dwelling and does not qualify as 'improved property' exempt from condemnation.

There is no basis for this National Park Service position either in the language or the legislative history of the Cape Cod National Seashore.

The National Park Service is trying by various legalistic technicalities to deprive me of this historic house and to destroy it.

This litigation is damaging to the conservation movement.

It has already caused considerable publicity.

The granting of a homesite exemption on the Malicoat property with similar facilities in the dunes in Provincetown is a precedent.

I am sure there are other homes in the Cape Cod National Seashore, with facilities similar to mine, appropriate to their location, which have been granted homesite exemptions and/or have received certificates of suspension of condemnation.

There are, I feel, certain other homes in other national parks with facilities similar to mine which have been accorded the rights given to "improved property" in the individual acts creating these parks.

My dwelling has always been well maintained.

I believe that the best means of preserving this historic home is for it to continue in private ownership, with the maintenance responsibility and expense being borne by me, and not by the federal government.

My detached one-family dwelling was built before September 1, 1959, and qualifies as "improved property" under the clear language and intent of the Cape Cod National Seashore Act and is exempt from condemnation, together with the land on which it is situated and which is in my ownership, The federal government did not have the authority for the "taking" of my "improved property."

I believe that, in fairness, the Department of the Interior should promptly file a motion to have this portion of this case dismissed with respect to my dwelling and the land on which it is situated and which is in my ownership; and a certificate of suspension of condemnation should be issued on my "improved property" as provided in Section 6 of the Cape Cod National Seashore Act (P. 87-126)

The U.S. District Court case number is #67-988--N. The U.S. Court of Appeals case number is #88-2029.

Thanking you for your fair consideration of this matter. I am
Very Truly yours,
Grace E. Bessay

Although Grace sent copies of her correspondence to Lujan to both Massachusetts senators, Edward Kennedy and John Kerry and to representatives Gerry Studds and Joseph Kennedy, the impact of her logic was far from initiating any corrective action. The mythic battle in which she was engaged, using only the slingshot of her determined will to force an adversary of overwhelming proportions to recognize the individual rights of one subject in its care, continued. Coverage of her case was ongoing in the local press and in the *Boston Globe*. On May 2, 1989, *The Cape Codder* had printed remarks by Acting Superintendent James Killian, in the absence of Superintendent Herbert Olsen, regarding a statement that had been made by Jeffrey Axelrod that "the park was not intended only to be preserved as a wilderness, but as a way to curtail over-development and preserve 'the human elements as well as the national scenery.'"[8] Killian was quoted as saying, "Any property that does not meet the improved property requirements is not eligible for a certificate of suspension of condemnation." Concerning the pending identification of Bessay's cottage and others for national registration as historic landmarks, He also remarked that the Park's list of such identified structures did not include Bessay's. Of course, he failed to say that the Park's list prepared by the NARO in 1987 didn't include any of the shacks, reflecting an egregious breach of research that I had pointed out with extensive evidence on August 26, 1988, at the Massachusetts Historical Commission's hearing in Provincetown.

As it turned out, the Registrar of the National Register of Historic Places completely countered Killian's remark ten days later on May 12, identifying every cottage within the Dune Shacks of Peaked Hill Bars Historic District as eligible for registration. In the same article, Killian expressed the opinion that the Park Service also contended that Bessay cannot prove ownership of the land underneath the cottage. The facts were, however, that Grace Bessay did have adverse possessory title to land on which her shack was constructed by a determination, through the appeal process, of the United States Court of Appeals for the First Circuit.

By the fall of 1989, the circumstances of Bessay's case were relatively improved, except for the one major component of her case still to be decided: the failure of her cottage to be identified as having the protection of "improved property" status. In relation to this issue, she took the last legal step by presenting "The Petition for a Writ of Certiorari to the United States Court of Appeals for the First Circuit In the Supreme Court of The United States, October Term, 1989."

For a private citizen of a considerable age with no special source of financing to pursue such a case over a twenty-one year period had to be unusual, even in America, and Grace Bessay truly was unusual. Hardly surprising was the Supreme Court's refusal to hear her case, but, in the process of presenting the writ of certiorari, Bessay's lawyer Jeffrey Axelrod made an extraordinary presentation. He cited a broad spectrum of deceits in relation to habitations within areas of the National Park system that had routinely forced the issues of habitation into unacceptable and often questionable actions on the part of the Park Service, in direct contradiction with their own expressed and mandated methods of management and goals of operation. In this regard, he suggested the statistics pertaining to National Parks, which had effectually eliminated supposedly protected resident populations and historically viable ethnicities, were rather alarming, and indicated that patterns and systems of operation were often in direct violation of Section 110 of the National Preservation Act. He also argued that they were in contradiction of the whole concept that had established, under Chapter 1 of Title 16 of the U.S. Code, a designation of "National Parks, Military Parks, Monuments and Seashores" that were essentially created after the example of the Cape Cod National Seashore in 1961, the model for all the park systems under Title 16 characteristically within already inhabited areas of one kind or another. As a result, the expansion of this kind of National Park Service operation within the Department of the Interior in a variety of circumstances had created significantly adverse results for the resident populations, sometimes disastrously so.[9]

And here we arrive at a moment to compare the initiation and promotion of the preservation initiatives of the late nineteenth and early twentieth century. These were founded upon the creative dedication and extraordinary efforts of some few far-sighted environmentalists and naturalists and resulted, among other achievements, in the saving of the Yellowstone and Yosemite Park areas, especially, and in setting aside such natural wonders as the Grand Canyon. These were extraordinarily important accomplishments of which we, as Americans, can be justifiably proud. The saving of nearly complete wilderness tracts in the West, particularly, is well known and documented and unnecessary to remark upon, because these reserves have long been a recognized and precious national legacy. The ideology that spared vast areas of environmental treasures continues without appreciable change in management operation and yields many beneficial results to everyone. We owe much to the vision and determination of those who enabled such an environmental task to become a functional reality and to those who have ably retained and managed such a resource within the Department of the Interior.

What has subsequently come into view is an issue and a challenge that has never been reckoned with on a large scale or addressed with an overall concept, except negatively, as in relation to the scourging of the American Indian tribes in the nineteenth century and the deliberate elimination of their habitat and their way of life by the government. Failing to understand the complexity and dire consequences of such a policy in the rush to populate the middle and far West and to exploit our rich natural resources, we established a mindset that has carried forward into the twenty-first century. It evidences an astonishing lack of understanding of the diverse elements that make up such a variegated texture as the social and historic legacies imbedded within the fabric of our nation. The valued imprimatur of unspoiled and uninhabited wilderness has become our definition, almost a religious one, of the preservation of the environment, but the sacred ethic of "wilderness" preservation is no longer a viable reality in many areas across America. In these places, the philosophy of "pure" nature may not be pursued without doing serious and sometimes irreparable damage, even to the other species that inhabit the environment with us.

The Cape Cod National Seashore was originally declared as a totally new and creative piece of legislation, meeting the challenge of addressing this problem; understanding the necessity to incorporate preservation within historic patterns of habitation and to develop implementation that would prevent a "trail of tears."

The original, local residents of Buffalo National River Park in Arkansas, some families claiming residency since before the Civil War, represented a pure "hillbilly" culture. Indigenous handcrafts in areas like this are among the most ancient and derivative of primitive methods of survival of any of our traditional cultural patterns, both here and in Europe and Asia. Weaving, spinning, basket-making, chair caning, the art of the forge and the smithy, and folk music had been long maintained with originality and a richness of cultural references. All these fundamentally revered aspects that an isolated ethnic entity produces and maintains were not considered as important when weighed against the pristine, physical aspect of the Ozark Mountain ranges. If a philosophy like that expressed in the founding of the Cape Cod National Seashore had been applied historically, the superimposed disruption and eventual removal of the inhabitants of the Buffalo National River Park would never have happened. They would never have been asked or forced to abandon their homes, their ancestry, or their "way of life." Instead, the Park removed 1,008 of the original 1,010 families over a period of fifteen years.[10]

This attitude of management needs to be exposed to the advancement of preservation concepts. We need to understand what value there is in ethnicity and the skills and values that it can teach us, which will be lost forever without their practice, by at least a few, and to appreciate what that may mean to us a a people, now or in the future. History shows us the result of the loss of those survival skills when we are in the face of crisis and dire necessity and experience the sudden or permanent deprivation of modern technology. Just as importantly, there is enormous interest in being in touch, even minimally, with the expression of a cultural identity, especially for those who are isolated by suburbia and driven by the worst aspects of daily conformities. A habitation expressing diverse skills and attitudes, as over against a standard ethos, has marvelous ability to influence, to inspire, and to refresh a stale vision of the universe, even that circumstance we do not share, or infrequently come upon or, perhaps, never see, even though we know it is there. As Ross Moffett said in his letter to the *Provincetown Advocate* newspaper before the Cape Cod National Seashore was established: "There are more people hankering after the sight of a wild swan than we realize." There are also more people who wish they knew how to spin a thread or sing a song connected with their past than is ever acknowledged by the prisoners of technology.

By misunderstanding these tenets, the National Park Service has deliberately destroyed a number of communities in the act of "preservation." In its rigid adherence to the re-creation of wilderness, it is often not even able to put that policy in effect, because the circumstances it has inherited will never, in fact, fit its interpretation.[11] That the "natural" environment has been affected by humanity, either minimally or hugely, is such a truism that very few argue the point. It is no longer a question, in most cases, of a "pure" natural environment. It is a question of an impacted environment that may be made less so by intelligent regulatory standards that take into account the immensity of man's pollution of the planet and the need to encourage and preserve a way of life that will enable civilization to survive without polluting it more, at least, or polluting it less. The principle is, of course, not "all" or "nothing," but "something" that regulates our bad habits, forbids our worst habits, and promotes the understanding of the complexity and synergy of life on earth.

In a letter to the *Provincetown Advocate* newspaper dated August 9, 1989, I touched upon this moral dilemma after the annual scuffle of the bass fishermen with the National Seashore over the nesting season of the plovers on the Great Outer Beach:

> The unique character of the Cape Cod National Seashore was established at the beginning. It was the first park in the country to be created within an already heavily occupied area that allowed improved property to be deeded in perpetuity under specified conditions. Bitter opposition from the occupants already here could not be reconciled. They could not concede to the preservation of certain of these lands as a wilderness area. This, they argued, was an usurpation of their domain. In time, most have come to see that the marriage of man to nature is possible, even desirable; that the Cape Cod National Seashore represents man in nature and not man and nature. That was the great achievement after all, that a place on earth was conceived where man could learn that his environment was

not to be totally fouled, that predation could be controlled and where he might observe the beauties of a sunset over Race Point and respect the life cycle of a nesting plover. The plover was never meant to be separated from us. Both they and the terns, however, were to be respected. The lessons were legion. We started learning and we were doing pretty well.

Then the idea began to grow that man in nature was too much trouble and that the plovers and the rest of us had to be separated. Not only was it necessary to the survival of an endangered species, but,believe me, it was cheaper. To supervise man in nature is a headache and a pain, besides, it costs a lot more money; hence the effort to eliminate the dune cottages and to return the land to beach status. When the forces of use and occupancy became troublesome and costly, the policy of the park became obdurate and the fishermen and the dune cottage occupants and others were locked in combat with the Seashore and the U.S. Department of the Interior

Naturally, they lost, but only temporarily. Unlike the completed history of the American Indian, this story does not end just yet; the dune cottages have been declared eligible for National Landmark designation and the fishermen have regained a small portion of the beach to traverse for a time. A few more plovers and a few less fishermen might or might not be a good thing, but plovers and fishermen, eagles and mice, deer and hunters and dune grass and its ancient antagonist, an angry ocean storm, will always be with us like the rise and fall of the tide.

By September 1990, Grace Bessay's fight was still at an impasse, neither side agreeing to resolution. The U.S. Supreme Court had refused to hear her final appeal and the Park Service had given orders for her eviction to take place on September 20. It was suggested, however, that a settlement might be in the offing and that Bessay might be allowed to remain in the dune shack for a time uncertain. Undaunted by either good or bad news, Grace Bessay went on with a new lawyer in place, Nancy Kaplan. A discussion in the *Cape Cod Times* newspaper, of September 22, 1990, briefly presented my position on the matter at the end of the article entitled "Dune Shack Resident Gets Reprieve." They were essentially the same views it had presented in an expanded version in a letter to the Secretary of the Interior dated September 13, 1990. I reminded him of the contradiction of the current management of the shacks and their proscribed protection under the Federal regulations, which the Park Service and the Department of the Interior were mandated to uphold. Part of the long exegesis contained the following:

> In reviewing the role of the Department of the Interior in the future management of these back shore landmarks, you certainly will be mindful of the language of the enabling legislation which specifically addressed the "unimpaired use and enjoyment for varied cultural, scenic, historic, scientific and recreational purposes." Such language more than implies the responsibility of preserving the cultural and historic legacy embodied in these cottages for future generations. Their preservation as an empty structure, however, will not fulfill this responsibility. These dwellings eviscerated of a human presence will mean nothing, for it is the way of life within these back shore dwellings that is the cultural and historic legacy. [12]

Copies of my letter to Lujan went to Congressman Gerry Studds, to Mike Perel, Provincetown's representative on the Seashore Advisory Commission, and to Grace. To Grace, I remarked: "May this help a little, if only in joining your great effort by bringing up a reserve at the last battlement. I think there is such a thing as justice in a way." The overall response to this was the expected outcome: Grace rejected the reprieve and the newly appointed Regional Director of the North Atlantic Region Gerald D. Patten wrote me on behalf of Secretary Lujan assuring me that: "The National Park Service shares your concern and has planned to address the future of these shacks in the formulation of a new General Management Plan." Like the refrain of the Walrus and the Carpenter in Lewis Carrol's *Alice Through the Looking Glass*, it was the same old threnody: "Will you, won't you, will you, won't you, won't join the dance" of the General Management Plan designed to eliminate the shacks—"every one."

Grace Bessay's case now became a matter of great public interest. The Park's original order to vacate her shack had been given to Bessay in March 1990, but negotiations had continued and the final eviction notice was now set for September 20, 1990. Articles appeared in the *Cape Cod Times* and *The Cape Codder* outlining the dilemma. Joyce Johnson's article in *The Cape Codder* dated September 28, 1990, reiterated the case for the Park Service, which defended its right to evict Grace Bessay based on the salient and central argument of their position, once again, that she did not have facilities that qualified her cottage as "improved property." In a *Cape Cod Times* article of October 3, 1990, it was reported that she had been offered another twenty-five years of the use of her shack, but she refused the deal for what she felt were justifiable reasons. The Park had made a laundry list of stipulations far more severe than she cared to risk, believing strongly, as she did, that signing on would subject her to constant and dangerous opportunities for the Park, once again, to evict her from her cottage, because she had not strictly observed all their infinite stipulations. "Why would I sign a termination clause with a termination clause?" she asked. She also refused to sign an agreement because of the amount of compensation offered by the Park, should it evict her prior to the agreed duration of her tenancy; it was only $400 per annum, an amount for a broken contract that could not even signify as petty cash to the government, and which was less, by approximately fifteen times that amount, than an agreement previously signed by a neighboring dune resident.[13] The inequity between the two contracts representing similar, if not identical, termination conditions, was enormous.

The old shibboleth always lurking in the Seashore's duffle bag of their *modus operandi* also surfaced in the *Cape Cod Times* article of October 3: "Until they were designated as a historic district, the Seashore had planned to take the shacks down as each use and occupancy permit expired, allowing the area to return to nature."[14]

As this long and somewhat detailed history shows, the suppositional "natural state" of the Great Outer Beach could not be said to be totally without man's presence for about one thousand years prior to the Cape Cod National Seashore's inception. It had been a focus for fishermen from foreign climes, used by indigenous American Indian tribes, and encountered by explorers. Their temporary settlements had been present on the Great Outer Beach, coming and going with the pelagic varieties of fish and of wild game, over centuries. By the very nature of the fishermen's profession and that of the seasonal hunter, the human footprint had been minimal and transitory, so that man's use had been in reasonable harmony with the environment, though it could not, however, be categorically described as "wilderness."

On the dunes for my birthday in October 1990, I was close to completing the biography of my dear friend Ross Moffett, with whom I had shared the months, weeks, and days of effort to assist in the creation of the Cape Cod National Seashore Park from December 1959 to July 1962, when the Province Lands had finally been turned over to the Park, enabling the incipient tract to begin to function as a viable entity. Almost immediately, Ross was selected as the first official archaeologist for the Seashore. The distinction was highly appreciated by this man whose research and writings had done so much for the discipline of archaeology on Cape Cod and who received great recognition from the Massachusetts Archaeological Society, not only in his lifetime, but long after his death.[15] I was nearing the end of the 500-page biography; it had occupied twenty years of my life from November 1970, just before Ross Moffet's death in March 1971 to the present moments of that fall.

As I watched the mist condensing on the french doors of Frenchie's shack and listened to shingles crackling in the stove, all was well. The mice came and went with our presence and our absence. We understood each other and left their routine alone; ours seemed timeless and uninterrupted as of old, but there were changes not to be ignored—the loss of family and of friends and, most of all, of time. The previous fall, in 1989, I had come out to the shack regularly to systematize all of the correspondence that needed to be identified and incorporated for the last time in the biography as it related to the intercalation of the chapters. It was a task requiring much patience, and I had completed it in peace and quiet beside the sea's reassuring breath of eternity and next to my loyal companion of some twenty years, our little dog Eurydice. Fondly nicknamed Dice by Sal and myself, she was a comforting presence in the place of Sal, who had been in Italy for a month attempting to settle affairs of his ancestral connection in Ischia. I would lift her into the old Chevy truck, for she could not leap up to the seat as of old, she was so lame. We would ride out together each day and settle into our routine, she in her old chair and I in mine, looking out to sea. Some six months later, Dice abandoned her chair and her lameness to leap across the divide between the quick and the dead. Her devotion, a memorial to love and affection, never left us, however.

My thoughts came back now to those fall days the year before and to Ross and his particular strength and fortitude, his vision and determination in the face of often impossible odds. What we had believed in was still there, and the strength of his clear vision still exampled what I strove to emulate. In that frame of reference, I composed a small tribute to him, which I entered into my journal six months later on June 17, 1990.

Fragment of Brick from the Roman Town of Verulameum, St. Albans Abbey

I have not gone there;
I may never go, but
The artist, archaeologist has sent me
This fragment of brick from a distance
Beyond death to last beyond mine.
It lies on my desk
Enveloped with a clear script
To mark a reverence for earth, for art,
Bringing St. Albans Abbey back to me, to you,
to someone.
Charging the memory with man's account of time.

The Bessay case now stalled for another year, as the central issues were discussed on both sides. At last, Grace Bessay, age 79, was given the final ultimatum to vacate her cottage in November 1991. As the end drew near in this developing saga, one of the most important documents relevant to the entire issue was a letter from Judith McDonough, Executive Director, State Historic Preservation Officer of the Massachusetts Historical Commission, to Gerald Patten, Regional Director of the National Park Service North Atlantic Regional Office, dated October 31, 1991. The letter was titled "Dune Shacks, Cape Cod National Seashore, Provincetown and Truro, MA." The letter immediately addressed the policy that should have been instituted from the beginning, i.e., reuse occupancy by the lessees who would maintain the shacks at no cost to the Federal Government and whose reuse would be sanctioned by the Massachusetts Building Code, giving the shacks exemptions from compliance as "improved property" standards, as defined by the Park, because of their designation of eligibility as National Registered Landmarks in the "Dune Shacks of Peaked Hill Bars Historic District." She further took the Park Service to task for allowing demolition by neglect in the case of two dune shacks, those of Leo Fleurent and Peg Watson, after the decease of their owners, in direct violation of the "adverse effect criteria" of Section 106 of the Federal Preservation Act.[16]

The process of reuse occupancy was, of course, what the Park Service did not want and which it had taken great pains to avoid consistently, counting on the eventual demise of all the shack owners, their heirs and assigns, and any residual influence of their lives on the dunes, so that that wonderful nirvana they had so looked forward to, a landscape empty of human habitation in the dune environment could finally become a reality. Such a landscape, however, was not the one that they had inherited in 1961, nor what they had packaged in glowing terms as a good deal to the resident population. In spite of the support of the Massachusetts Historical Commission in the matter of registration of the shacks as National Landmarks and the specific recommendations for corrections of mistaken policy and deliberate violations of the Federal law by preservation officers such as McDonough, the chances were poor that the giant would fall to reason and practicability or that Grace Bessay would deliver little more than a glancing blow to Goliath in the closing chapter of her case, but she stood her ground unflinching.

When it became apparent that the date of Bessay's eviction from her cottage, November 20, 1991, was not going to be delayed, I prepared a kind of amicus brief to draw attention to the major elements of the dilemma one last time and to focus on the most essential aspects, with the intention of presenting the statement, in person, at the Seashore Advisory Commission meeting scheduled for November 22. In anticipation of that occasion and wishing to contact as many officials as possible, I sent out twelve copies of the full statement between November 11 and 16. On the second page of a nine-page statement, I summoned the philosophical principle on which the whole mater was based

> I emphasize that the Bessay cottage is one star in the constellation of cottages on the back shore of the Great Outer Beach. If the light goes out, whether kerosene or candle, the overall radiance is diminished. The country will not be able to renew this source of light in the future, for it is from another time and age. The American people no longer live by this light, but they yearn for its glow, and a small preservation effort here will symbolically extend the philosophy of Thoreau and others who

"Dune dweller Josephine Del Deo addressing Cape Cod Seashore Advisory Commission, Friday," Joyce Johnson: *The Cape Codder* "Park's Advisers Agree To Take Another Look at Dune Shacks." Tuesday, November 26, 1991, p. 5

understand what it meant to live within the natural environment in the most minimal terms and who chose, deliberately, to do so. There are some of us who still choose to do so. Grace Bessay is one of them. Must she be denied this unobtrusive privilege in this day of awareness of the importance of such a concept when Thoreau was allowed to realize his in the absence of such awareness? [17]

The newspapers again weighed in on the situation, of course, and in a November 19 article in *The Cape Codder,* journalist Joyce Johnson quoted Bessay as saying: "I am fighting for the principle as well as because I love the shack and being there." Of course, none of this made much traction with the Seashore and, as the deadline approached, *The Boston Globe* gave one last reminder of where the Park Service was, had been, and intended to be: "The government's original intent was to reach accommodation with owners for life or set-term occupancy permits, negotiate each cash settlement and when all was said and done, allow the shacks to disintegrate or take them down and let the area revert to its wild state." [18]

The National Park Service had been guilty of serious intended destruction of structures within its jurisdiction almost as soon as the Park was created in 1961 and of further "demolition by neglect" in clear violation of its mandate under the National Historic Preservation Act. This is not a matter to be lightly glossed over, for it signified the resolute determination of the Department of the Interior to accomplish its objective and to use every available means to do so. None of these factors could realistically be brought to bear at this last moment in time, but they had to be reiterated for the record. Grace Bessay, however, was not in a position to continue a legal struggle with the Park, having expended her life over a period of twenty-four years and all of her financial resources on the basis of principle. Fortunately, she was granted a reprieve on November 22,and her tenancy was extended for another twenty-five years, but Grace knew it was a pyrrhic victory and that, in the end, the issue that she had fought to resolve once and for all, was still pending. She had maintained her position through every adversity and had exhausted every resource. Her premise was direct, simple, and reasonable. As she left the territory she had occupied as a living symbol of what we, as dune dwellers, also held most dear, she delivered one last salvo of sense and sensibility to the Cape Cod Seashore Advisory Commission on January 31, 1992:

Grace Bessay at the "Grail" (1995). This was one of the last pictures of Grace at her beloved dune shack. Grace died in October 1996. *Courtesy of Peter Clemons and Marianne Benson*

To turn any of these vital, living quarters into mausoleum-like museums would be a mockery of the intent of the Cape Cod National Seashore Act which was to preserve the way of life on lower Cape Cod...These cottages should continue to be lived in so that they may be preserved...The Cape Cod National Seashore has been called the Crown Jewel of the national parks...Properly understood and appreciated, these historic cottages are the jewels in the crown of the Cape Cod National Seashore...

Respectfully submitted, Grace E. Bessay.[19]

CHAPTER IX

Lighting the Lamps

1992–1997

FROM JANUARY TO June of 1992, I served on the Dune Shack Subcommittee of the Seashore Advisory Commission to assist in finding a solution to the long-term use of dune shacks within the Dune Shacks of Peaked Hill Bars Historic District. On the inside cover of my archive of the subcommittee, I wrote the following:

> It seems essential for people to believe in their government in order to have one, and to the extent that they disbelieve, to that extent is a government weakened and diminished. In the final analysis, a great nation is nothing more than a fundamental and abiding faith.

Josephine at the Typewriter (Frenchie's Shack) by Salvatore Del Deo 1995; watercolor on paper, 7½" x 6". *Collection of Berta Walker*

In all the deliberations, therefore, regarding the issue of the dune shacks, I kept faith in what I had written. It was the same faith that Grace Bessay had invoked in her long fight to retain her shack, and it was the banner she carried, invisibly, as she approached every engagement with her government, believing not only in herself but in her nation. Success does not always reward such belief, but it is always inherent in the dialogue of democracy, no matter in what form, for without it no sound resolutions ever take place.

The statements made by both Grace Bessay and myself at the January 31, 1992, meeting of the Seashore Advisory Commission regarding the dune shacks were extensive and communicated, almost in one breath of accord, the principle of retaining the "way of life" of the dune cottages on the Great Outer Beach. My statement underlined the case and then enumerated the steps that would be necessary to maintain that way of life in a proposal of three pages. I include my initial statement here without the following proposal:

> In discussing the future of the dune cottages within the Historic District at Peaked Hill and environs, it is clear, from both a practical and environmental point of view, that substantial individual ownership of the cottages must be retained. Future public use of the cottages, even of the most prescribed kind, will never equal the "survivalist relationship" previously enjoyed by the owner occupants of the dune dwellings. Since it will never be possible to build new cottages within the Historic District, and rightly so, no new bond similar to the peculiarly intense and strong relationship experienced by the original dune dwellers who built and or maintained these cottages will ever be possible. In fact, as time goes by, the experiences of dune dwelling will change and mutate and the type of ambiance available in this century will certainly require increased rigor to retain in the next. We have, therefore, to approximate the original conditions,which is to maximize, as much as possible, the sense of individual place and full owner responsibility and minimize the idea that the cottages are simply a time-share or rental unit.
>
> No matter how fair or legally correct a public use by lottery or other carefully orchestrated egalitarian method of choice of inhabitants, such administrative management and subsequent use will always be anathema to the single owner-occupant of the dune cottages and essentially counter to the very reason why they are eligible for preservation as unique outposts of the individual human spirit. Hard as this is to explain, it is even harder to defend, but the truth cannot be honestly avoided. Those of us who understand this look upon any management as best when least....
>
> The dune dwellers fought early, and a few very long indeed, as we saw from the case of Grace Bessay, to retain their resident status as provided by the original Cape Cod National Seashore Park legislation. In an age when individual privacy is under total siege, the dune cottages still offer us that priceless possession, or they did. I believe we are gathered here today to renew the assurance that the springs of solitude will refresh the next generation .but such assurance is still in jeopardy.
>
> On the door of Harry Kemp's cottage was tacked a firm warning written in a wavering hand: "Please do not break windows or doors. There is nothing of any value here except a little solitude."

Immediately, a subcommittee was appointed to address the issue of the dune shacks, which included three members of the Advisory Commission: Richard Philbrick from Orleans to serve as chairman; Mike Perel from Provincetown, and attorney William Hammatt from Chatham. Dr. Julie Schecter, director of the Peaked Hill Trust, and myself were added as members to represent the dune shack community. This subcommittee was given front-page coverage in *The Cape Codder* newspaper of February 4, 1992, with an article entitled "Future Looks Brighter for Historic Dune Shacks" by Joyce Johnson.

> A unique opportunity, new to the Seashore and new to the National Park Service, was formed between the Commission and dune shack advocates who will work out a management plan for the shacks for consideration by Seashore officials. The

> long-term plan of the Seashore, at least until 1989, when the shacks were designated eligible for inclusion on the National Register, had been for their destruction, as owners died or their lease agreements ran out. "Since 1989, we have had to do a 180 degree turn," Seashore Superintendent Andrew Ringgold said Friday. A cooperative shack policy would be the result of a new plan of the National Park Service (NPS) to promote partnerships to attain some goals that otherwise are beyond its financial reach. ...The first step in the partnership was taken by the Commission when it invited long-time dune dweller and author Josephine Del Deo and Dr. Julie Schecter, representing the Peaked Hill Trust, to meet with a newly appointed Advisory Commission subcommittee.

The first meeting of our subcommittee took place on February 18 and was largely devoted to a "philosophy of use" in response to a questionnaire from the NPS to which the subcommittee members responded individually. The issues we faced were multiple and difficult, but our resolve to succeed in establishing workable solutions was firm. Results of our February meeting put us in forward motion as to in-depth formulations, and the month of March was intense, with an exchange of specific questions and answers in regard to the long-standing use and historic leasing options.

The essentials of the discussion, which Chairman Philbrick had suggested in a letter to subcommittee members on March 2, had concerned eight items. Of these, I considered the last three the most important: "the need for a mechanism to determine who will occupy," "how should performance of occupancy be monitored?," and "what about renewability of occupancy?"[1]

Working out special stipulations relative to the Federal Directive 82-12 concerning Historic Property Leases and Exchanges proved daunting, and so, in a determination to précis some of the endless detail of clauses relating to the special directive,[2] I prepared a memorandum for our subcommittee meeting scheduled for March 25. The synopsis I provided consisted of seven pages of pertinent matter that capsulated, on page one, the relative sections and suggested that: "if historic leasing is the vehicle for the future protection of the dune shacks, the following might be relevant." The overview of seven pages was followed by three pages of comments specifically related to Title 36.[3] I have mentioned such detail in order to emphasize that the Dune Shack Subcommittee did not make their decisions in a general manner, but were specific, and that, when it was presented to the Park, our proposal came from intensive scrutiny and informed organization of the available material. At the time, we never doubted that such commitment and effort would be taken seriously by the CCNS, and I myself always worked on this principle, believing that the variations we attempted to put into effect, adjusting the particular situation of the dune shacks, would be appreciated and incorporated with the overall existing bureaucratic addenda, which was a one-size-fits-all formula. As it turned out, we were completely mistaken.

By April, our work had progressed to the final phase, and the April 10 meeting of the subcommittee identified the separate elements that still needed our attention and resolution. After that meeting, Dr. Schecter provided a list of eighteen points she felt important in a letter to Chairman Philbrick dated April 16, and I composed a letter to all the shack residents that summarized our work to date and requested their input. I sent this letter by certified mail to each dune dweller, for we needed to be sure the summary reached the constituency. As their responses came back to us, they differed in certain aspects, but all expressed an identical devotion to their dune dwelling and to the dune environment, some touchingly so:

From Murray Zimiles, nephew of Boris Margo:

> Since the birth of my son eight years ago, I have taken him to the dunes every summer. I wish to pass on to him not only my family history, but the experience of silence, of living with nature, of truly experiencing the sunrise and the sunset, of knowing that living on the dunes in a simple manner can act as an antidote to the harshness of our consumer-oriented society, and of being in a place of profound beauty that may influence his sense of values and his pursuits as an adult. This is the heritage and one of the greatest gifts my uncle Boris Margo has given me. I love him for it and feel it my duty to protect and transmit this heritage to future generations. [4]

Prior to the presentation of our completed plan to the Park, the Subcommittee had to work its way through the framing of an introductory "Philosophy of Use" and further to establish a resolution at the end of the document. The resolution we finally adopted was extremely brief, however and was labeled Resolution I:

> That as existing arrangements for use and occupancy of the dune shacks expire, CCNS return them immediately to the traditional use and occupancy by the Park Service's process of historic leasing, adapted to the unique characteristics of the shacks along the following lines.[5]

There followed the specifics of the leasing arrangements we had meticulously crafted and reexamined over the months between January and May 1992. The provisions were conceived and phrased in the context not only of our members' positions, but of the dune dwellers themselves from their many years of experience in the shacks in the past, and also in terms of the recent history of occupancy provided by the Peaked Hill Trust's system of use since 1986, the year of its incorporation. Even now, nearly twenty years after this exercise in seeming futility, I believe the rest of the members of the Dune Shack Subcommittee would agree that the exertion had been justified.

Although it appeared at the end of the six months after our proposal was presented to the Park Service and subsequently lay dormant for more than a year while the same gambit of a "General Management Plan in progress" played out, we believed that something significant had been attempted in order to manage the spiritual as well as the historic and cultural legacy of the dune shacks. Our proposal began:

> That the Cape Cod National Seashore be guided in its management of the dune shacks by the following:

Philosophy of Use:

> The individual dune cottages located within the "Dune Shacks of Peaked Hill Bars Historic District" form a constellation of cottages eligible for listing in the National Register of Historic Places. This constellation of the Great Outer Beach of Provincetown and Truro, Massachusetts, extends temporarily from the several fisherman's huts of over 150 years ago to the dune shacks of the present time, embodying a continuous legacy, both social and cultural.
>
> The Keeper of the National Register found "significant associations of the dune cottages with the historic development of American art, literature and theater."

> They have further significance as structures conveying continued "use of the dunes seaside setting over time." While the area may be historic because of the noted artists and writers who worked there, those occupied in more ordinary pursuits contributed to the structures themselves, and to the environment that proved so inspirational, as is the case in other historic districts.
>
> The dune cottages at Peaked Hill Bars offer the rare privilege of experiencing a survivalist relationship with nature. Only thoughtful guardianship of this way of life will keep it from disappearing from its unique place in the American landscape.
>
> Their use should derive from this history. [6]

By mid-June, 1992, Julie Schecter and I were exchanging letters of guarded expectations that our completed efforts had been somewhat successful, but a considerable amount of time passed after the acceptance of our proposal by the Seashore Advisory Commission. The September 1992 issue of the *Newsletter of the Peaked Hill Trust* contained two items that were disturbing: "No word from the CCNS" and "CCNS intends to Remove the Newest Dune Cottage." The first item emphasized the fact that the proposal we had presented in June had disappeared in the undergrowth of bureaucracy for the time being. The second item was far more disturbing, for it showed, once again, the way the Park had failed to communicate and integrate ongoing changes and procedures by returning continually to the old, established way of dealing with its historic mandate, which, in the case of the dune shacks was to isolate their importance solely as historic "structures" and to ignore the concept of a "way of life" that emphasized the traditional cultural aspects that needed to be preserved. The "newest cottage" to which the article referred was the Ofsevit cottage, which had been placed on the list of cottages eligible for listing on the National Register. The Ofsevit cottage had been rebuilt by the Peaked Hill Trust after having been burned down by vandals, and this rebuilding was done with permission from the Park and with the greatest care to follow the exact dimensions of the original footprint and former architectural elements. Nonetheless, a letter from the CCNS to the Peaked Hill Trust (PHT) dated August 7, 1992, said: "The Ofsevit shack will be removed when the use and occupancy reservation which allowed it to be rebuilt expires." The directive continued: "Historical leasing is to perpetuate historical structures." In short, the PHT was alerted to the fact that "once a cottage falls under the ownership of the CCNS," a fire can remove it forever.

The Park's statement was an example of its continuing insistence on the "structure," or, as Superintendent Maria Burks later described it, the emphasis on "planks and nails" instead of on the "way of life" represented by the structure and its cultural, social, and historic legacy. The fact that the CCNS was making such a statement after it had received our proposal to address historic leasing, which had specifically provided a clause on page 4 that read: "7. The leasee may rebuild, relocate or otherwise repair or replace the present structure in case of fire, erosion or vandalism," underlined the disconnect of the Park Service's bureaucratic inefficiencies in this regard, especially at this juncture when an officially approved committee had just completed its deliberations and offered a leasing proposal to be taken under advisement. Further augmenting our anxieties, there appeared in the October 21, 1992, edition of *The Cape Cod Standard Times* the following: "Dune Shacks Future Threatened...Park Service says if rundown shacks are rebuilt, they won't be historic." After quoting a brief rebuttal by me concerning this latest broadside, the article went on: "but Commissioner Richard Philbrick, who served as chairman of the Advisory Commission's Dune Shack subcommittee, considered the memo 'ominous.'"

Above: *Boris Margo's Shack at Peaked Hill* by Salvatore Del Deo, 1992. *Collection of Connie Banko*

Left: The Wood End Life Saving Station in Provincetown built in 1896, J. W. Dalton, *The Lifesavers of Cape Cod*, p.91

This article highlighted the serious manner in which the National Park Service continued to institutionalize its long-held precepts, which appeared to be exempt from review or change. This was to the great detriment of many historic properties, parks, and monuments under Title 16, which had come under their mandated preservation in the reinterpretation of previous standard practice when "The Cape Cod Formula" was created with the establishment of the Cape Cod National Seashore.[7] For instance, as soon as the CCNS was official in 1961, one of the first actions of the Seashore had been to burn the Wood End Coast Guard (Life Saving) Station built in 1896.[8] It razed the beautiful home of former State Ranger Henry Helmer, the last supervisor of the state-owned Province Lands, shortly after the deaths of Helmer and his wife. That structure represented elements of artistic craftsmanship by Helmer, whose association with the Provincetown art community was extensive. The house could have been used for Park personnel, because it was in the Province Lands and was demonstrably related to the community. The dune cottage of Charlie Schmid was bulldozed immediately after his death in 1982 and his personal effects scattered to the wind without even a moment of time given to his friends to retrieve valuable or intimate belongings that might have meant something in a number of ways. Finally, the cottage of Tony Vevers and his family was destroyed by a Park ranger in the spring of 1967, as we have seen, without regard for the deeded private property and with no notification given to the Vevers that the Park intended to destroy it.

As my disappointment with lagging events concerning the work of the Dune Shack Subcommittee subsided in the early months of 1993, other more rewarding events crowded the calendar in the spring, temporarily eclipsing the nagging worry about the fate of our proposal. Salvatore was to receive a major retrospective of his work at the Provincetown Art Association and Museum in May, which was a fitting recognition of his forty years of painting in Provincetown, not to mention the strong ties he had developed with every aspect of the community's life. These included being chairman of the school committee, initiating children's art classes for grades 1 to 6 at the Provincetown Art Association, the establishment of the Fine Arts Work Center, and many more public and personal commitments that enabled him to interpret Provincetown's extraordinary daily drama with such vigorous, yet intimate, reflection.

Salvatore came out of the tradition of Charles W. Hawthorne through his first teacher here, Henry Hensche and later Edwin Dickinson. He fulfilled a mantra similar to that of his distinguished predecessor, not only in sheer painting virtuosity but in his overall immersion and love of the fishing community, which both Edwin Dickinson and Ross Moffett, as two of Hawthorne's favorite students, had also shared and carried forward in their time. What Salvatore had learned from all three of these mentors continued the legacy that Hawthorne had initiated, to which the young artist Salvatore had committed himself with years of devoted interpretation of the same ambiance.

The retrospective which opened on May 28, 1993, featured a number of stunning paintings of the back shore and the dunes, which reflected his love affair with the landscape of Provincetown, especially, and of Truro. The cover of the catalogue for the exhibition featured a portrait of Manuel Pahliero, a cod fisherman, whom Sal had chosen to paint while Manuel was ashore in the winter of 1968.[9] The painting, entitled, *Manuel Doryman*, has since become an icon of the community and rightly so, for it features the inscrutable calm and weathered endurance of a fisherman from the ancient tradition of hand-lining. Charles W. Hawthorne and Ross Moffett were the only other artists who had captured, so consistently, the classic essence of the fishing community with such rugged metaphor.

Looking through the catalogue again, I am reminded of the sincere admiration his peers had of Sal as a painter and as a person, represented by the several statements and comments they phrased to accompany the paintings and enrich the representation of his artist's life:

Varujan Boghosian

Commitment, integrity and passion
Drawing and the sweet labors of painting
composition and color- all of these
ingredients are combined to make the face
and being of the artist Salvatore Del Deo
From his love and observation of the sea in its many nuances...from his
knowledge of the landscape and still life
he has given us, through his unique voice,
a memorable record of time and place.[10]

Sal painting on the back shore, 2003

The Artist in Residence by Salvatore Del Deo, 2001; oil on canvas, 14" x 20"

During the summer and fall of 1993, we were out at the shack as often as life would permit, and, of course, by October, it was time, once again, for my birthday celebration. My journal begins:

Most of my birthdays since my marriage have been celebrated here with the great ocean at my back accompanying the inner song of joy and gladness that I am alive and well. This year, Salvatore accomplished such a splendid birthday celebration for me in his genuinely thoughtful way. Not only did he think of everything down to a perfectly silly and adorable card, but he timed each lovely gift and moment with precision. We left late on Sunday and slept in our deluxe bed which is the best in the world. Rising with the sun, more or less, Sal made the coffee and served me in bed after which I was given two beautiful gifts which he had long before purchased in Orleans and had wrapped in high style. One was a nightgown in blue, feminine yet warm, and the other was a satin, blue pair of Isotoner slippers, quite the thing for traveling. After a favorite breakfast of eggs and potatoes, I was quite at liberty to delve into the forbidden territory of Somerset Maugham, as an absolutely unrelated adjunct to my reading list, in the pursuit of *Of Human Bondage*.

Sal went in to check the possibility of Romolo's gift and, sure enough, it had arrived. It was a surprise to find that the dear boy had bought me a juicer. I was mighty pleased, being so lovingly cared for on every front. Sal also arrived back at the shack with 13 oysters for the evening repast which turned out to be a seamless meal beginning with the oysters and progressing to liver wrapped in sage and bacon, a delicate butternut squash from the garden and our wonderful tomatoes, also from the garden. The piece de resistance, however, was the cake which Sal had had made for me and which bore in modest but elegant script the greeting of the day: "Auguri" (Happy Birthday) Impresario of birthdays is Salvatore. One is lucky to have such a husband to provide such loving and thoughtful tribute. The benefits of such love, however, are not just realizable on my birthday, but every day.

The day did not end, however, with the cake. It continued to provide me with unexpected and happy returns in the satisfaction I received from trumping Sal at Scopa, Briscola and even pick-up-sticks. Such a clean sweep, I seldom achieve and coming on my birthday, of all days, it was memorable.

The candle flickered as we prepared for bed. No mice were apparent, but the boats fishing on the horizon dotted the sea with star-like consistency. They seem always to be there from one year to the next. From our bunk, we can see the faint glimmer, one here, one there, and they reappear mysteriously like phantoms of celestial seasons, making the sea a reflected constellation of the sky. So, the year ends or begins. Nothing changes—the chair, the stove, the playing cards are in place. The Dorcorder box with our sheets and clothes is never touched by nibbling mice, its exterior too tough, even for them. The batteries in the radio never seem to run down. The coffee is always the best, no matter how old the coffee grounds. We two seem to get it right somehow; we don't put a strain on the place, and she rides true for us, not shifting much with the changes in weather. We keep a steady hand at the wheel and don't ask for a quick passage. We're content with the slow progress of our days together here, knowing we must enjoy what we can, vaguely sensing the fall in our lives, but, like my birthday, the best time of the year.

Frenchie's Shack at Night by Salvatore Del Deo, 2005, oil on canvas, 14" x 20"

Even though the date for receiving proposals for the three shacks that had been offered by the Park for long-term leasing was September 10, the October newsletter of the Peaked Hill Trust discussed their own application for the cottages in some detail. At the same time, a new management plan was underway in the Cape Cod National Seashore, one that would require another three years of planning. Heading this process was Mark Tabor, the Seashore's "on-site planner" as a newspaper article in *The Cape Codder* indicated. The difficulty with which the CCNS was particularly concerned at this point, and which had been apparent for some time, was that private properties that fell within the boundaries of the Park and were also subject to local zoning law, lacked appropriate zoning to control over-development in many cases. It was Tabor's job to take the case to the various communities and ask for support and a tightening of their zoning in order to control the tendency to exploit and overbuild. When he arrived in Provincetown, however, the issues were quite different and the citizens were only too eager to tell him what they thought of the Park's General Management Plans.

In an article entitled "Seashore Planners Get Earful of Complaints" in *The Provincetown Advocate* and another in *The Cape Codder* newspaper—"Provincetown Roasts Seashore Planner"—there was little doubt, after the citizens aired their complaints, that the talk of a new management plan was eyed with dubious and cynical disbelief:

> Town officials and citizens, one by one, complained about the Seashore's management history....They criticized the Seashore for limiting the access of fishermen and ORV operators to the beaches, for taking away rights enjoyed for centuries to use the beaches and the dune shacks. They complained about being denied access to old picnic and bathing areas, of being charged money to go to the beach on foot or on bicycle, and of being hassled by park rangers for such "crimes" as picking beach plums or of falling asleep fishing late at night....They complained about the deed that created the Seashore in which the Province Lands were turned over to the National Park Service, with the understanding that Provincetown would be assured, in perpetuity, an airport and a dumping area.
>
> The plan as presented made no mention of the airport, Dr. Len Alberts, chairman of the airport commission, said. "I'm confused as to where the airport stands in relation to this management plan....I don't see the airport mentioned in it once and I've read it twice..."
>
> Dr. Charles "Stormy" Mayo III urged the Seashore to include a provision for conflict resolution in the plan. Tabor mentioned that cooperative partnerships were a goal of the plan.
>
> "You will forgive me, but most of us are struggling with airports and landfills, as you do in your community," Mayo said. "When we read something like cooperative partnerships, it sounds good, but it doesn't have much meat on the bones."
>
> Tom Murphy, a sports fisherman and ORV user said he never received a survey, nor was he mailed a copy of the management plan newsletter. Murphy deplored the Seashore's erosion of user rights, saying that residents of Provincetown and surf fishermen have been the most impacted by the Seashore's restrictive management policies. "The Seashore has engaged in a program of deceit, duplicity, mismanagement and harassment..."
>
> Mary-Jo Avellar said she was not surprised, nor did she or her husband receive a copy of the Seashore newsletter on the management plan, which was mailed out last month to more than 2,000 residents... "The problem with the survey is that

> it is not designed for the users of the Seashore or the people of Provincetown," Avellar said. "It is designed for the bureaucrats who have to run the Seashore, the bureaucrats who are trying to compartmentalize every aspect of our lives so that they can run the place without problems. That's not the way it was supposed to be."[11]

It seemed obvious to everyone, in other words, that this new management plan was just another mechanism to delay any real initiative on the part of the Seashore to cooperate with the town of Provincetown on issues vital to its residents.

After the local community had had a chance to express their dissatisfaction with the Park's management plan, the Massachusetts Historical Commission weighed in on the proposal. In a letter dated November 19, 1993, Secretary of State Michael J. Connolly wrote to Superintendent Andrew Ringgold that:

> The historic Dune Shacks located in the Cape Cod National Seashore are vitally important to the citizens of the Commonwealth. Every available effort should be made by your officer in concert with the private sector, to preserve them and continue their occupancy. Occupancy of the dune shacks has, undeniably, led to their upkeep and the continued recognition of a pattern of life unique to the Cape Cod Seashore. I was dismayed to see no reference to them in the Fall, 1993 issue of the *General Management Plan Newsletter.* The Dune Shacks are a unique historic resource that requires special attention in order to insure their survival, and should be afforded special recognition in the master plan of the Seashore, etc.

When the dust cleared, Provincetown had its way, and the airport and the "dump," which subsequently assumed the preferred title of "transfer station," survived to accommodate fundamental needs of the community. It had been a long and stressful fight and one that never should have transpired, but the Park had chosen, instead, to "remove the meat and leave us the bones," as Charles "Stormy" Mayo had characterized their procedure, not taking into account that, on any given day, Provincetown could produce a cadre of informed citizenry that refused to be hoodwinked into acceptance of a slippery, elusive policy under any auspices.

In November 1993, Salvatore and I were approaching our fortieth wedding anniversary in a unique manner. I was finalizing, at that moment, the last editorial oversight of my manuscript *The Life and Times of the American Painter Ross Moffett—1888–1971* for the publisher. This writing marathon had taken me twenty years to bring to completion, and it would now become a completed reality in a matter of months. The work load had been enormous, and I was working six to eight hours a day to prepare all the several aspects of the massive detail that would be required by the publisher. I had not anticipated the complexity of this process, and it was only through the loving support and encouragement of my husband and the faithful and efficient typing skills of my daughter Giovanna, who prepared the final draft, that I was able to finish the task. The last phase of this endeavor had overlapped, somewhat, with the six months of my participation in the work of the Dune Shack Subcommittee, which, fortunately, had been completed in 1992.

The biography was launched, with resounding success, at a book signing at the Berta Walker Gallery in Provincetown in July 1994, and, by the end of the year, about a third of the small edition had been sold. I learned a great deal about the governance of time and the necessary precepts associated with keeping a schedule at a professional level of competence throughout the publishing experience, but, to me, the biography represented the satisfaction of expressing my earnest passion for painting and for the career of Ross Moffett, in particular. The reward of realization was worth the dedication necessary to bring forth his presence in the world of art. In presenting his life and work, I had also emphasized his commitment to the environment and his extremely important contribution to the establishment and the early years of the Cape Cod National Seashore. (see Chapter Two).

The January 1994 newsletter of the Peaked Hill Trust expressed the deep regret of Director Julie Schecter that the organization had lost the bid to acquire any of the three leases available on the Fleurent, Schmid, and Jones shacks and examined, in some detail, the possible reasons why. In a letter to me dated February 15, 1994, she admitted that she was "overwhelmed" by the turn of events and that she was not certain how to proceed from that point. Her letter went on to discuss the various options we had previously reviewed in formulating the leasing process, and she agreed that the Park had probably chosen appropriate occupants for the leases of the three available shacks. I certainly felt that to be the case as well and didn't agree, completely, and never had, that the non-profit approach of using the shacks was the best option. This was the point at which our basic philosophies of use differed, but with great respect for the other's opinion.

The development of the General Management Plan, introduced in 1993, continued its snail-like pace across the agendas of meetings and discussions in 1995 and 1996. The idea that our original 1992 Dune Shack Subcommittee proposal should be reviewed and perhaps restated with new or revised material also became part of the discussion. Former Chairman Richard Philbrick reconvened the subcommittee with several new members at the request of Superintendent Burks, and, in May 1996, this re-invoked committee pretty much came to the opinion that the original Dune Shack Subcommittee proposal was still pertinent, only highlighting certain elements and reemphasizing, basically, the conclusions we had made in 1992:

> Because we are convinced that the great preponderance of our 1992 report is valid today, we have chosen not to write a new report from scratch, but rather to affirm that report (copy attached) and to emphasize or clarify and interpret certain sections. (page one, dune shack report 5-31-96). The last remark suggested: "that some form of the subcommittee should continue to serve as an affirming entity for dune shack uses."

The subcommittee also praised the work of the Peaked Hill Trust as having instituted "good management skills," which was a tribute to Dr. Schecter for her defense and advocacy of the capabilities of the non-profit organization.

In the summer of 1995, I was occupied with the publication of my Italian short stories and travel sketches entitled *Passaggi-Passages*. Another felicitous occasion of a book signing at the Berta Walker Gallery was reason enough for celebration. As I now look back on that moment, I realize it was a mutual achievement for myself and my daughter Giovanna, as her illustrations for the book garnered as much praise as my writing. I am reminded of the intense creative energies of every member of my family and how that energy has been nurtured, in no small part, by the experience of life on the dunes in both subtle and lasting ways. On October 1, 1995, my granddaughter Linnea was born, just three days before the date of my own birthday. I was inspired to contemplate the prospect of a new chair at the old table on the porch of Frenchie's shack, where she might be as privileged as we had been to count the boats on the horizon at night and gaze upon the moon lighting a lunar landscape of sand. Therein lay much of my heart's endeavor, to make possible the philosophical prospects of such solace for yet another generation.

In May 1996, Grace Bessay died, having left the balance of her twenty-five year reprieve to her close and devoted friends Peter Clemons and Marianne Benson and their family, who honored her contribution to dune life by a fitting memorial service. They assumed the diligent and tender care of her dune shack known as the "Grail," which she had so loved and in which she had placed her determined quest for the uncomplicated and unencumbered life.

The elements of the latest Seashore Management Plan had been made public along familiar lines in July 1996. The documents detailing the plan known as the Draft General Management Plan and the Draft Environmental Impact Statement, taken together, constituted about three hundred pages. It was conceivable that someone would take the trouble to access this library of rules and regulations, but the average citizen was not in that rare stratosphere and thus comments, acceptable for 60 days, were bound to be few. Copies were made available at the headquarters of the CCNS and at town offices, but guessing the response was not hard to predict: both positive and negative critics would doubtless give up and go to the beach.

The superintendent who had replaced Andrew Ringgold and who was presenting the plan was Maria Burks. She was measured in her response to issues and became known as an able and straightforward administrator with a disposition to some positive consideration when it came to the dune shacks, repeating the concept that they weren't just an accumulation of "planks and nails." Regardless of these positive qualities, from the standpoint of the dune dwellers, her job, under Park Service directives, followed the familiar pattern of operation, which was to insert a new management plan at prescribed intervals, the latest of which she had effectuated with that familiar emphasis on "finally" solving problems. I sent a long letter to her on February 12, 1997, regarding Lawrence Schuster, the tenant in the Braaten cottage, who had been the year-round occupant of that shack for a considerable period. In it, I made the case, once again, for long-term residency. (Partial excerpts follow):

> In all of this, the underlying premise of the dune dwellers has never changed: a continuance of occupancy by the residents, their heirs and assigns which is the ideal response to the preservation of the historic dune cottages, the natural environment which surrounds them and, most especially, the spiritual essence of the individual survivalist relationship with nature. Unfortunately, bureaucracy seems unable to accommodate to such a premise and, therefore, has attempted to impose a bureaucratic solution on a non-bureaucratic phenomenon. The Park Service has chosen to break with the past and to impose, instead, a simulacrum of the historic life of the dune dwelling experience at Peaked Hill. Such a course seems an exercise in futility, since the deliberate dismantling of an original in order to put in its place, a replica of itself will always and inevitably defeat serious contextual meaning.
>
> In the case of Lawrence Schusteer, however, the Cape Cod National Seashore might yet take advantage of an opportunity to preserve an outstanding example of a priceless historic process. Through summer and winter, hurricane, heat and hiatus, he has experienced a daily life on the back shore on the dunes at Peaked

Lighting the lamp in early evening at Frenchie's shack

> Hill........He has not established his residency by time-bites or by career convenience, but by dint of commitment and a preference of absolutely wishing to live, as much as possible, as nature dictates. If his tenancy is summarily snapped, it seems to me that all that such a tenancy represents will eventually be lost.[12]

Although it is far too difficult to predict the fate of the dune families attempting to maintain their residency on the Great Outer Beach, the lights have not gone out as yet. Deprived of surety, but still expecting to retain our rightful place at the edge of eternity, it is perhaps appropriate to invoke the poet Emily Dickinson:

The poets light but lamps,
Themselves go out.
The wicks they stimulate,
If vital light
Inhere as do the suns,
Each age a lens
Disseminating their
Circumference.[13]

CHAPTER X

Circumference

1997-2003

THE THIRD GENERATION of the Del Deo family had firmly established itself at Frenchie's shack by 1998 with the birth of our grandson Luca. Now, a second chair at the old table on Frenchie's deck was put in place next to the one for his sister Linnea. Events were moving rapidly along for our son Romolo, not only with the birth of his two children but in his career as well. In the last half of 1998, he submitted a design for the competition for the doors of the Church of the Transfiguration being built along the lines of a sixth century Byzantine basilica by the Community of Jesus in Orleans, Massachusetts. Not so remarkably, but fortuitously, Romolo's *bozzetto*, or model, was chosen as the most interesting and best adapted to the idea the doors were to represent, which was Adam and Eve before the "fall of man." The doors were to be fifteen feet high and approximately nine feet across, each door to measure four-and-a-half feet. Cast in bronze, these doors would certainly appear to be a monumental undertaking, and, in fact, they proved to be so.

By September 1999, Romolo was throwing up the large, clay figures in Gino Giannancini's Pietrasanta Fine Arts Foundry in Greenpoint, Brooklyn, where the foundry had moved from Bleeker Street in Manhattan Unlike Ghiberti's doors in Florence,[1] these were to be two massive single units, not a series of jewel-like representations in bas relief. The choice of a subsequent foundry big enough and providing enough expertise to do the casting, however, was not easy. Romolo finally selected the Polich Foundry in Rock Tavern, New York, as having the best setup for the execution of the whole bronze-casting project from beginning to end. This foundry was also the one Frank Stella had chosen to fabricate his sculptural experiments; he occupied a large space there devoted to his work. From the fall of 1999 to April 2000, the doors were completed in clay, moulds were made, and the waxes finalized in the foundry adjunct of Polich in Long Island. This saved traveling back and forth, two hours each way, to Rock Tavern, but when the waxes went to the central foundry at Rock Tavern for casting, he had to make this round trip daily. On April 8, Sal and I also made the trip to see the foundry ourselves. We were amazed by this airport of a space in which Romolo's large doors took up but a small fraction of the immense working area.

The date of the dedication of the church was to be June 17, so, in the interim, the completion of the huge project had to be accomplished down to the last detail. A crew of five men were sent to Orleans in May with the steel framework needed to hold the doors—some 6,000 pounds of bronze. Romolo, of course, supervised the entire installation. At the end of the dedication ceremony and fete to dedicate the church in June, we went back one more time to see the doors in the reflective evening light. Our progress over the short distance, between the dining tent and the church, was constantly interrupted by the sisters and brothers of the Community who stopped us many times to express their appreciation for the achievement of our son, so that it took over half an hour just to walk about one hundred and fifty yards. We were very touched by this tribute and we knew that, in fact, something unique in the art history of the country had been created by Romolo. These doors were reputed to be among approximately half a dozen individually commissioned bronze doors in the United States.[2]

During this period of excitement over Romolo's artistic achievement and the great joy of having two healthy grandchildren, I developed one of the symptoms of my advancing age—a condition of heart arrhythmia that appeared to worsen between 1998 and 2000. Diagnoses were not definitive, however, and I spent considerable time trying to solve the erratic rhythms of the heart that were diagnosed variously by many able physicians and clinics. The temptation was to sweep the problem temporarily from the scene and to assume it was minimal and could be solved eventually without invasive procedures. Having cast caution to the winds, in this matter, I approached my granddaughter's birthday and mine, which were only days apart, with the greatest anticipation. As she was in New York City, we couldn't share the occasion as we did in later years, but even so, Sal and I went to the dunes with our familiar routine still in place:

From my journal:

October 4, 2000

After Linnea's birthday comes my own. The years pass like unseen waves upon the surface of life until one becomes acutely aware of the breakers on the shore, or the longer infinities of the great ocean's swells which have little to do with the quieter rhythms of one's existence. It is better not to note the extremities of time, but to continue to feel protected within ritual, for the infinite will take care of the cycle all too easily at last and dismantle our secure stronghold of habit.

In this regard, our long-term ritual still prevailed in this millennial year, and we were out at the shack again—lighting the Coleman lantern, fussing with the kerosene light, cleaning up the mice's residual extractions from the great, old chair which loses its stuffing every year to this activity and which, by now, has exposed bare wood on the arms. The edge of the dune where Frenchie's palace still rides at anchor has advanced toward us at a disturbing rate. Sal estimates approximately 10 to 20 feet have been lost over the last two summers, and the drop to the beach is precipitous. Of course, we wait for tide and wind to reverse this process as it usually does. This location, which is that of the 1915 Peaked Hill Coast Guard Station, was never really too precarious and may have been relatively secure, even in 1931 when the older and original Life Saving Station (O'Neill's habitation) went into the ocean in January; however, we gaze at the menacing wash of the tide's encroachment with some dismay.[3]

The shack is in good condition except for the porch which badly needs propping up and a new roof. All else is tip-top—trim painted, main roof fine, birdhouse in place, outhouse riding very well with a magnificent view to the broad sweep of dune and water. We are in a cozy hollow. The pump performs with one glass of water, thanks to Willie Hapgood's repairs, and all is well. Rosehips, collected this year, made about ten jars of jam. No beach plums available. Scott Dunn gave us cranberries from his large store.

Lawrence has made the Braaten cottage a first-class residence dune style. Superintendent Maria Burks has endorsed his renewable lease on an annual basis and thus he has been the recipient of a policy of a rather wise and sensible superintendent, one of the few we have had who has been able to balance National Seashore dictates and the personal character of the dune shacks and their residents. Burks, not always on the side of traditional occupancy; nevertheless, has left some things alone. Our 1992 subcommittee setting up original guidelines for historic leasing of the dune cottages, was able to put a sufficiency of sensible and fair values in place to establish the modus operandi so far. The Peaked Hill Trust has admirably carried on its commitment to its form of operation with a volunteer corps of group users and members, although, this has never been my idea of the best approach.

Hazel Hawthorne died this summer, and with her disappears the epoch she represented. Thalassa and Euphoria prevail still in the care of the PHT. As to my celebration, it largely consisted in being there with Sal and modestly enjoying what we have always enjoyed: overlooking Portugal and Spain 3,000 miles away. Several days of my birthday week were not sunny, but overcast. This was fortunate in a way, as Sal did some excellent studies on the grey days as he always does. His many dune landscapes crowd his little studio, so many truly rich and redolent of the sea and the shack. He had occasion, as soon as our first day, to put his studio in order. This is a process that never ends and is essential to the place.

The second night, we grilled fresh bass on our outside fire pit. JB. (John Browne) had, once again, timed the delivery of a magnificent bass, which landed on our doorstep wrapped in a tinfoil tunic. Sal, of course, had the tedious job of cleaning, scaling, and preparing all for the table. It takes a good deal of time, but no complaints, as this fresh treasure from the back shore is priceless.

The summer of the year 2000 was idyllic with our grandchildren close by, watching their exuberant and headlong rush into life; Luca prancing up and down the path between Romolo's domain and ours, Linnea flitting on the same leafy trail like a wraith of perennial spring, and both bubbling in and out of the little rituals of beach and backyard, bathing and chasing the ducks, and delighting in the garden. Luca saying to Sal, "Come Nonno, Come Nonno" and holding out his hand imploring him to follow and to share his glee and joy in the adventure of all the wonder he was discovering. Three years later, they transferred the same joyous routine to the world of the back shore and Frenchie's shack, Linnea saying matter-of-factly to Romolo: "Papa, this is where I want to live."

Three Generations at Frenchie's Shack

A year later in 2001, Romolo had begun another large standing bronze for a real estate developer in Newport News, Virginia, who wished a major sculpture to be placed in the central square of a residential complex he was creating called Port Warwick, named in honor of the writer William Styron, whose work he so admired. This twelve-foot bronze would be approximately twenty feet high when installed on a large marble pedestal. Romolo was excited to begin this new commission, and he returned to New York City with his family in early September. As he prepared to celebrate his twelfth wedding anniversary on September 12, the tragedy of the World Trade Center intervened and

Romolo and Giovanna at the shack, 1983

Linnea, Sal, and Luca coming off the beach

Luca picking rose hips, 2003

Sal and Jo with Luca on the porch of the shack

Sal and Jo at the shack, 1988

enveloped the life of the family in ways that would never be forgotten. My journal reads as follows regarding this experience:

> Their apartment at 151 Hudson Street was only ten blocks away from "ground zero," but, thankfully, the location was two blocks outside the cordoned-off area of the center of destruction and fall-out. Sal and I were having breakfast on the porch in our screened-off area when the phone rang about 9:15, as I recall. It was Romolo calling to tell us a plane had just struck the tower of the World Trade Center, but that he was all right. I had to have him repeat what he said several times, as I had no idea what he was talking about at first, as the news had not yet come over the radio or on TV. Quickly, he said goodbye. "I've got to go and get Luca," he said. "I love you."
>
> At that moment, as he told us later, he had no idea if the plane that struck the tower was carrying nuclear material and so the farewell. Luca was in a day-care center one block away from the World Trade Center and Linnea was in PS234, about two blocks away. After locating Sine in the melee and confusion of the street and retrieving Luca, together they went to get Linnea. At Linnea's school they collected a number of friends and their children who couldn't connect with their families. After regrouping behind a concrete barrier of some construction site about halfway to their apartment they closed ranks to join together for the rest of the race to get to the relative sanctuary of Romolo's loft.
>
> Once Romolo got his family safely into he apartment, he went back out into the street to do what he could to save lives. He was convinced from his knowledge of metallurgy that the tower was compromised by the heat of the fires and would come down. He wanted to warn as many as possible adjacent to the towers that they were structurally failing. At that point, the debris from the devastated tower was raining down like snow and he watched in horror as countless trapped victims above the impact, with no avenue of escape, plummeted to their deaths. Romolo saw much more, and will never be able to forget those images of death and destruction. He said his life will never be quite the same.
>
> The second emergency for Romolo, after getting his family safely home, and convincing the schools to evacuate, was to buy bottled water, food, etc., in case of the failure of services. At that point New York seemed like a city under attack by a first wave. He had no idea what lay in store for him and his family. As he came out of the deli where he picked up several necessities, the North tower collapsed, and he said the impact of the crash and the total atmosphere was exactly like an immense earthquake—terrifying, in fact. He stopped in the doorway of the deli as the wave of ash and debris washed up the avenue from the impact of the tower like a tsunami. When the air cleared, he rushed home.
>
> Friends in the neighborhood and closer to the World Trade Center were desperate, as they had had to evacuate without any place, literally, to go to at that moment in time. Many had pets which they had to leave in apartments. Romolo, being a good Samaritan, as usual, offered to put up his friends for the night. They slept on the floor and were grateful. Having just returned to New York on September tenth from the summer here, he had ample provender from our garden and also had a supply of the wine of the house, "Il Tramonto," to make the situation less stressful for all. Though he couldn't help thinking how different things might have

been had they decided to spend a few more days in Provincetown, still he gave thanks that his family was safe and thought of all those so very much less fortunate that night.

The days following were so full of fear and uncertainty that the family actually took a friend's offer to stay in a midtown hotel overnight and they spent at least twenty-four hours away from the terrible aftermath of the turmoil of 9/11. After some weeks, Romolo went back to working on "Melpomene," but he didn't like what he had done and took large sections of it down to the armature. As he worked on what was left, the whole approach changed. What turned the piece into a new challenge was the attempt to express the sense of real and immediate tragedy, not just the mythical symbol of tragedy in general

Throughout October, the impact of 9/11 continued to disrupt the family's life in New York. The outpouring of non-stop assistance, courage, and heroism shown by the firefighters, police, and volunteers in clearing the debris in those early days after the collapse of the towers will certainly remain one of the great heroic moments in the city's history. Mayor Giuliani distinguished himself, as well, with a tireless dedication to his city and his people. Whatever may be said about his political life and conduct under normal conditions, the attributes he demonstrated of organization and courageous leadership were magnified a hundred times by the awesome debacle he faced. He rose to the occasion and his leadership, at that moment, will doubtless remain remarkable in its frame of reference. The unforgettable sacrifice of the hundreds of firemen and police who gave their lives and many more who put themselves at risk to save others is, of course, beyond compare. The Muslim terrorists had succeeded in creating, contrary to their intention and to a degree far beyond their understanding, a strengthening in the resolve of the Christian faith to rise to the full challenge of its religion.

The fall days of 2001 also proved ever more difficult for me, as my resources gave way under the diminished capacity of my heart to provide a successful delivery of a normal blood supply due to the dysfunction of the mitral valve. We periodically went to the shack for renewed spiritual support, the world there giving sustenance, perspective, hope, breathing room, and release from the constrictions that man has made as part of his daily life. November always astonished us with its deep, mahogany colors flung across the darkening landscape. What color there was stood out with close harmonies and became ever more vibrant as fall moved, inexorably, to winter and the bayberry, poverty grass, cranberry hollows, and drying rose hips clinging still to their ubiquitous, bristling bushes reminded us that, in all things, nature was the master choreographer. Often, as we drove back from the shack at any time of year, but somehow more frequently in the late fall days, the circling hawks captured Sal's wonderment and would cause him to exclaim "the hawk," with a kind of awe and fascination, as if some preternatural presence had just appeared from another geological age. Startled, I would temporarily imagine the worst possible event out of sheer surprise at his ejaculation. In time, however, I accommodated to this sudden jolt of recognition and, attempting to capture Salvatore's hawk, wrote a poem in which he might soar in any season without extraneous remark.

Salvatore's Hawk

The hawk returns each day for your discovery,
Suddenly soars a silhouette as jet against
the sky,
Swooping invisible mice down hollows, dune sides,
Hovering, motionless, in flight,
Waiting for the tremble of betrayal.
And you, of course, startle the diurnal rite,
Exclaim again, "the hawk," as in profound surprise
that death is life.

In January 2002, I underwent open-heart surgery to repair the mitral valve. I experienced the rebirth that such medical genius has provided to persons like myself who, otherwise, would lose the "last of life for which the first was made," as Browning so rapturously reminded us, without taking into account the uncongenial path that far too often faces that "last of life" so fraught with peril as is the "first" of life. Recovering slowly but with enormous gratitude for the extraordinary skills of my surgeon at Beth Israel Deaconess Hospital in Boston, I began a series of sonnets entirely devoted to my youth growing up in Michigan. I completed the series of twenty sonnets, which I called "My Michigan Stove and Other Sonnets," the following year in 2003. Somehow, those of us who experienced the Midwest of America in their growing years, have benefitted by the enlargement of perspectives totally unavailable to the Eastern attitudes. The middle of the country holds firmly to the genesis of the country in many ways; not the original settlement, of course, but that first euphoria of spirit which promises unlimited space and unheard of opportunities, and backs these up with a vigor still palpitating in that atmosphere of "going West." Michigan, like Ohio, Indiana, and Illinois, is hardly West, but it is germinal in some ways to Provincetown's early genesis as a painting community. It produced some enthusiastic students of Charles W. Hawthorne, such as George Yater, Philip Malicoat, Bruce McKain, and John Frazier from Kansas, and Ross Moffett from Iowa. When undertaking Moffett's biography, therefore, I came to it with my own sense of the Midwestern landscape and of the temper of its people. I understood the farm land and the farmer's sense of his place. We have yet to lose this completely in America, but it is fading fast. The essentiality of place cannot be overemphasized. It carries with it an indigenous purity of thought, related not only to who your ancestors were, but to how you are largely defined by that inherent relationship with your own physical reality, which is securely established in the early years of one's life. Thus my sonnets carried some of what I had temporarily inherited in Michigan and gave me a scope I might never have had if I had grown up in the East, in northern New York where I was born.

Gaining strength gradually, as the time slowly passed toward the fall, I experienced the pleasure of seeing the completion of Romolo's "Melpomene," that sculpture of somewhat soaring proportions, the winged muse of tragedy. Working in rain and heat, he completed the patina on scaffolding and ladder, and, in September, she was ready for shipment to Virginia. The process of bronze casting had been accomplished at the small but astonishingly adequate foundry of Digby-Veevers-Carter in Truro, Massachusetts. Digby found a way, even with somewhat limited space, to cast a nearly flawless "Melpomene." So was the muse of tragedy made somewhat whole and palpable for a few more generations, at least. It was a moment in which to break out a bottle of champagne as Sal and I, with Berta Walker, Digby, and Romolo, exerted ourselves to wrap the sculpture in bubble

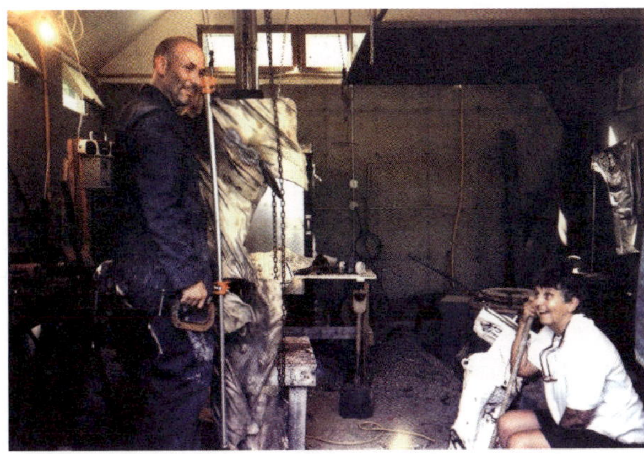

Romolo discussing his casting of *Melpomene* at Digby's Foundry with friend and mentor, sculptor Joyce Johnson, 2002

Melpomene arising fresh from being cast at the Digby Vevers-Carter Foundry in Truro, Massachusetts, September 2002 (Romolo in front kneeling)

wrap and heavy plastic. Lowering her to her prepared bed of an old mattress for safe traveling, we saluted the muse of tragedy, of art, and of the historic process of casting sculpture in bronze—so unyielding and so intractable, and yet so timeless as the art.

October 2002:
There was time then to withdraw a bit and to refresh the spirit at the shack. We took Berta Walker with us. It was her first trip to the shack after many promised forays. Tommy went with us also, and we celebrated my birthday, not with a full course dinner, but with a special pastry that Berta brought from Angel Foods and with a sip of clear, dune water, heavenly food and drink, indeed. Quiet, but restoring, was the day. I neglect to count the years. They wink at me from some spiteful landscape known as old age and insist on coming into view in spite of my admonishments to mind their own business. I am fortunate to be able to rail at time and fate, but I try not to out of respect for what has been done for me to spare my life and to make more pleasant the retrieved days snatched from eternity for my sake.

All too soon, in January 2003, the Seashore sought yet another Dune Shack Subcommittee report through the Seashore Advisory Commission. Once again, for the third time since and including our 1992 report, comments were sought from the dune families and dwellers. Still fighting for their rights, the dune shack community responded, often with indignation and alarm, but always with that remarkable empathy for their way of life. Selected examples of their comments follow:[4]

Mildred Champlin, Mission Bell, April 3, 2003:

We notice in the sheaf of subcommittee papers we picked up at that meeting (March 1)—the first time we had seen the material—that one of the major objectives of the Seashore is to make sure good communication will be maintained for the next generation of dune shack dwellers, hand-picked by the Seashore, as contrasted with the current and original) population.

It was clear from Champlin's complaint that the dune dwellers had been sidelined at the March 1 meeting, and that the message they were being given, albeit indirectly, was that they were being consigned gradually, but firmly, to oblivion.

Susan Pomerantz regarding meeting of Seashore Advisory Commissioin and potential evictions:

Dear Maria Burks, I am writing regarding the shacks (Thalassa and Euphoria) that used to belong to my grandmother, Hazel Hawthorne Werner. I did want it to be known that, to my knowledge, Hazel expected the family to have access to the shacks for limited periods of time while she was alive, in her arrangement with Peaked Hill Trust. (I am unclear about arrangements after her death, but I'm sure it was meant to be fair.) I used the shacks well before she made arrangements with PHT, but never attempted to get a week thereafter. That doesn't mean none of us were interested. My brother, Lou Pomerantz of Vermont, tells me he tried for years through the lottery system of PHT, both before and after Hazel's death, to get a week, but never succeeded. Thank you. Sue Pomerantz

God Help The Fragile Dunes

To all whom it may concern;
I, Schatzi (aka) Chanel-Schnell, in behalf of the "Dune Dwellers": Renters will not protect the dunes—wild life or true life. Renters will not see to the upkeep of the shacks nor the surroundings simply because they are Renters. They don't and never will know that it is: TRUE LOVE of what is seen: TRUE FEELING for what is alive and TRUE COMPASSION for the love of what GOD is presenting. Will renters know that walking up or down a Dune will loosen a ton of sand that will never again mold together? Will renters know that a fire will have smoldering embers that will be alive for 30 years (roots are 30 feet or more into the dunes). There's so much more. HOW CAN ANYONE HAVE THE AUDACITY TO TRY TO REVOKE the written promise of President John F. Kennedy?

A nostalgic postscript—Frenchy Chanel (my mother) was instrumental in marking and fencing off the nesting areas and eggs of the terns. Before your thoughts turn commercial, PLEASE give some concern to the ones that LOVE GOD'S GIFT.

Most sincerely, "Schatzi," Owner of Frenchy's Shack"

Murray Zimiles to Superintendent Burks: regarding the Boris Margo Shack, May 5, 2003:

Perhaps you remember our meeting and the letter I wrote a number of years ago concerning the dune shack I inherited from my uncle Boris Margo. In our meeting and letter, I spoke of our family history with Provincetown and the dunes. I spoke of how, in order to retain life tenancy, Boris and Jan were "forced" (intimidated) to sign the property over to the Seashore. This coming summer will be my 60th continuous year on the dunes. The fact that I can no longer control or have any say in how my shack is used continues to rankle.

Prior to the time Peaked Hill Trust took over the formal managing of Boris's shack as agent for the Seashore, I allowed the same organization the use of it for many years never asking for or receiving a single penny in compensation. I only asked that they help maintain it and schedule others around family usage. In my previous letter, I pleaded with the Seashore to allow me a long-term lease as I not only helped Boris construct the present shack but have lived on that spot all my life; my first trip out there was when I was two years old.

When the National Seashore took over, I was quite shocked not to be given a 25-year lease, especially since I still have the knowledge and resources necessary to maintain the property. The fact that leases went to total "strangers" was outrageous. The Peaked Hill Trust, an organization that I admire and belong to, has remembered my largess and has continued to allow me a week on the dunes (it used to be two weeks). The rest of my family have not received time. As the Seashore deliberates future policy, I would, once again, ask that I receive a long-term lease or, if possible, ownership of the property that I helped construct and lived in all my life.

When Boris Margo died, the shack was being maintained and used by The Peaked Hill Trust and was subsequently delivered, via a new agreement, to yet another organizational consortium called the Outer Cape Artists' Residency Consortium,[5] which still included the PHT as manager and as a partner of usage in that the Trust retained fifty percent of the available shack time for its lottery winners in exchange for management. There was never any consideration given, I believe, to Murray Zimiles's plea for a long-term lease.

Also forthcoming, in addition to these and other personal responses, was the official position of the Provincetown Board of Selectmen regarding the Dune Shack Subcommittee Report to the chairman of the Seashore Advisory Commission Brenda Bolyn in a policy statement dated May 14, 2003. This statement was six pages in length and constituted a well-researched position with extensive documentation. Essentially, it embodied the fullest possible discussion of the dune shacks in their relation to the Park and cited pertinent government references that supported the selectmen's opinion that the dune shacks had exceptional cultural and historical value. The full text of this statement is worth careful review, but I shall include here only several salient points.

Provincetown Board of Selectmen: May 14, 2003:

The Provincetown Board of Selectmen believes that this community is remarkable as well: for the courage its members have shown in building and living in such basic homes at the edge of the backshore, for the tenacity of its members in ensuring the community's continuation through storms of climate and politics,

> and for their continued desire to remain a community set somewhat apart, despite the encroachments of modern life and government regulations all around us.
>
> In view of the significant issues, the Provincetown Board of Selectmen voted on May 12, 2003, to request that the Advisory Commission remand the January, 2003, report back to the Subcommittee for further review and public input.
>
> We reserve the right to continue to participate in the process when a formal public comment period begins pursuant to the requirement of law... [One of the complaints, as voiced, for instance, by Mildred Champlin's letter of April 3, 2003, was that the dune dwellers had been side-lined by the March 1, 2003 meeting and not invited to participate; therefore necessitating the remanding clause requested by the selectmen...]
>
> To date, research undertaken by our Cape Cod National Seashore General Management Plan Implementation Advisory Commission (IAC) indicates that relevant congressional and National Park Service statutes, regulations, rules, guidelines, procedures, protocols, and other materials appear to support the concept that some, perhaps all, dune shack dwellers are a protected cultural resource, and that the Cape Cod National Seashore (CCNS) has legal obligations to manage this cultural resource in the way that best maintains, perpetuates, and strengthens this cultural group's continued access to and use of the dune shacks in which they live.
>
> The IAC research indicates that, subsequent to the time that various settlements were finalized among various occupiers of the dune shacks, the NPS was charged with new, refined, and expanded legal obligations that require CCNS to take a careful and fresh look at the dune shack dwellers themselves as a protected cultural resource. [Quoted from page 1]
>
> As early as 1990, the NPS was engaged in a major expansion of cultural resources management (CRM), especially those areas known as "traditional cultural properties" (TCP). The NPS National Register Bulletin titled "Guidelines for Evaluating and Documenting Traditional Cultural Properties" (known as Bulletin 38), defines TCP as: (a place) that is eligible for inclusion in the National Register because of its association with cultural practices or beliefs of a living community that (a) are rooted in that community's history and (b) are important to maintaining the continuing identity of the community. [A co-author of Bulletin 38 has written that TCP protections actually predate the 1990 Guidelines; that they are not limited to Native American sites; that they are not limited to ethnic communities, and that they protect even areas without continuous use.]:[6] King, Thomas, *Thinking About Cultural Resources Management.* AltaMira Press, 2003, pp. 112-19 Quoted from page 3]

This extensive presentation and thorough analysis concluded with the assumption that the issue of the dune shacks had been incorrectly assessed by the NPS and that the Park Service should feel obliged to change their misguided policy. The last sentence of their letter ended: "We look forward to a continual dialogue with you and the public on this essential part of our local ways of life."[6]

This full statement by the Provincetown Board of Selectmen left no stone unturned in an attempt to be specific about its principles in regard to the dune shack community, a position which it still maintains and has been true for the entirety of habitation on the Great Outer Beach. Just as the essential relationships of the Coast Guard personnel in their several stations were tied to their families in the town, so the dune dwellers are tied to the residents of the Provincetown community in myriad and very meaningful ways, not just as symbols of a "way of life" but as fellow participants who are still connected by a philosophical umbilical cord linked to the total protean environment that Provincetown continues to resonate as its culture. Dawn Zimiles, the niece of Murray Zimiles, responded to the request of the Park for dune dweller comment.

Dawn Zimiles's Response

> The taking of these small houses from the families that built them represents a great loss to the individuals that have a personal history there, as well as the spirit of this area that will be lost if the descendants are denied the right to carry on the simple and beautiful life created out in the dunes by their families....The spirit of Provincetown lives in these places and is being lost forever...[7]

This is why, perhaps, the struggle to resist the dissolution of a connection that is a vital and life-giving union has been so intense: the child cannot be severed from its mother and vice versa. In the end, all the passion of dissent and disagreement with the forces which the Cape Cod National Seashore has brought to bear on this issue have produced an unnatural and contentious result, a result, I might add, that is unnecessary. The repeated threnody of the dune dwellers has been one of declared endorsement of protections for the natural environment, hope for sensible regulations of use, a desire to cooperate in pursuing those regulations and a commitment—financial, physical, and moral—to maintain their properties in a manner that is in conformity with environmental standards necessary for the Park's survival and the essential elements of its management.

In spite of all this, the Cape Cod National Seashore has unflinchingly sought the elimination of the shacks, before and after 1989, and has sought to eliminate their inhabitants and their "way of life" based on an inappropriate philosophy of use and interpretation of the original legislation. Added to the inappropriateness of this approach is the enormous cost of repeated funding for management plans and an incursion of obligations to maintain and repair the shacks in the future, an unnecessary cost to the American taxpayer. What needs to change, therefore, is the Seashore's idea of "the philosophy of use" and, with it, all the baggage of a prior era in which National Parks were basically "wilderness" parks, blessedly free of man's intrusion, for the most part. Man's intrusion in every possible space has now become endemic and increasingly toxic, but the solution is not to get rid of man in nature, but, where amenable circumstances can be instituted, to accept his presence and enlist his services in the massive and never-ending effort to clean up the world's most frightful mistakes and prevent unacceptable environmental risks. The Cape Cod National Seashore needs to do this with their fractious and determined dune dwellers, who were and are equipped to assist the Park Service in this new approach, which was essentially mandated when the CCNS was created. It may be a case of revisiting the *Merchant of Venice,* wherein Shakespeare has posed the ultimate question as to how to achieve a verdict acceptable in the courts without killing the accused and making untenable the future life of the accuser. The "letter" of the law must accommodate to the "spirit" of the law without destroying either and thus invoking the larger tenets of a truly civilized society

Compass Grass by Salvatore Del Deo, 1953; pen and ink drawing

Ancient Historian

The compass grass still carves and sweeps
Its histories on tomes of sand
The wind's direction and abandoned reach
Of endless cycles on an unread beach.

Appendix

Part I

The Dune Cottages at Peaked Hill Bars—A Survey

Foreword 2012

The original survey of *The Dune Cottages at Peaked Hill Bars* contains basic information, still relevant at this time to the historic background regarding the cottages, which I assembled in 1986.[1] This more recent survey includes certain material that has become available to me since, not to mention the fact that time has altered life and death dates of occupants and many other factors of life in the shacks. I have, therefore, revised the survey to accommodate the most pertinent material and to correct whatever has seemed unclear or proven to be inaccurate in the first survey, adding further description as necessary and removing information which now occurs in the body of the text of this memoir and which would be a duplication in the Appendix.

With all this in mind, it is important to understand that no study of these "temples by the sea" may ever completely encompass the true moving and living history of the dune shacks. The best that may be accomplished is to take the known facts and incorporate them in the recounting of a way of life that is both fluid and, at the same time, fixed and to which generations have expressed exceptional devotion.

The Author

Acknowledgments

The original dune cottage survey, completed for the Cape Cod National Seashore in 1986 entitled *The Dune Cottages at Peaked Hill Bars—A Survey* at the request of the then-Superintendent Herbert Olsen, acknowledged several sources of particularly pertinent information which I received, firsthand, from Coast Guard personnel stationed at the Peaked Hill Coast Guard Station in the 1920s and 1930s, namely Philip S. Packett and Louis "Spucky" Silva, and from John Corea, former chief of the Wood End Station. Other sources which I used at the time were standard references and a great deal of material from my own personal archive and from intimate association with fellow dune dwellers over the years. One of these was Ray Martan Wells, who was extremely helpful in sharing with me her personal knowledge of dune life during the 1930s, especially, and beyond. Her long and productive life continued to be a marker for us all until she died in 2011 at the age of 103.

Today, in updating this 1986 survey, further acknowledgments are necessary in order to thank those who have generously given their knowledge, time, and interest to assist me in securing the most accurate information possible in capturing a fleeting history which often cannot be defined without the process of comparing disparate sources. I am indebted, therefore, to the following persons for their contribution to this portion of the updated survey which covers the shacks still extant in the officially created historic district of "The Dune Shacks of Peaked Hill Bars Historic District."

Marianne Benson and Peter Clemons for their sustained support of my work and making available to me the Great Beach Cottage Owners Association archive plus other records, maps, and extensive material regarding the traditional way of life on the dunes. These papers constituted a collection of resources unavailable anywhere else, and I would have found it impossible to attempt the more volumetric overview I have documented without them.

Cape Cod National Seashore Park Historian William Burke, whose corroborative and informational material made more complete several historic references in this survey.

Gail Cohen, official historian of the Hedgerow Repertory Theatre Company of Rose Valley, Moylan, Pennsylvania, for providing valuable information regarding many of the dune dwellers of the past and their interconnecting histories, and for her energetic interest in this memoir.

To Mildred Champlin for the particular references pertinent to the Champlin cottage known as "Mission Bell" (1953 to the present).

To Marcia Adams and Sally Adams for the extensive documentation of the Adams cottage and the life of their family on the dunes (1953 to the present).

To Connie and David Armstrong and their family for the time given me on several personal visits to their cottage to provide vital statistics of their life on the dunes from 1948 to the present, and especially to Connie Armstrong whose recollections of the Eastern Group of shacks in the Truro area and the full trajectory of her family's seasonal habitation, without which, the confirmation of certain personal histories, associations, and dates of habitation would never have been possible.

To Dr. Robert J. Wolfe for his thorough ethnological study entitled "Dwelling in the Dunes: Traditional; Use of the Dune Shacks of the Peaked Hill Bars Historic District of Cape Cod," August 2005, which work brought to light, with insightful construction, the peripheral and integral aspects of both impersonal and personal facts emphasizing and making plain the "way of life" of the dune dwellers at Peaked Hill during the major part of the twentieth century.

Joyce Johnson, sculptor, visionary, community leader, journalist, and founder of the Truro Center for the Arts, whose commitment to the environment as a devoted dune dweller, working to save the beauty and the essence of the way of life in the dune shacks, was unfailing. Joyce died shortly before the publication of this book, but her remembered presence among us will be a lasting endorsement of its message.

To the Massachusetts Historical Commission, which has so consistently supported the preservation of the dune shacks of the Outer Cape and the "way of life" they represent.

Existing Cottages

The shacks listed in this updated survey, as in the original survey, which I have referred to in the Foreword, are numbered in sequence from the westernmost shack in the "Dune Shacks of Peaked Hill Bars Historic District" to the easternmost still extant. Shacks no longer extant are separated from this listing in the present survey and are discussed in a separate category following the main inventory, as I have indicated in the Acknowledgments of Part I.

The first number given with the named identification is the assigned number of the Cape Cod National Seashore listing dated December 12, 1985. The second number, or map number, indicates the aerial map number from the series of aerial photographs compiled in August 1964 by Arthur L. Sparrow Co., Registered Land Surveyors, in South Orleans, Massachusetts, for the U.S. Department of the Interior, Northeast Region.

04-8713(Map 201-4)

Lawrence McCready & Robert Abramson

Jean Miller Cohen Burns (present assigned name)

This cottage was originally constructed by Eddie and Albert Noons, c. 1940, on a site near the Race Point Coast Guard Station, and is the westernmost shack of all the shacks in the Historic District and the only one whose location was in the Province Lands owned by the State of Massachusetts and turned over to the Cape Cod National Seashore in July 1962.

Circa 1950–1951, it was sold to Howard Lewis and, in 1958, was purchased by Jean Miller Cohen and her friend, the artist John Grillo, a student of Hans Hofmann and Mark Rothko. Grillo, a recognized artist on Cape Cod and throughout the country, is still alive at this writing. Subsequently, Jean Miller Cohen, herself an artist and also a student of Hofmann's, together with her then husband Donald Burns, purchased Grillo's interest in the cottage. Sometime later, after 1969 (no exact date available), Cohen and Burns sold the cottage to McCready and Abramson, and this ownership lasted until 1993. Artists who occupied the cottage separately during the period between c. 1955 to 1958, were Marcia Marcus and Jan Muller, who were also Hofmann students.

In 1993, when the McCready-Abramson stipulation with the Cape Cod National Seashore expired, an organization called the Provincetown Community Compact formed an agreement with the Park to run a residency program for artists and others which constituted three-week artists' residencies in the summer, the artists being selected by jury review. The balance of the year, in the spring and fall, community residencies were made available for one week stays selected by lottery. There is a sliding scale for all residencies except for one $500 artist's fellowship. This program has been under the supervision of Jay Critchley and Tom Boland from its inception and is still in operation at this writing.[2] The Cohen shack was moved to its present location in 1978.[3]

04-1052 (Map 202-4)

David Adams

The Adams cottage was built by Jake Loring and Dominic Avilla in 1935, according to Marcia Adams, from scrap wood and salvaged beach wood which the locals called "monkey wood." The shack was used for family gatherings by the Loring family until World War II, when the government forbade its use, as well as that of other shacks, because of the danger of lights identifying habitation along the coastline, which could be spotted by submarines. During this period, the shacks were abandoned and much vandalism occurred. In 1953, David and Marcia Adams purchased the Loring/Avilla shack from Dominic and Al Avilla. At the same time, Nathaniel and Mildred Champlin and Francis and Patsy Villemain had purchased their shacks, suggesting to the Adams couple, that they buy a neighboring shack. Thus, the mutual friends began life in close proximity on the dunes for many seasons to follow. Both Champlin and Villemain were professors in the disciplines of philosophy and education at New York University at the time, and David Adams was a graduate student seeking his doctoral degree there with Nathaniel Champlin as his adviser.

The Adams's first dune experience in their 1935 Chevy converted to a beach buggy involved Howard Lewis who assisted them in the midst of a novitiate's buggy breakdown, and who offered them, as well, shelter in his cottage, which he later sold to his friend Leo Fleurent in 1963. Life on the dunes went on for both the Adams and Champlin families in much the same way, involving repair, maintenance, and, sometimes, major moving such as that entailed after the February winter storm of 1978 which brought David and his son Tom through the same storm system from Kalamazoo, Michigan, to save their shack hanging over the edge of the dune that had been washed out from under it. They were assisted in saving the shack by the skill of Warren "Pinky" Silva who brought it back from the brink with his bulldozer and placed it on a metal I-beam to a position where it could be secured later.

David and Marcia Adams raised their family in the summer months in their dune abode in constant contact with the dune environment. They had four children, each of whom pursued entirely different careers. Tom became a marine engineer, Sally pursued a career as a lawyer, and Jonathan has had a career in fiber optics; Kenneth died in 1975. All four experienced the routine hardships and adjustments of keeping their two shacks (the second, a kind of small service building for various purposes) viable through constant repair and adjustment to the whims of nature. They learned about the lore of fishing through their friendships with the MBBA (Mass. Beach Buggy Association) families, enjoying their generous donations of fish for family gatherings and parties. They all credit their experiences with making them much more resourceful in meeting the exigencies of life. David Adams died in 2009. The many pleasures of his life on the dunes included recording his love of the natural environment through the medium of watercolor.[4]

In terms of this property, as well as in the case of all the dune shacks attempting to establish rights of residency without the government's willingness to apply appropriate language for residency, which is framed under the category of homes protected as "improved property" described and guaranteed in the law creating the Cape Cod National Seashore, the history is long-standing, and much of it is contained in this memoir. These dune shacks, are now duly registered as historic properties, on the National Register of Historic Places.[5] and the resident dune dwellers are continuing to maintain them and the traditional way of life they represent.

04-1053 (Map 202-4)

Nathaniel Champlin

The Champlin cottage became known as "Mission Bell" from the time that a large Michigan school bell arrived at the Champlin's shack in 1956. Mildred and Nathaniel Champlin bought the "Mission Bell" cottage in 1953 from Dominic and Al Avilla, and thus began a long trajectory of life on the dunes for nearly sixty years, at this writing. Nathaniel Champlin was a professor of philosophy at Wayne State University and also a professor of aesthetics at Cranbrook Academy, both institutions located in Detroit, Michigan. Champlin received his doctorate from New York University after World War II, having benefitted from the G.I. Bill, as did many other veterans. In the same disciplines of education and philosophy, a former fellow student from Pratt Institute, Francis Villemain, became associated with the Champlin shack as part owner in 1953, which interest lasted until c. 1970, when the Champlins bought out his share.

At the same time that Champlin and Villemain established their interest in the shack in the back shore, they alerted David Adams to the possibility of acquiring a shack close to theirs (see Adams cottage history). Following the close friendships of shack owners in this part of the Historic District, one should mention Leo Fleurent as a member of the society of friends helping each other in that area of the dune shack community and sharing responsibilities of maintaining their shacks, both physically and spiritually. In the early days of the Park's management, this meant engaging in an ongoing fight to keep their shacks from being eventually eliminated. The dune shack sodality and the determination to protect their way of life is securely in evidence in the Great Beach Cottage Owners Association Archives and elsewhere, as this memoir certainly establishes.

The original shack of the Champlins was built about 1937 by Dominic Avilla, according to Mildred Champlin. When the Champlins acquired it from Dominic and Al Avilla in 1953, they spent an enormous amount of time and effort to improve it, gradually, to a residence on the dunes worthy of remark as to the way in which imagination, hard labor, and artistry can transform a rough abode into a working and efficient dwelling. According to notes of Marcia Adams, Champlin knew a lot about building, because his father had been a contractor in Newport, Rhode Island.[6]

When the severe winter storm of 1978 hit "Mission Bell," the Champlins, as in the case of the Adams cottage, had to move the cottage back from its location with the help of "Pinky" Silva who was able to save it from oblivion and move it to its present location. Similarly, three separate storms in 1991 took 75 to 100 feet of the shoreline, leaving "Mission Bell" only twelve feet away from the brink again. This time, however, the sand built back, as it often does, and the cottage was saved.

The Champlins have three children, all of whom have careers shaped in some way, it seems, by their early youth as dune dwellers: Mai Champlin Peck is involved in the Cuyahoga River Watershed River Restoration and Wetland Preservation Project in Cuyahoga, Ohio; Andrea Champlin studied at the Boston Museum School of Art and is a painter and teacher; Paul Champlin directs wildlife management for the Newport, Rhode Island Navy Base. The Champlin family, as in the case of the other families of traditional dune dwellers, exhibit the one element necessary for dune life survival: a passion and commitment to a way of life almost unobtainable elsewhere in modern society.[7]

04-1051 (Map 202=4)

Leo Fleurent

The Fleurent cottage was constructed in 1938–1939 by Eddie and Albert Noons and Edward "Jake" Loring of Provincetown for the use of Albert Noons. In plan and scale, the cottage is similar to the Adams cottage, which was built by Loring and Dominic Avilla. Around 1950-1951, the cottage was sold to Howard Lewis, during whose occupancy, the cottage was known as "Lewis Camp." By approximately 1960, the cottage was occupied by Leo Fleurent who became a year-round resident after 1967. Fleurent, who was not an artist, resided in his shack year-round until his death in 1984,[8] thus becoming the second year-round occupant of a dune shack, together with Charlie Schmid, prior to Lawrence Schuster's yearly occupancy of the Braaten cottage which began in 1983.

Fleurent was affectionately known to his friends and fellow dune dwellers as the "Colonel" and was exceptionally devoted to his dune life and to his home on the dunes. After his death, however, Fleurent's shack was allowed to deteriorate to such a degree that it was identified as a clear case of "demolition by neglect," a condition which was in direct violation of The National Preservation Act of 1988, Section 110 (revised).[9] Photographs taken in 1991 reveal enormous neglect and deterioration and it was not until the Park's awarding of Fleurent's dune shack to Emily Beebe and Evelyn Simon of Wellfleet, at the same time as two other twenty-year historic property leases were awarded to the former shacks of Randolph Jones and Peg Watson (Schmid), by the Cape Cod National Seashore that any remedy took place.[10] The rehabilitation of the Fleurent shack began in 1994 and was completed in 1998. The exceptional care of both Beebe, an environmental engineer, and Simon in accomplishing the restoration of the shack is noteworthy and demonstrates the particular sense of devotion to the historic elements and the ethos of the shacks in the flow of residency from one generation to the next.

04-8618(Map 202-4)

Conrad Malicoat

The Malicoat family is one of the most important resident families of artists in Provincetown. Philip Malicoat, father of Conrad, a painter from Indiana who studied at the John Heron Art Institute in Indianapolis, came to Provincetown in 1929 to study with the famous painter and teacher Charles W. Hawthorne, founder of the Cape Cod School of Art, the first major summer art school in Provincetown. Malicoat later studied briefly with Henry Hensche who kept Hawthorne's school going under a new name, The Cape School of Art, and with Edwin Dickinson, one of America's most distinguished painters. Malicoat eventually established his own private teaching career and was widely recognized. He was, for years, a leader in the affairs of the Provincetown Art Association, the second oldest Art Association in the country, dating from 1914 to the present.

Philip Malicoat's wife Barbara Brown Malicoat was the daughter of Harold Haven and Florence Bradshaw Brown, both of whom were directors of the Provincetown Art Association; Harold Haven from 1928 until his death in 1932, and Florence Bradshaw from 1932 to 1936. Barbara Brown Malicoat was a gifted graphic artist and contributed, together with her husband, a great deal of time and energy to the affairs of the Provincetown Art Association and to the community at large. Philip Malicoat was a member of the first faculty of the Fine Arts Work Center in Provincetown together with Karl Knaths,

Henry Hensche, and Jack Tworkov. Conrad Malicoat, his son, the present owner of the dune cottage, is a graduate of Oberlin College and a sculptor and artisan. Martha Malicoat Dunigan, his daughter now deceased, was also a graduate of Oberlin College and a graphic artist and teacher. Anne Lord Malicoat, Conrad's wife, is a graduate of Radcliffe College and a sculptor and ceramicist. Granddaughters Robena Malicoat, a painter, and Breon Dunigan, a sculptor, continue the family's artistic tradition.[11]

Philip Malicoat built his first dune shack sometime between 1948 and 1949. According to his son Conrad, it was very small, about 12 x 16 feet, and was located on a piece of property he owned that was approximately 75 feet wide and extended from Bradford Street to the Atlantic Ocean. Due to an unfortunate incident which occurred while the Malicoats were in Europe around 1955, the shack was burned to the ground during occupancy by a friend who had been allowed to use it. Conrad and his father and the painter Bruce McKain, a close friend, rebuilt the shack sometime before 1960.[12] This property is listed on the December 12, 1985, inventory as "Private Property—Homesite 3.0 acres"They sold the remainder of the property to the Federal Government and were protected from condemnation by the "Homesite" listing.[13]

08-1049 (Map 201-8)

Hazel Hawthorne Werner: "Euphoria"

Hazel Hawthorne Ufford Werner's two cottages known as "Euphoria" and "Thalassa" are on the West and East flank, respectively, of what I refer to as the Peaked Hill complex of cottages, which were built near and around the two shore-ward Coast Guard stations at Peaked Hill. The cottage here referred to is known as "Euphoria" and is on the West flank of the Peaked Hill complex, approximately 1,050 feet or 450 strides from the nearest cottage to the east of it, which is that of Boris Margo and Jan Gelb.[14]

The shack "Euphoria" was built by James Meads, a Provincetown builder, for Cora F. Holbrook in July, 1936.[15] According to Hazel's drawings of the lineage of shack constructions and placements that she prepared for Andrew Fuller and Grace Bessay and the Great Beach Cottage Owners Association in 1971, and which are reproduced in this Appendix for reference, Hazel's notations indicate she purchased the shack from Cora Holbrook in 1943. A later notation remarks that in around 1952 she moved the shack back from its location about 70 feet.[16] Both Cora Holbrook's signed statements and Hazel's corroborative drawings and information combine to give us, in this case, an exact physical history of the shack's construction, placement and ownership

Hazel Hawthorne Werner was a dune resident for a great many years dating from circa 1920 (from her own statement given at the December hearings to create the Cape Cod National Seashore Park [17]) until a chronic condition diagnosed as Parkinson's Disease prevented her from occupying her shack in her later years. Her life and times in connection with dune life are portrayed in two reliable sources: Edmund Wilson's memoir of the thirties and William Brevda's biography of Harry Kemp.[18] Both these books discuss life on the dunes in connection with Hazel and her milieu and establish the picture of her times. She entertained and/or rented to some very important personages in the art and literary circles of that period including: Edmund Wilson, E.E. Cumings, Peter Blume, Edwin Dickinson, Claire Leighton, Curt Valentine, Norman Mailer, and many others. Hazel Hawthorne was the author of a novel about Provincetown called *The Salt Box*, long out of print, I believe, and a number of other literary works which include several pieces published in *The New Yorker Magazine*.

Hazel was an active member of the Great Beach Cottage Owner's Association from its founding in 1962 until its dissolution c.1978, and worked assiduously to try to save the dune shacks and their way of life throughout the period of the organization's active life. Her valuable inventory of drawings and notations referred to and reproduced in this survey, which covers the placement and brief historical references to the shacks in the Peaked Hill complex from 1920 to 1960, were given to Andrew Fuller, cochairman of the GBCOA in April 1971.

After the nonprofit organization known as The Peaked Hill Trust, established to manage dune shacks no longer maintained by a traditional dune dweller for various reasons, was formed in 1986 by agreement with the Cape Cod National Seashore Park, Hazel turned over both her shacks to the Trust which manages their care and rental on a lottery basis, during the summer and fall seasons.

08-1040 (Map 201-8)

Boris Margo/Jan Gelb

Boris Margo was an artist of international note, having exhibited widely in this country, especially in New York galleries and, of course, in Provincetown ,for more than fifty years. He was one of the original group of Surrealists and is in many important collections. Boris's brother David Margolis was also a well-known painter, having studied mural painting with the Mexican muralist Diego Rivera. His mural for the Bellevue Hospital in New York was unfortunately destroyed during the McCarthy era. Jan Gelb, Boris Margo's wife, was a painter and spent a large part of every summer on the dunes, where she evolved a unique approach to that environment over the years. Murray Zimiles, Margo's nephew, is also an artist of note in many genre and a teacher, and Dawn Zimiles, Boris Margo's great niece continues the tradition of art in this three-generational family of artists who have consistently been attached to their shack at Peaked Hill in multiple ways with tenacity and devotion.[19]

The original Margo/Gelb shack was built by Boris and Jan in 1942.[20] This shack and a second shack were sequentially lost to erosion of the shoreline, and, according to Murray Zimiles, Boris's nephew, the present shack is the third shack on the site and was built sometime between 1967 and 1971.[21] The shack is very near or on the site of the original Peaked Hill Life Saving Station built in 1872 and which was owned by Eugene O'Neill, beginning in 1919, and where he lived and wrote until c.1924 The station slid into the water in January 1931 [22] (see also Chapter 5, p. 69).

This, then, is the closest we can come to the memorial site of the old Peaked Hill Station and, by association, with the abode of Eugene O'Neill. I have carefully paced distances between the site of the "second" or Peaked Hill Coast Guard Station built between 1913–1914 and the site of the old station.[23] The Coast Guard Station is clearly visible in the distance in the photograph as the furthest building outlined against the horizon. This building has a high watchtower and is occupying what later has become the site of the Jeanne Chanel cottage. The confusion which surrounds "the station," on occasion, is one of nomenclature; the Peaked Hill Life Saving Station, was later replaced by the Peaked Hill Coast Guard Station built on its new site. All of the Life Saving Stations were renamed and reclassified in 1915 when the Life Saving Service and the Revenue Cutter Service became the U.S, Coasat Guard.[24]

We see, therefore, that if one stands on the site of the Margo cottage and glances eastward to the Chanel cottage, one glimpses the trajectory of vision seen in the photograph of the old station sliding into the ocean as follows: (paced distances)

(West to East) Boris Margo to Rose Tasha (Harry Kemp) 432 feet (more or less); Rose Tasha (Harry Kemp) to Chanel, 773 feet (more or less); Boris Margo to Chanel, 1,205 feet, (more or less)

The Margo to Chanel shack represents the distance between the first and second stations, more or less, and this distance can be said to be approximately one quarter to one half a mile.

The Peaked Hill Life Saving Station was decommissioned in 1914 and sold to Sam Lewisohn a wealthy NewYork financier, art patron and a friend of the painter Maurice Sterne Lewisohn shared the use of the building with Mabel Dodge who oversaw the conversion from life saving station to residence at his expense. During this period when Mabel Dodge occupied the station sporadically between 1914–1915 and again in 1917, she completely renovated the interior with the help of Robert Edmond Jones, creating a spectacular setting for the friends of her New York salon. Ray Wells remembered well the remarkable blue of the interior created by Jones.[25]

Samuel Lewisohn sold the building and land to James O'Neill in 1919 who gave it to his son Eugene O'Neill and Agnes Bolton as a wedding present. Ten years later, in 1929, O'Neill divorced Agnes and married Carlotta Monterey, and, in 1930, O'Neill gave the building to his oldest son Eugene O'Neill. It is not possible now to name the full list of famous or notable personages who came and went in the station before it fell into the ocean. The list included the members of the Provincetown Players and it can be confidently said that the old station either housed or hosted a stellar cross section of American intelligentsia at that time between 1914–1931. Edmund Wilson, of course, was the last of these.[26]

The Peaked Hill Bars Coast Guard Station in a new location, c.1932, after it had been moved 660 feet inland from a shoreward position following the severe storm of 1931. *Photo courtesy of David Mayo*

Ray Wells also provided a valuable recollection of some of the other structures surrounding the station c.1930 when I spoke to her in preparing the original survey in 1986, remarking that among these buildings was a small shack owned by the Chief of the Station Frank Mayo, which, she said, went into the ocean at the same time as the Peaked Hill Life Saving Station in 1931.[27] Also extant was a rather palatial cottage that later became the Ofsevit cottage and a very small outbuilding built by a Coast Guardsman named Cadose. and later owned by Coast Guardsman Frank Henderson. Ray herself lived in this shack in 1931–1932 and then it was given to Harry Kemp by Henderson.[28]

Chief Frank Lothrop Mayo standing next to Coast Guard Surf Boat at Peaked Hill Bars, August, 1935 (see also, footnote 30). *Photo courtesy of David Mayo*

In a fascinating aside, John Corea, former chief of the Wood End Station, with whom I also consulted in 1986, recalled his early impression of Eugene O'Neill on the dunes in 1917 when John was just a young boy. His memory of O'Neill was of a particularly fascinating figure, because, at that time, according to Corea, he was living in a kind of hut constructed of beach grass and found materials, which seemed to a child's mind something like an igloo. Corea was part of a small group of children taken on an excursion to the dunes by a woman by the name of Edwards, who had been teaching them how to do wood blocks. John recalls that it was an exhausting trip, but one he would never forget.[29]

To complete the historic cycle of Coast Guard (formerly Life Saving) structures at Peaked Hill, we need to add the final description and disposition which was that shortly after the devastating storm of 1931, the Coast Guard became nervous about the safety of their new station and moved it back 660 feet inland to a safer location. They also moved back, at the same time what became listed on the Park's inventory of 1985 as The Abandoned Boat House.[30] The station building on this third site was used until the hurricane of 1938; after that, for two years, it was put on watch, the full crew of the Coast Guard Station having been moved to the Race Point Station. Philip Packet and Frank Henderson, Coast Guardsmen, alternated watches at this station until 1939. In 1940, it was sold to a doctor for $200, but was never used by him to any degree. When World War II prompted much vigilant activity on the back shore, the government paid $27,000 to get the station back again and it was used as a lookout station to spot enemy vessels, planes, etc. After the war, c.1945, the government turned it back to the doctor who had previously owned it This ownership was largely in absentia, and the station was severely vandalized. In order to stop further depredation of the building and surrounding area, the State of Massachusetts burned it in the late forties.[31] The poured cement foundation, as opposed to the Barnstable brick foundation of the shoreward station, can still be seen at the site. The painter Bruce McKain painted the remaining structure in 1933–1934 as a commission from the WPA project. This ancillary discussion of the Peaked Hill stations and history connected to the Margo-Gelb and Chanel shacks and also to the Tasha-Kemp and Ofsevit shacks in proximity is intended to provide a volumetric depth of view

Returning to the discussion of the more recent history of the Margo-Gelb shack, during the troublesome years of the late 1970s and beyond, the National Seashore was in the process of closing off the traditional dune dwellers' access and use of their shacks by exacting compliance with signed stipulations. Jan and Boris protested through the Great Beach Cottage Owners Association against the taking of their shack, but to no avail. When Boris died in 1995 and his life estate in the shack came to an end overnight, the Park turned the shack over to the management of The Peaked Hill Trust and the entire family of Margo-Gelb-Zimiles were denied access to the shack except for a two-week seasonal summer visitation. Eventually, even this time was shortened to one week and then eliminated altogether. At the present time, the Peaked Hill Trust and a similar nonprofit group, The Outer Cape Artist's Residency Consortium are combined in the management of the shack, each sharing half the available time between their constituent memberships.[32]

08-1043 (Map 201-8)

Rose Tasha (Kemp)

A substantial overview of the history of the Tasha (Kemp) shack was provided to me by Ray Martan Wells in my interview with her on October 16, 1986, as has been discussed in this survey under the Boris Margo(-Gelb) shack history. This established the Tasha (Kemp) shack as originally part of the Peaked Hill Life Saving Station complex. The several buildings in this complex were variously service buildings connected with the station and/or small cottages constructed, from time to time by the Coast Guardsmen themselves for use by their families in the summer months. The Coast Guardsman who built the original Tasha (Kemp) structure was a man by the name of Frank Cadose, and it was this cottage that Ray Wells rented in 1931 and 1932 for the sum of $3.00 per week. During the period of her stay there, she was associated with the novelist Hartwell Shippey and the playwright B.S. Bercovici. The Cadose building, prior to Well's occupancy, had been acquired by another Coast Guardsman Frank Henderson, who, like the first owner, was a member of the crew of the Peaked Hill Station.

Henderson was a most colorful Provincetown figure. In 1916, he acted with the famous Provincetown Players together with artists and professional actors.[33] He was known for his strength and acrobatic abilities and his great integrity of character. He accompanied Rear Admiral Donald B. MacMillan to the Arctic in 1926, and it was during the defense of his good friend MacMillan's sterling character and reputation that Henderson suffered a cerebral hemorrhage and died on the floor of the Provincetown Town Hall. Henderson was a firebrand of a civic leader, and one of the selectmen who spearheaded the initiative to establish the town manager form of town government in 1954. He turned his cottage over to Kemp, according to Wells, sometime around 1935, but the date given in William Brevda's biography of Kemp was 1932.[34] What Kemp wrote in his dune cottage is a matter to be usefully studied in Brevda's biography, especially in chapters 12 and 14 and in the bibliography of the book.

The amount of writing accomplished by Harry Kemp on the "back shore" was impressive and included the controversial novel *Love Among the Cape Enders*, although this novel was probably written in the Ofasevit cottage between 1927–1929, the period of Kemp's stay there (see Ofsevit history in this survey). Kemp's output during the time he occupied his own dune shack, approximately twenty-eight years, included a prodigious amount of poetry, many tracts and articles, and, in general, the major part of his writing during that time frame, although he did not return to Provincetown on a truly year-round basis until the 1940s, alternating between Greenwich Village and the Cape. He also completed a novel entitled *Mabel Tarner: An American Primitive* (New York, Lee Furman, 1936). Edmund Wilson's journal of the period of the 1930s, already referred to in this survey under the histories of the Hazel Hawthorne's "Euphoria" shack and the Margo-Gelb shack, colorfully illustrates accounts of some of Harry Kemp's worst and best moments on the dunes in the earlier days.

In the late forties, Salvatore Del Deo developed an intimate friendship with Harry, and Harry became his spiritual godfather. Details of their close relationship are recounted in Chapter I of this memoir, "Between the Sand and Stars." The person who gave Harry so much spiritual and temporal support, however, especially in his later years in Provincetown was "Sunny" Rose Tasha. She was an inspired and devoted proselytizer of his several dreams and the actual enactments of some of them, such as the annual reenactment of the Pilgrims' First Landing in Provincetown, which Harry sincerely believed would change the error of the history books that insisted that Plymouth was the place. Eventually Harry Kemp's success in this endeavor was made annually possible by "Sunny's" organization of the entire event (see Chapter I) In general, "Sunny" Rose Tasha watched over the health and welfare of Harry Kemp, building him a small cottage of refuge on her land, with the help of friends like Alan Dodge, and offering him, thereby, a sense of security when he could no longer make the daily trips to his shack on the back shore. In 1977, after Harry died, she also built a replica of his dune shack in the Provincetown Heritage Museum,of which I was chairman at the time. It contained what he loved best: as many books as could be crowded on the shelves, a kerosene stove (actually Frenchie's), an old coffee pot, his jacket with a flower in the buttonhole, an empty wine bottle, some notebooks, and an uncompleted poem in his portable typewriter. A simulated window opened on a dune landscape painted by artist Harvey Dodd, and the physical circumstances of his dune life were defined. I like to think that my own profile of Harry, contained in a series of portraits that I entitled *Compass Grass Anthology* and published in 1984, fills out some of the congenial metaphysical aspects as well.

Today, the Tasha-Kemp cottage is maintained by Rose "Sunny" Tasha's son Paul. He adheres to the principle that Harry, and subsequently "Sunny," always insisted upon, which was to leave it open (unlocked) for "stranded seamen" in case of disaster. This was the principle established by the Coast Guard's half-way houses on the dunes over decades, providing a shelter for the injured, the stranded, and even the dying, who could at least take cover from overwhelming natural circumstances. It is a place for the gathering of friends and family, and it also carries an artistic legacy in the name of Carl Tasha, "Sunny's" oldest son, who was an artisan of exceptional ability in several disciplines, especially jewelry and smaller bronze sculpture. The ultimate disposition of the Tasha-Kemp shack is yet to be made clear at this writing.

08-1041 (Map 201-8)

Irving Ofsevit-Zara Malkin Ofsevit Jackson

A colorful and detailed history of the Ofsevit cottage was provided to Andrew Fuller, co-chairman of the Great Beach Cottage Owners Association on March 13, 1971, by Zara Ofsevit Jackson. She begins with the history of the ownership and construction.

> My mother's cottage was built about 1918 to 1920 by a town clerk who acquired (or drew up himself) the deed to the land. My mother mentioned the name of Rogers, I think Charlie, although the deed was not in his name...Nick Wells has a certified copy of the deed itself. [Nick Wells was co-chairman of the Great Beach Cottage Owners Association, together with Andrew Fuller, at the time the letter

was written]. The cottage was definitely occupied at the time my mother (Alice Malkin) bought it in 1929. Among the previous tenants was Harry Kemp.

I remember going out to Peaked Hill for the first time at the age of five (1929) to live there for the summer. Our cartload of furniture my mother had purchased at an auction of the old lighthouse was pulled in a horse-drawn wagon

The chief of the Peaked Hill Coast Guard Station at the time was Mr. Mayo; his mate was Joe Morris. Manuel "Greeney" Silva was the cook, his daughter was Victoria. Those early summers at P.H., if we were lucky in our timing, we hitched a ride on the Coast Guard wagon pulled by a nasty-tempered horse named Betsy, for our weekly shopping trips. Otherwise, my mother carried groceries home in an onion sack slung over the shoulder, on a path of wooden planks stretching from the Station to the paths in the wooded part of Snail Road. From there, we climbed aboard a 1918 model bus that regularly made the round trip around Provincetown.

During our first summer, I remember there being only my mother's cottage, a rather remarkable fishing shack belonging to Mr. Mayo, and another cottage in which Harry Kemp lived at different times.[35] Our first introduction to Harry was when my father burned garbage too close to the beach grass in front of our cottage and Harry ran over carrying a basin of sand to help quell the fire.

I remember that Hazel Hawthorne Werner being on the dunes during the summer of 1930, because I was six, her daughter Nancy was five years old, Jane was ten, and Sally was one and a half.(somehow, figures at that time were very important)

I believe it was 1931 when severe storms hit the Cape all summer. One night, I remember waking to find our cottage full of people, all keeping up their spirits while they worried whether the storm would abate before the cliff was washed into the ocean. The next morning, we awakened to find the cliff edge perhaps only three to four feet from the porch door. Captain Mayo's fishing shack was left hanging half off and half on the bluff. To "save" it, a rope was looped around it and attached to the Coast Guard tractor. As the tractor slowly moved back, the rope pulled taut and the shack crumpled like a house of cards and pitched down the cliff into the sea. I remember that earlier there had been a fire in the old Coast Guard station (called the O'Neill station) and, at the time of these severe storms, this too was washed into the sea."[36]

Watch Tower of Peaked Hill Station, built c.1938–39, as an observing lookout during World War II and placed on the shore, as the main station was too far inland to observe the beach and shoreline (see Hazel Hawthorne's map p.4 and also Zara Ofsevit references of this survey; see also, footnote 38). *Photo courtesy of David Mayo*

The Coast Guardsmen and our neighbors emptied our furniture through the windows of the cottage in preparation for the same operation as for Mr. Mayo's place, but fortunately the storm subsided and we lasted the summer on the same site. During that winter the storms continued and my mother received a telegram from Joe Morris, who stated, as caretaker for our cottage, that it was necessary to move it back from the cliff as far as was practical on rollers. Because there was a rolling dune immediately behind us and she evidently didn't think it advisable to place the cottage on top of a hill, the distance it could be moved back was very limited.[37]

The following summer (either 1931 or 1932) she decided to move the cottage beyond the reach of the storms and cliff erosion just as the same decision was made for the Peaked Hill Station. This meant, in the case of the Station, that, during the World War II, a small watch house was built on the bluff so that the man on watch could have a direct view of the beach and ocean. A telephone connected the tower to the main building. When the Station was on the original site, its cupola tower was used for the Watch because the station was close enough to the beach for the view to be possible.[38]

My mother's cottage was moved by the same man who moved the Coast Guard Station—Jesse Meads. Cut into sections, these were loaded one at a time into a horse-drawn cart to the new site...600 feet directly in back of the original location. My mother and Joe Morris were very careful to place it within the boundaries cited in the deed. The cottage was placed on a line with the new site of the Coast Guard Station, in approximately the same relationship as the previous sites. During the years the Coast Guard Station remained open until 1938 or 1939 (I believe), Joe Morris acted and was paid by my mother to act as a caretaker, making any necessary repairs.

By 1930 or 1931, three other cottages were built behind our original site, one built by Louis "Spucky" Silva (Hazel bought this), one by Phillip Packett, and one built by Raymond Brown and later sold to Al Fearing.[39]

The year that the crew was removed, and for either one or two years following, Frank Henderson lived in the Station and acted as caretaker to maintain the property. It was completely closed and empty for a year or two after that and then it was sold at auction.[40] My mother bought the boathouse from the original purchaser with the stipulation that it be moved from the government property onto hers. She died in 1943, before she was able to do this. In 1942, the Station was reopened because of World War II. Instead of the local men who used to be at the station, young men who had enlisted in the Navy were very chagrined to find themselves marooned in the middle of "nowhere." A Chief Warrant Officer, Mr. Ireland, was in charge of Race Point and Peaked Hill Bars. When the old crew of the Coast Guard Station was disbanded, my mother asked Jimmy Thomas (Jonathan's father) to take care of the maintenance of the cottage for her. After her death in 1943, he took care of it for me also.

Zara Ofsevit diverges, at this point to recall her summers in the cottage with her husband Irving and later with her one-year old daughter. Among the friends she rented to during the period 1943–1954 were: Jan Gelb, Margo's younger brother, and his wife, Peg Watson's friend Edwin Denby,[41] Bradley and Claire Burch, and others. She remarks that Nick Wells rented the shack for her after 1954 to Robert Baker for several years and then to Jonathan Thomas, both of whom maintained it and made necessary repairs in lieu of payment. In later years, the Ofsevit shack was occupied, at various times, by the painter Frank Milby, occasionally by the sculptor Joyce Johnson, who was also the founder and first director of the Truro Center for the Arts, Castle Hill, and by Barbara Baker, a later and a following director of Castle Hill.

It is seldom possible to obtain statistics such as these from a distance of more than fifty years, but the letter is clearly accurate in every reference that can be checked against it from other sources and is especially valuable from the standpoint of this survey..The Ofsevit shack was transferred to The Peaked Hill Trust sometime after the Trust's agreement with the Cape Cod National Seashore in 1986, but it burned to the ground due to vandalism in 1990, thus necessitating a complete rebuilding of the structure which the Trust undertook with full observance of Park regulations, which included no expansion of the original footprint. Even with this observance of the Seashore's prescribed standards for rebuilding, the Park attempted to remove the shack from the list of dune shacks eligible for inclusion on the National Register as part of *The Dune Shacks of Peaked Hill Bars Historic District,* the eligibility for which had been in place since May 1989. Its eligibility, however, was later restored and the Ofsevit shack was eventually included in the officially registered historic district.

08-1044 (Map 201-8)

Stanley and Laura Fowler

Stanley and Laura Fowler were two of the older dune residents who lived in their dune cottage, as they preferred to call their shack, six months of every year from 1949 until 1991. They were remarkably dedicated to the health and welfare of the dunes throughout their long sojourn there, admonishing those who littered, disfigured in any way, or abused this precious reserve by the sea. They became experts on the movement of every blade of dune grass and the flight of every variety of sea bird in the course of their dune life, and although the outward expression of such love may have seemed excessively vigilant, like the other dune dwellers who have inhabited their back shore residences for such a long time, they might have been said to have been the generals of that army of preservationists that all we foot soldiers joined in company against the ravages of man.

Stanley Fowler's admonition,s contained in his brief history of their residency, state it well: "Erosion was recognized by our forefathers as one serious problem if Provincetown was to be saved. It was with great sacrifice in money and labor that they imported and planted African beach grass for this purpose. This grass grew from shoots rather than from seed, as the greater portion of seed is blown around by the winds before it can germinate and take root. We have proven that hordes of people trample the grass and vehicles crush it; the grass dies and will not be replaced for at least two years, if ever, The sand moves where the grass is killed and erosion starts again" [42]

Laura Fowler added to this in a letter to me dated April, 27, 1992, during the work of our original dune shack subcommittee research: "No one knows the comings and goings of the people who lived in all the shacks in the Peaked Hill District better than ourselves (the Fowlers), having lived there for forty-one summers, six months of every year." She goes on to recount their attention to order and preservation of the shacks. "Jan Gelb, Peg Watson, and Laura Fowler kept law and order in regard to trampling grass, fires, and vandalism. Some of the shacks still stand because of our care." [43]

> Stan and Laura Fowler started construction of their cottage in 1948, several years after their first visits in 1940-1941 when they met their friends Al and Dorothy Fearing. They camped on the dunes for several years prior to starting construction

of their cottage which was concluded in 1949. They had a signed agreement and bill of sale with E. Jeffe Beede to buy the land they were building on. Mr. Beede had a heart attack several days before the signing and was unable to make the arranged meeting. The resulting delay in the purchase of this site was the reason the Fowlers were unable to establish clear ownership of the property prior to the cut-off date mandated by the Park which was 1959. The process of the building of their shack was arduous by any standards:

At this time, they were living in Plymouth, Massachusetts and much of the construction (sizing and cutting) of the original cottage was done at their home in Plymouth. They were both working full time jobs during the week, but on Friday nights, they would pack the car with lumber and supplies and drive to Provincetown. Upon arrival late Friday night, they would walk across the dunes from old Route 6 carrying their young son and as much lumber as they could carry on their back. After one trip to the shack site, Stan would return to the car at midnight or later and get another load of lumber to bring out... They worked on their shack full days on Saturday and Sunday and then drove back to their home in Plymouth on Sunday night. Stan was proud of the construction skills he had and very proud that the lumber he used in this well-built cottage was new and first quality.

Stan and Laura gave Peter and Marianne Clemons the use of their cottage in 1990, because at the time, they were both 80 years old and the trips to and from their home in Florida each summer were too difficult for them. Stan had also been diagnosed with skin cancer They sincerely hoped to sell their interest in their property to the Clemons family but were told by the Federal Government that they could not, given the previous life estate stipulation terms. Stanley Fowler died in 2000. Laura Fowler died in January 2005. Peter and Marianne Clemons had maintained the Fowler cottage for fifteen years, but the Cape Cod National Seashore sent them a 30-day eviction notice in early June 2005."[44]

Today the cottage is being run by the Outer Cape Artists' Residency Consortium.

08-1050 (Map 201-8))

Abandoned Boat House

(see Ofsevit history)

08-1045 (Map 201-8)

Grace Bessay (Andrew Fuller)

Hazel Hawthorne Werner indicates that it was Raymond Brown who built the Bessay (Fuller)-Fearing cottage by the placement on her 1933 diagrammatic page (page 2) of cottage locations.[45] The date 1931 is also verified by her accompanying notes. In a third historical reference, Ray Wells and her map indicating cottage construction and placement, Raymond Brown is also identified as building the Fearing cottage. It seems clear, therefore, from proof by Hazel Werner and Ray Wells, and by a corroborative reference from the National Register's researchers and Park Historian William Burke, that Coast Guardsman Raymond Brown built the Bessay (Fuller), originally Fearing, shack in 1931–1932. The following material, provided by Peter Clemons and Marianne Benson, succinctly encapsulates the shack's history to the present:

Cottage of Stanley & Laura Fowler, 1984. (In background, cottage of Andrew Fuller and Grace Bessay)

The cottage sits on the original site, but the dune under it was restored after serious erosion issues threatened the building in the early 1950s. Mr. Brown sold the property to Ann Kleiman of New York City (possessory title in land and building) in 1934. Ann Kleiman sold the cottage and land to Dorothy and Al Fearing of Winthrop, Massachusetts (deed dated November 25, 1939, deed book 802, p. 123) in 1939. The Fearings met Andy Fuller and Grace Bessay when the Great Beach Cottage Owners Association was being formed in 1962. Dorothy and Al Fearing sold the cottage and land to Andrew Fuller of Brookline, Massachusetts, in 1969 (December 12, 1969).

Andy Fuller was the founder and co-chair of the GBCOA, assisted by his friend and partner Grace Bessay of Cambridge, Massachusetts. They were devoted dune shack advocates and worked hard with other dune dwellers to keep the historic dune shacks from being destroyed by the Federal Government. Andy and Grace had many friends among resident dune dwellers, all of whom were highly appreciative of what they were attempting to accomplish in trying to preserve not only the shacks but the very way of life on the dunes. In 1975, Marianne Benson and Peter Clemons met Andy and Grace and were invited to use the dwelling as their guests, helping with repairs and caretaking. They were also introduced to Stan and Laura Fowler at that time. Andrew Fuller died in 1981 and left the property to his partner Grace. For the next fifteen years, Grace and the Benson Clemons family enjoyed the "Grail," the name of the dune shack. In 1991, Grace Bessay was forced to accept a twenty-five-year use and occupancy stipulation or would have been denied any future access to the "Grail." When Grace died in 1996, she left her beloved shack to Marianne and Peter and their family.[46] (See also Chapter VIII "Bessay and Goliath")

The Clemons family relationship to both the Fuller-Bessay shack and the Stanley and Laura Fowler shack thus epitomizes the closely knit texture of the dune shack society and the profound friendships that develop over time. This connection is not casual but goes deep into the core of the way of life among the dune dwellers; one's commitments by word of mouth and by deed suffice to clarify a trust and a promise of responsibility. The Clemons family have demonstrated this code over many years. Peter Clemons is a professional graphics designer and conducts an art shop in Provincetown. Marianne Benson has spent many years cataloguing and preserving records of both Grace Bessay and Andrew Fuller as well as the entire span of the Great Beach Cottage Owner's Association activities involving a time frame from 1962 to 1978. Their two sons, Thomas John, an artist, and David Andrew, a novice screen writer, carry on the family commitment to the dune shack way of life.

08-1047 (Map 201-8)

Jeanne Chanel

The Chanel cottage was constructed on the site of the Peaked Hill Coast Guard Station, built in 1913–1914, between 1945 and 1946.[47] Jeanne "Frenchie" Chanel came to Provincetown as a chorus girl from *George White's Scandals* on a vacation with, so the story goes, Bette Davis. Davis enjoyed the Provincetown visit and then returned to her career; "Frenchie" did not. She fell in love with Provincetown, especially with the dunes, and stayed permanently. She began determinedly to build her shack upon the site of the Coast Guard Station, built between 1913-1914 after the Life Saving Station built in 1872 had been decommissioned,[48] and her dedication to dune life began. My remembrance of that life is amply referred to in this memoir and also in a collection of Provincetown profiles, *Compass Grass Anthology,* which I previously cited in the discussion of Harry Kemp in the Tasha-Kemp shack.overview.

Through the years, the friends who came to visit "Frenchie" included many Provincetown artists and more than a few mendicants who lived for a time at her Peaked Hill abode. Her generosity of spirit occasionally overtook her common sense, and she sometimes found herself supporting diverse visitors with the few dollars she earned here and there by selling small paintings and decorated clamshell ash trays Among the artists who periodically found their way to the "back shore" and to "Frenchie's, was the artist Howard Mitcham, who wrote a number of exceptional Provincetown cookbooks that were treasured for his linoleum and wood cut illustrations and his cryptic local humor, which accompanied the fish recipes The artist Arthur Cohen, our close friend, also delighted in the shack's environment and in photographing, especially, "Frenchie's domain."

Frenchie, of course was a painter in her own right, a naif whose work has found its way into many private collections as well as the permanent collection of the Town of Provincetown. My husband, Salvatore, first visited Frenchie in 1948, and my own acquaintance with her dates from our meeting in 1953, when Salvatore and I were married and began the sojourn of our seasonal occupancy of the shack for the next sixty years. Adrienne Schnell, Frenchie's daughter, was a professional singer and entertainer who entertained thousands of troops as she traveled everywhere with the USO bands during the World War II years. In later years, she, too, returned to Provincetown and stayed with her mother in her Provincetown cottage until Frenchie's death in 1983. "Schatzi," as Adrienne was always known to us, generously accorded us the continuing privilege of using the shack as was our custom after her mother died.

Our maintenance of the dune cottage was continuous over the years. In 1976, for instance, we raised the cottage up, as it was being buried by sand, and, in 1985, we received a building permit from the Seashore and the town of Provincetown to reconstruct the previous existing bedroom extension on the new level as a closed-in entryway and small studio. This 1985 renovation was done by Sal and our good friend Richard Meads. In 2003, a severe northwestern storm struck the back shore in winter, almost completely collapsing the porch on the ocean side. In 2004, it was carefully replaced and re-braced by Scott Dunn, lessee of the Jones shack, who is now deceased. During the reconstruction done in 1976, there were revealed some old Coast Guard metal cots and a good deal of foundation brick. This establishes further the location of the shack as being on, or very near, the site of the Peaked Hill Coast Guard Station built in 1913–1914 (see references in Ofsevit-Tasha, Margo-Gelb and Hazel Hawthorn's diagrammatic sketches in this appendix dated 1939–1946)

These facts, however, are not the relevant details that begin to describe our life on the dunes in the Chanel cottage with which this memoir is descriptive throughout. It has been for us, a refuge, a source of creative energy, and a leavening of our life in every respect. I cannot reasonably cite the work I have written here except to present categories, such as short stories, plays, a novel, anthologies, poetry, and a portion of the extensive biography of the artist Ross Moffett. My husband Salvatore has executed, over the years, numerous oil paintings, and hundreds of watercolors, drawings, and sketches, and has found never-ending inspiration for his art at all times of the year. Our daughter Giovanna experienced the inspirations that accompanied life in the shack in her early years and has continued her skills as an artist and a writer. Romolo, our son, has extended his earliest impression of the dune ambience to his career as a sculptor,lifelong. Now, a third generation of our family, in the persons of our granddaughter Linnea and grandson Luca, clearly appear to have been inspired by life at the shack, each in their own creative way.

08-1042 (Map 201-8)

Hazel Hawthorne Werner ("Thalassa")

This is the cottage known as "Thalassa," whose present location is approximately 450 feet east of the Chanel cottage. According to the information given to me by Louis "Spucky" Silva in an interview of his recollections of Peaked Hill that I taped in 1979,[49] he built the shack c.1931–1933; it was a structure 9 feet by 12 feet. The windows that he put in it were from the Eugene O'Neill cottage (The old Peaked Hill Life Saving Station, which had fallen into the sea in January 1931). He sold the cottage to Hazel Hawthorne Werner in 1936 for fifty dollars.[50] Louis Silva also mentioned that a number of his "shipmates" at Peaked Hill built similar cottages; these men would have been Philip Packett, Joe Medeiros, P.C. Cook, and Morris Worth. These Coast Guardsmen are discussed also in connection with the Bessay-Fuller (Fearing) shack and with the Schmid-Watson and Theodore Braaten shacks. Reference to Raymond Brown, also a Coast Guardsman in this group, should be included in this list. A typed memo from Hazel Hawthorne, (probably sent to Andrew Fuller) describes the further disposition of the cottage in 1949 to its present location.[51] "Addenda to above [sale of Thalassa]: This cottage, Thalassa, was moved from the dune where it had been constructed, a point about 30 to 40 feet west of Fearing's cottage, to a point just west of the Whitehead pit line in the summer of 1949. I am absolutely certain of this date, as I wrote a story for the *New Yorker* while the men were making the move, and its sale paid the bill for their work almost to a cent. Too bad this picturesque anecdote can be of no use to us."[52]

The fuller discussion, more or less of Hawthorne's life on the dunes was given in the *précis* of her shack "Euphoria."

08-8655 (Map 201-8)

Theodore Braaten

The Braaten cottage was built by Coast Guardsmen Joseph Medeiros and P.C. Cook in 1931 and sold to Theodore and Eunice Braaten, c.1933, for use as a seasonal residence.[53] Sometime in 1946, it was moved to its present location by Provincetown artist and resident Oakley Spingler.[54] During World War II, the Braatens leased the shack to the U.S. Navy for use as a mine testing station.[55]

The Braatens were from Norwich, Connecticut. Eunice Braaten was born in 1897. She graduated from Radcliffe College in 1921. While there, she was a member of the famed George Pierce Baker play-writing class as was Catharine Huntington, who was a founding member of the Provincetown Playhouse on the Wharf in 1939–1940. Eunice Braaaten's career was many-faceted and unique. She wrote children's plays and was the director of children's plays for the Norwich Players. Her adaptation of a Hans Christian Andersen story, "The Tinder Fox," was produced throughout her lifetime. During World War II, when the Braatens leased their cottage to the Navy, Eunice was Assistant Director of the Bay State Service Club, which produced entertainment for the servicemen on Boston Common, as well as serving in other organizations affiliated with wartime charitable activities. From 1917 to 1946, she was a reporter for the *Boston Herald Traveller*. This intrepid woman was a direct descendant of William Eddy and the vicar of the Church of England in Cranbrook, Kent, England, whose two sons John and Samuel, came to America in 1630, settling in Plymouth, Massachusetts. Eunice Braaten's lifelong passion for her shack, which was a legend in Provincetown, lasted until her death at the age of 96 in 1993.

Theodore Braaten was general manager of the Public Utilities of the City of Norwich, Connecticut and, during World War II, both he and his two sons served with distinction in the United States Armed Forces. Later, his son David was national syndicated columnist Jack Anderson's associate for many years and he also wrote for *The Washington Times*. David Braaten has two children and three grandchildren. His brother, Theodore Jr., has three grandchildren. Theodore Braaten, Sr., lived to about the age of 103. The Braaten family always maintained their deep, personal connection to their shack and their way of life in the dune colony at Peaked Hill.[56] In March 1987, when the intense pressure to preserve the shacks was underway, David Braaten wrote a long and definitive letter to the Cape Cod National Seashore concerning the ongoing review of the cottages. It is worth quoting a brief paragraph here to show the intensity of his empathy for the cottage and the way of life:

> It's the intangible values represented by the dune cottages, though, that make the strongest argument for their rescue, I think. They are the last survivors of a time and place and philosophy of life that was probably unique, and certainly will never be duplicated. Artists and writers could find the solitude and serenity they craved, within easy walking distance of a town that offered not just groceries and a market for their daubs and scribblings, but a live-and-let-live attitude that must have encouraged whatever creative genius these undeniably eccentric dune dwellers possessed.

Theodore and Eunice Braaten of Norwalk, Connecticut, in front of their shack at Peaked Hill from *Yankee Magazine,* 1975, *courtesy of Marianne Benson and Peter Clemons and the archive of the Great Beach Cottage Owners' Association*

At some uncertain date, however, the Braatens had signed a release of the property on which their shack was located to the Whitehead Sand Co., who owned a large tract of land that included the Braaten parcel. The Braatens did not file adverse possession on this piece. In December 1968, they signed a five-year lease with a special use permit with the Seashore, and in August 1969, they withdrew their membership from the GBCOA.[57] The special use permit for the Braatens was renewed until 1988, when then Superintendent Andrew Ringgold told them to remove the shack from the property, in spite of the fact that all the shacks had, by this time, become eligible for registration on the National Register of Historic Places.[58]

During a period of difficulty and uncertainty experienced by the Braatens in their relationship with the Seashore, Lawrence Schuster contacted Eunice Braaten and they came to a mutual agreement that Schuster would be caretaker of the shack in exchange for residency, with the stipulation that David Braaten would have visitation privileges at agreed times of the year. David Braaten came with his son in the summer for a visitation period twice, but eventually gave up any time at the shack. After Theodore Braaten, Sr.'s death, Schuster negotiated a special use permit with The Cape Cod National Seashore for the use of the Braaten shack, where he has been living full time since 1983.[59]

08-8654 (Map 201-8)

Charles Schmid/Peg Watson

This cottage known as Peg Watson's was constructed in 1931–1932 by Philip S. Packett and Morris Worth, Coast Guardsmen stationed at Peaked Hill. They rented out the cottage at first for $5.00 a week and paid $2.00 a year to the State of Massachusetts for squatters' rights. In 1934, they sold it to Norman Lowenstein for $180.00, and he, in turn, sold it to Margaret Watson some time before 1939. At the same time that the

Peg Watson's Cottage by Salvatore Del Deo 2004, oil on canvas, 14" x 18"

cottage was built, Packett built several stables for Lowenstein's horses in back of the cottage from telephone poles and sections of wood carried up from the beach.[60]

Margaret Watson, known to all as "Peg," occupied her cottage almost continuously from about 1939 to the time of her death in March 1972.[61] Her life on the dunes was remarkable, like that of so many dune dwellers, for its vigilance and love of all things that touched the sea and shore. In a letter written to Superintendent Herbert Olsen on January 5, 1986, Miriam Hapgood described Peg's persona and her shack with tender recollection:

> The shack I knew best, not far from the ruin of the Peaked Hill Coast Guard Station [that was the 1914 station which had been moved back from the shore in 1931] belonged to Margaret Watson. My husband and I often walked across the dunes to swim in the ocean and share lunch in her plain but charming room with its wide view of the dunes. Peg was a graduate of Radcliffe College and a social worker in New York,[62] where she lived in an ancient apartment on Union Square next to the S. Klein store and ice skated at Rockefeller Center on weekends. She was a witty, brave woman who loved nature and solitude. If she saw someone despoiling the dunes, disturbing nesting terns, or littering, she would sally forth like a defending lion. [63]

Because her friend and neighbor on the dunes, Charlie Schmid, had so kindly assisted her in maintaining her shack and by doing many personal errands for her in her latter years, as she became severely crippled by arthritis, Peg Watson left her beloved shack to

Charlie. For a decade, he continued to care for it and to make it available to friends such as the sculptor Joyce Johnson and the painter Toni Strauss.

When Charlie Schmid died, however, in 1982, the shack gradually deteriorated from neglect. It was not until a decade later that it was awarded a twenty-year historic lease to Laurie Schecter and Gary Isaacson and the deterioration was addressed and the shack brought back to stability. This historic lease had been effected through the efforts of the Dune Shack Subcommittee's proposal to the Seashore to save three shacks deteriorating by neglect: the Leo Fleurent shack, Peg Watson's, and that of Randolph and Annabelle Jones in deliberations in 1992 (see Chapter IX).

After long negotiations with the CCNS, the repairs of the Watson shack were undertaken. When extensive efforts to raise the shack to prevent its being inundated by sand were made in 2004, this difficult project was engineered with innovative skill and incredible determination under extremely difficult circumstances by Gary Isaacson and Laurie Schecter. Many friends came to their aid, however, and the assistance of such persons as Will Hapgood, Bill Fitts, and others from the Peaked Hill Trust, such as Genevieve Martin, neighbor Scott Dunn, and the Construction company of Winkler, enabled the project to succeed.[64] At this writing, the lease is still in place, but Gary Isaacson is deceased.

8 P-1036 (Map 203-8)

Nicholas Wells/Ray Martan Wells

According toe Ray Wells, this cottage was built by a Coast Guardsman named "Bunny" Ellis in 1935–1936, from material salvaged from the O'Neill Life Saving Station wreck. Its original location, when .Ray purchased the cottage in 1936, was on the shore, in line with and somewhat to the east of the Braaten cottage.[65] After her marriage to Nick Wells in 1950, she and Nick eventually moved it to its present location, placing it on stilts and expanding it considerably.[66]

Ray Martan Wells was the sister of Zara Malkin Ofsevit Jackson, and her early experience in the dune way of life began in the 1930s with her stepmother Alice Malkin, who had come to Provincetown to study painting with Charles W. Hawthorne. As a young woman, Ray Wells had traveled a good deal across the country, working in different disciplines, such as a script writer for MGM studios and as an editor for *Book Digest.* Because her early training was in the theater, having studied at the Stella Adler School of Acting in New York City,[67] she brought to her Provincetown connection and life with her husband a passion for the theater. In the early 1960s, she founded, together with the painter and printmaker Jim Forsberg, the Provincetown Theater Workshop. This thespian group was a vital reestablishment of the old tradition of original theater in Provincetown and excited the interest of many in the arts to join in the productions.

Nicholas Wells was an entrepreneur and real estate developer from Providence, Rhode Island, but when he settled in Provincetown, he directed a good deal of his energies to the arts and to the interests of his wife Ray. Together, they developed a number of properties, which essentially represented Ray's artistic vision. Nick Wells also incorporated his considerable legal adroitness on behalf of many civic endeavors such as the Provincetown Academy of Living Arts.[68]

Because of Ray's passion for the dunes and her shack, Nick joined the Great Beach Cottage Owners Association as co-chairman,together with Andrew Fuller, in 1962 when the organization was formed. The combination of Fuller and Wells went a long way in spearheading and directing successfully, for a time, the cause of saving the dune shacks at Peaked Hill. The extensive account of their mutual activities is preserved in the GBCOA archive. Ray Wells was also very active in civic affairs, and, after the death of her husband, continued her participation in such organizations as The Re-greening of Provincetown with energy and dedication. As an artist and painter, she was a founding member of the Provincetown Group Gallery established in 1964 and continued to participate in its activities until it closed in 1994. Although she was well aware of the famous and near-famous in relation to the dune shacks, she was critical of any history which excluded the very central fact that the dune cottages have sheltered the unknown communicants with nature and art to a great degree, and it is these unnamed appreciators who comprise, together with their celebrated compatriots, the complete portrait of this remarkable community.[69]

08-8644 (Map 204-8)

Randolph Jones

The overview of this small shack between 1944 and c. 1974 is better told by Annabelle and Randolph Jones themselves in a three-page, typewritten document among records given to the Heritage Museum (now the Provincetown Public Library) in 1994 by the Provincetown Historical Commission.[70]

> Since 1944, my husband and I have spent from three to eight weeks each summer in a shack on the dunes in what was supposed, at that time, to be Provincetown. The owner or owners of the dunes unknown. The shack was built in 1935 by Jesse Meads of Provincetown for a Loraine Catheron of Boston and sold in 1938 to a friend of ours who spent only a short time there because his wife did not adjust to the dunes.[71] From then until 1944, when we acquired it from the second owner, it was virtually abandoned, being used and misused by various persons and allowed to begin to deteriorate. We repaired it then and have maintained it in good condition since. Last fall, we contracted to have a sill and some shingles replaced. After work was started, it was discovered that two more sills needed replacing. A thorough job was done which included moving the shack forward about twenty feet onto new foundation posts, replacing the door, a new window and shutter in the rear, re-shingling two sides, replacing a section of the floor, painting new trim, etc. Total cost $394.39
>
> There were many rumors concerning ownership of the dunes, all unfounded, until 1953, when apparently the Hannahs were taxed for property on the dunes. After we learned we were in North Truro, on land owned by the Hannahs, we arranged with them to occupy the land and to pay taxes on the shack and personal property. We have renewed this arrangement annually. In about 1946–1947, a Quonset hut was erected on a dune close to our shack, occupied for about three following summers by the owners. It attracted people who broke into it either to occupy or ransack or steal or simply to wantonly destroy. We interceded many times, re-boarding and re-nailing, but had no cooperation from the owners. Finally, we arranged to lease the land from the Hannahs in order to protect ourselves and that of the other shack owners who cared.
>
> The dunes mean a great deal to us. Each day is filled with living in an environment that appears barren, but is actually rich. I have a collection of stones from the beach and have made an attempt to categorize them. We have looked for and found Indian relics. One productive high tide brought us enough lumber, "monkey-

wood," to build a two-foot square and twelve foot deep shaft which we sunk into the sand by the shack and with a pulley and rope made a dry well refrigerator for food. We enjoy what is edible on the dunes, such as wild peas, beach plums, cranberries, rose haws (rich in Vitamin C), blueberries, and raspberries. I have made unadulterated bayberry candles. My husband even considered experimenting with a windmill.

Erosion has always concerned us. We attempt to prevent it, but when it has taken place during the winter, we have started a rebuilding process during the summer, first on a small scale by staking whatever fish netting we could find on the beach on top of piles of weeds and brush. The netting halted the process and now the sand is gradually collecting and building."

Annabelle went on in her description of dune life to talk about growing a garden on the dunes, and described using leaf mold, compost, loam, and sea weed and decried the fact that their experiment, partially successful, was derailed by hurricane Carol. Although I have not reproduced Annabelle's full typed description, I have selected the main elements to give a sense of the personal history of the Jones's dune life, which, I gather from introductory remarks, was written in approximately 1962, when the shack owners in Truro were having a tussle with the Commonwealth of Massachusetts over their shacks. Other accompanying correspondence in the Jones file from Grace Bessay and Peg Watson and records of the GBCOA archives indicate the probability of this surmise.[72]

Because the name of Frank Henderson appears in the Jones correspondence with Peg Watson in 1962, it would seem that he was involved in caretaking of the Jones cottage off season. According to the survey referred to in note above, the shack was moved back from the shore in 1973–1974. Later, after their death (a date which I do not have but which appears to be subsequent to 1981, since they signed a stipulation with the Federal Government in that year[73]), the shack was used and maintained by the family of Edith Thomas, the wife of Jimmy Thomas who used it for some time.

In 1993, after the period of activity and final recommendations of our Dune Shack subcommittee, the eventual awarding of the Jones shack to Marsha and Scott Dunn in a twenty-year historic leasing process by the Seashore was finalized, which, as I have discussed, was replicated in connection with the Leo Fleurent and Schmid/Watson shacks. After the lease was awarded to Scott, a local carpenter, and Marsha, a resident of Welfleet, many improvements to the shack were made, and, today, .it is in good repair. Scott Dunn is now deceased, but Marsha's attachment to the shack and to the way of life she shared there with Scott remains a lasting memory, not only of their days on the dunes, but those of Annabelle and Randolph Jones as well, which Annabelle so poetically recalled in her journal.[70]

08-8647 (Map 203-10)

David Armstrong

The Armstrong shack is the last shack still extant in the group of shacks known as the "Eastern Group," as illustrated by Dr. Wolfe in his ethnological study.[75] From its position traveling further east, therefore, one encounters the shadowy and remembered community of several "lost shacks" which are presented with as much definition as possible in Part II of this Appendix. Shacks no longer extant, however, were not all in this area.

The construction of the original Armstrong shack dates from 1926–1929. It was built by Provincetown entrepreneur Pat Patrick and his friend Joe Oliver, who shared ownership with him, according to the Armstrongs. From Patrick, the ownership passed briefly to a priest by the name of John Craig (dates unknown). The Armstrongs took over the shack in 1948, coming to an agreement with the Hannah sisters, Junia and Elizabeth, who owned the land; they have dwelt in it continuously since that time. In 1983, however, they were forced to move it back from its shoreline position because of severe erosion. David Armstrong recalled the move as "six days of difficult labor."[76]

The occupancy of their cottage involved much dovetailing of family life and friends. Connie worked on a schedule of various activities all based on an academic school year, so that she could spend the summer months with her young children at the shack. David, however, was a radar and sonar engineer in the beginning of his career and then worked for Raytheon, developing the microwave oven. Some of these engineering skills transferred to the cottage on the dunes, affecting certain modest amenities of living without the onus of superfluous technology. In the summer, he worked a full week and came to the cottage on the weekends to join his family. Janet Armstrong called the cottage her "spiritual home" and recalled a childhood entirely lyrical in its freedom to explore nature. She later transferred her early experiences to her career as a professional designer of jewelry. Her formal training at the Boston University School of Art and Music, and later at the De Cordova Museum, as an artist in the medium of metallurgy and as a goldsmith was richly enhanced by her early experience on the dunes. Ruth Armstrong, her sister, chose a path quite diverse but still, one might say, based on principles learned at the foot of nature. She became a Unitarian minister after graduating from Harvard Divinity School and her children, like Janet's, benefitted from the nourishing tradition of the perennial contact with their shack on the dunes. The Armstrong family, I think, illustrates essentially, but not exceptionally, what the other traditional dune families regard and have maintained as a protean way of life.[77]

The Armstrong Shack showing the management of sand, c.2007–2008. *Photo courtesy of the Armstrong family*

Connie Armstrong was very firm in her conviction that living in the dunes over time created a sensitivity and insight unavailable in any other way. She touched on the verity of people who lived for decades in the dunes as "walking gently upon the earth."

Connie metaphorically expresses her deep connection to the environment of their habitation when she says: "If you make your home on the dunes, you have to become friends with the sand."[78]Although seemingly aphoristic at first reading, this remark contains the core philosophy of dune habitation. In the never-ending dialogue carried on by dune dwellers, and as exemplified here especially by Connie and her brother-in-law John Armstrong, now deceased, who tirelessly invented ways to establish the right balance between the sand and the shacks which have a propensity for, becoming overwhelmed by sand and, adversely, imperiled by the absence of sand in blowouts, sand must, in fact, be understood to enable the shacks to remain fluid in the sense of repair and maintenance, yet fixed over time in their sea of sand.

In closing this brief survey of the extant dune shacks at Peaked Hill Bars, which are now included, with one exception,[79] in the National Register of Historic Places, I believe it is very pertinent to cite the remarkably apt and farsighted analysis of Dr. Graham Giese, regarding the geomorphology of Cape Cod in relation to the dune shacks and as presented in Dr. Robert Wolfe's report, frequently referred to in this survey:

> Because of their low impact with the landscape, dune shacks represent a relatively unique experiment in human settlement on a barrier dune system...According to Giese, the typical approach on the Eastern seaboard has been to substantially modify coastal zones to accommodate human settlement...Impacts on sustainable natural systems have been huge...But Giese saw in the dune shacks, a uniquely different approach. Instead of modifying the barrier dune system, dune shack residents have built simple structures, attempting to fit them into their immediate surroundings without substantially altering natural systems. It represented a type of low-impact habitation rarely seen on the Eastcoast with a sustainable community... He stated that the dune shack society might be viewed as an instinctive, ongoing demonstration of compatible human-nature relationships with potential lessons for coastal dune ecologists... As Giese observed, an important feature of dune shacks as a general house type was the minimal infrastructure built to support the neighborhood of shacks. It was what a shack lacked as much as what it had, that defined it as a distinct house type... But the design was preferred over alternatives that transformed the natural landscape.

Diagrammatic Maps

Hazel Hawthorne Werner
1920–1960

These diagrammatic maps of dune shacks in the area of the Peaked Hill Bars Life Saving and later Coast Guard Station were made by Hazel Hawthorne Werner and given to Andrew Fuller in 1971. They represent a very accurate trajectory of the building, movement, and location of these cottages from 1920 to 1960. In a letter which accompanied the delivery of these maps to Andrew Fuller dated April 4, 1971, Hazel divulged some additional information which adds to the data she stated in her map sequence:

> Dear Andy,
> Here are the sketches of cottages within the Beede Tract between the years 1920 and 1960. Proportions and distances got out of hand sometimes I fear. I have no recollection of the dates when the Hills and, subsequently, the Fowlers, appeared. The former settled down on their site with a trailer ("mobile home") for a season or two. The Margos rented cottage #10 from me in the summer of 1940. I had bought this cottage from Joe Medeiros.
>
> My brother, who was at the c.g. station as a surf man through the winter of 1926–27, tells me he used #6 with O'Neill's permission, and that it later went over the bank. My own impression is that Hayward Canny used it—see note re #6 on the '33-'39 sketch. The Margos will fill you in on this point if it has any importance."

From Hazel Hawthorne's reliable recollections and observations, we now know much more than could ever have been verified by any other patchwork of information, and are in her debt for the care and diligence which produced her sketches and diagrams. They are reproduced without alteration except for a reinforcing tracing to enable their reproduction to be made more easily visible.

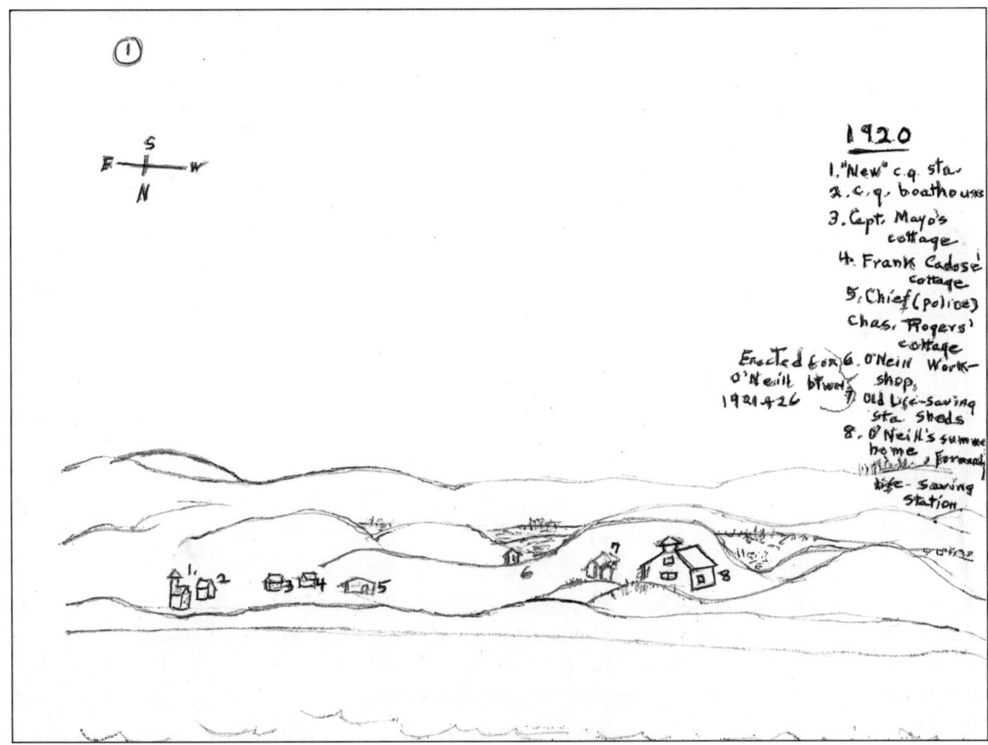

Page 1. 1920: 1.New c.g. Station; 2. c.g. Boathouse; 3. Capt. Mayo's cottage; 4. Frank Cadose's cottage; 5. Chief (police) Chas. Rogers' cottage; 6. O'Neill workshop (erected for O'Neill between l921–1926); 7. Old Life-Saving Station sheds; 8. O'Neill's summer home, formerly Life-Saving Station

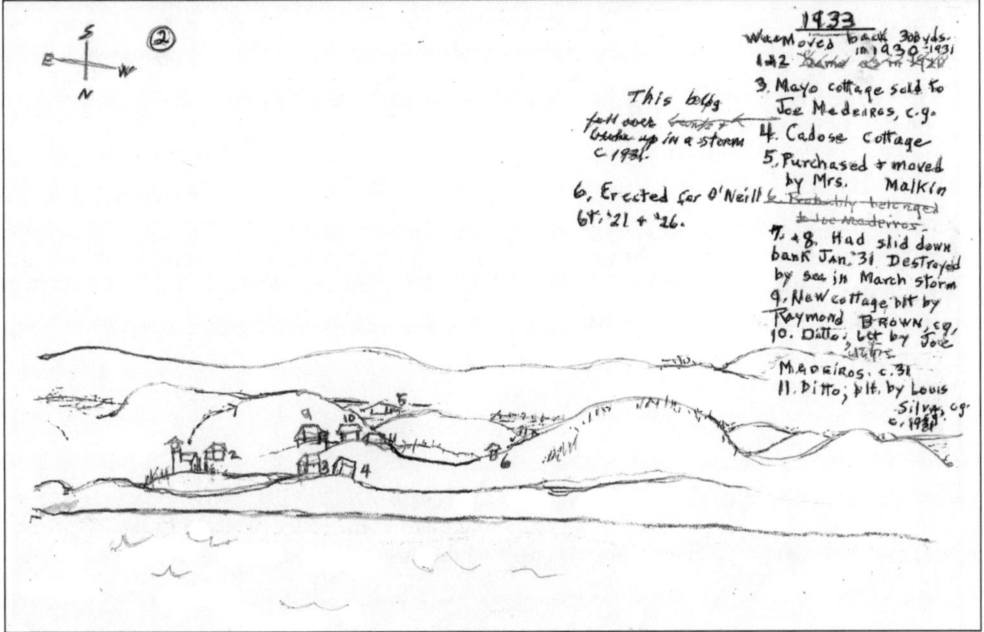

Page 2. 1933: 1 & 2. were moved back 300 yards in 1930-1931; 3. Mayo cottage sold to Joe Medeiros, c.g. This building fell over, broke up in a storm, 1931; 4. Cadose cottage; 5. Purchased and moved by Mrs, Malkin; 6. Erected for O'Neill (blt. 1921 & 1926); 7 & 8. Had slid down bank Jan. 1931. Destroyed by March storm; 9. New cottage built by Raymond Brown, c.g.; 10. Ditto blt. by Joe Medeiros, c. 1931; 11. Ditto blt. by Louis Silva, c.g., c. 1931

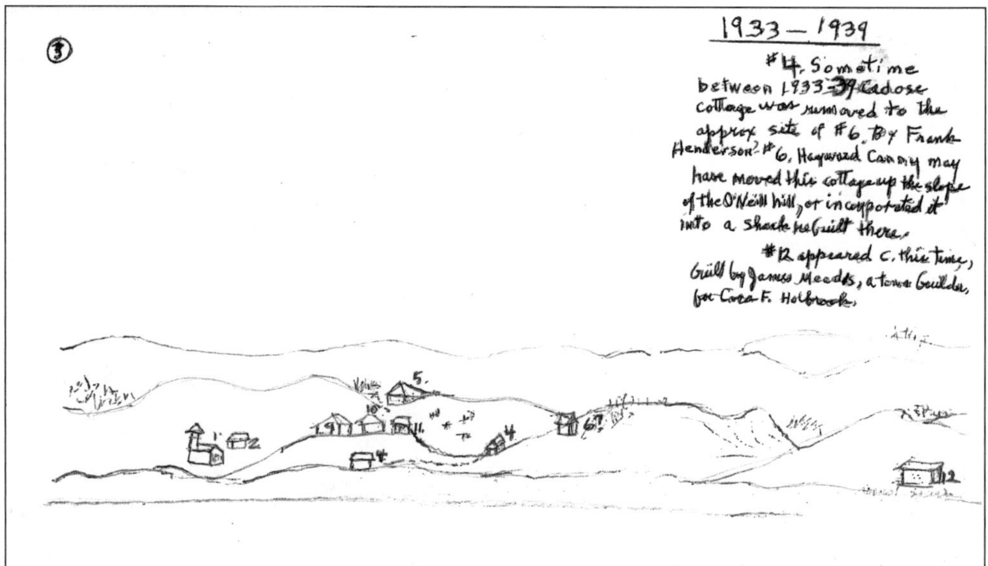

Page 3. 1933–1939: 4. Sometime between 1931 and 1939 Cadose cottage was moved to the approximate site of #6 by Frank Henderson; 6. Haywood Canny may have moved this cottage up the slope of the O'Neill hill, or incorporated it into a shack he built there; 12. appeared about this time, built by James Meads, a town builder, for Cora Holbrook

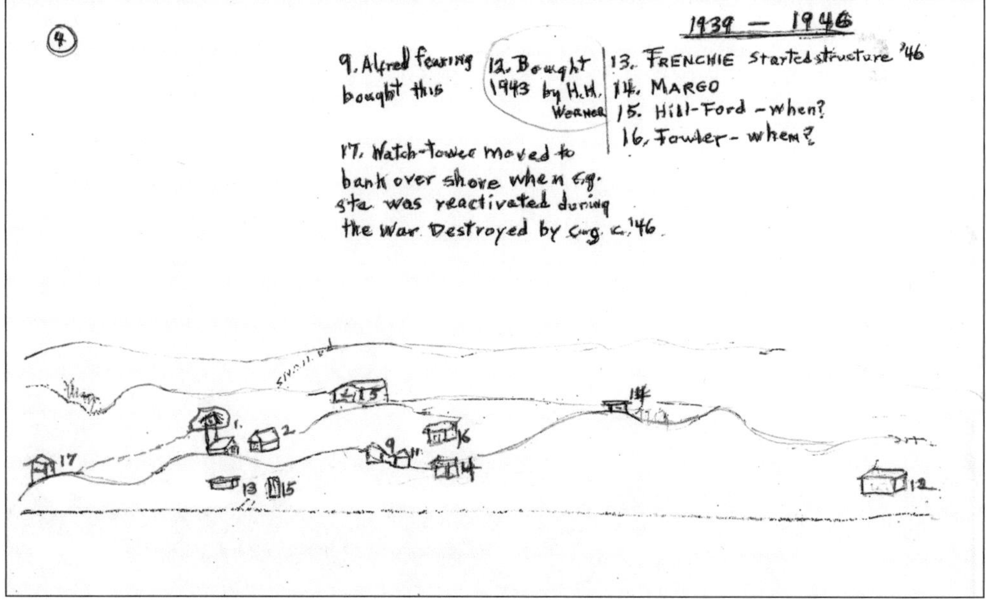

Page 4: 1939–1946: 9. Alfred Fearing bought this; 12. Bought 1943 by H.H. Werner; 13. Frenchie started construction, 1946; 14. Margo; 15. Hill-Ford (when?); 16. Fowler (when?); 17. Watch tower moved to bank over shore when c.g. sta. was reactivated during the war. Destroyed by c.g., 1946

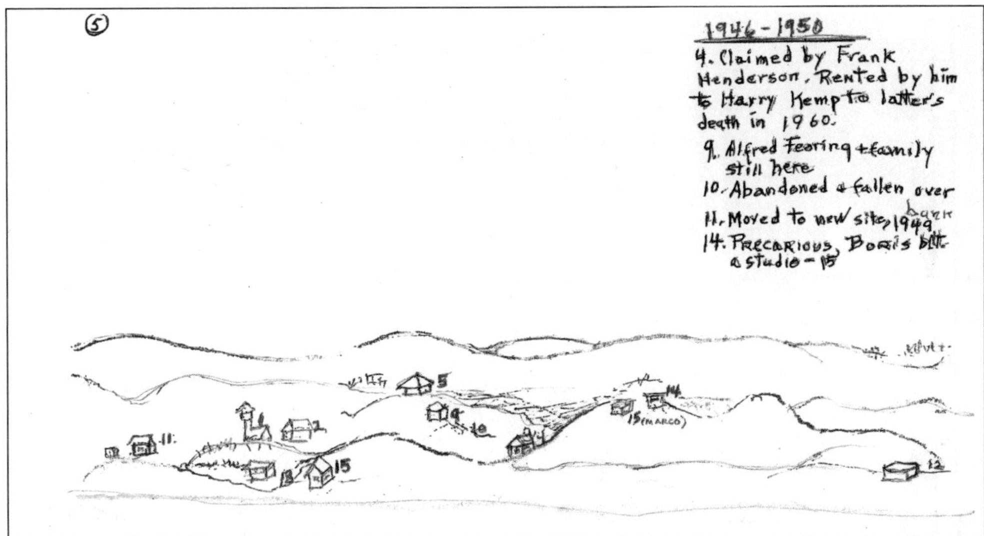

Page 5. 1946-1950: 4. Claimed by Frank Henderson. Rented to Harry Kemp until his death in 1960; 9. Alfred Fearing & family still here; 10. Abandoned and fallen over; 11 Moved to new site l949; 14. Precarious- Boris's blt a studio l5.

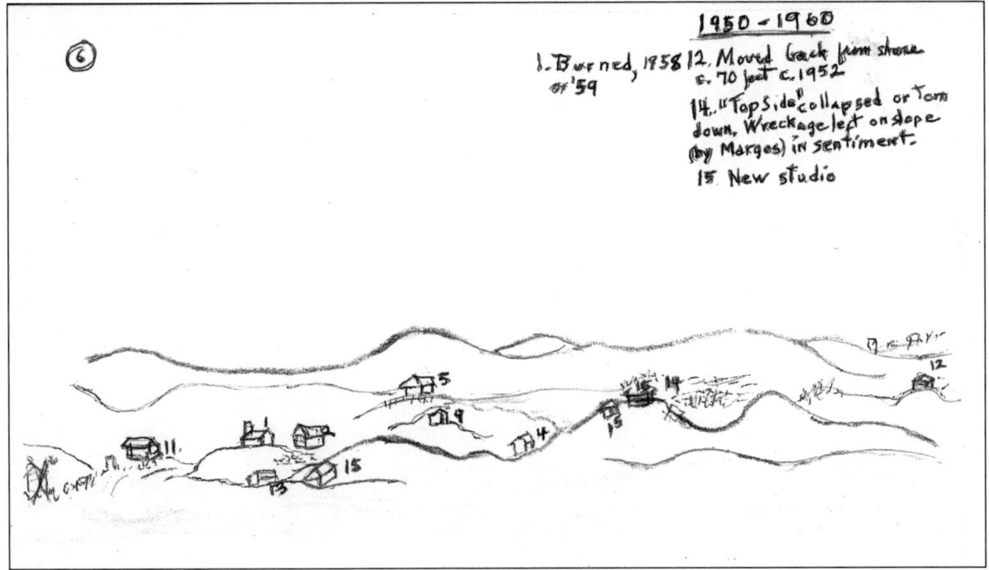

Page 6. 1950-1960: 1. Burned, 1958 or 1959; 12. Moved back from shore 70ft., c. 1952; 14. "Topside" collapsed or torn down—Wreckage left on slope (by Margos) in sentiment; 15. New studio

Part II

The Lost Shacks

Acknowledgments

A second part of the survey covers the "Lost Shacks" no longer in existence and for this particular research, I am also indebted to a number of persons, in addition to those mentioned in Part I, without whom the former and illusory presence of these "Lost Shacks" could never have been resurrected. The additional acknowledgments for Part II, therefore, follow:

To Kathy Besag whose mother and father Kathryn and Edward McCulley either built or found and refurbished a shack in the early thirties which has come to be called "The Red Shack." The McCulley family residence in the shack having lasted until c. 1937, Kathy Besag was able to provide both memories and significant photographic material to firmly document this shack. The security of this information has created substantial relevancy for the locations and time frames for several adjacent or nearby shacks in the area.

To Anne Gushee Arsenault whose summers between 1939 and 1957 spent with her family in the "Red Shack" she recalls with poignant clarity including recollections of other neighbors and, later, the specific time frame of the transfer of the shack to the third and last inhabitant Grace Bessay. This valued account is included in Part II of the Appendix.

To Robert "Bobby" Patrick who provided recollections of his father Pat Patrick's frequent beach-combing trips to the back shore seeking lumber to build various shacks and also his famous restaurant "The Flagship." He emphasized his father's love of the dunes and the ritual frequency of his beach-combing trips which never diminished even during the trying days of World War II. Such an exceptional view of activity on the dunes provided a distinct and sober perspective of an intense aspect of dune life with firsthand observation.

To Alan Dodge, artist and architect, for his sharing with me the history of his briefly famous concrete shack in the dunes, which has long been remembered for its astonishing concept and rather unique features. Without exaggeration, Alan Dodge's livable cement abode was a one-time structure featuring imagination, durability, and adaptability. In an environment in which these attributes commanded attention, Alan Dodge"s shack was thought to be at the top of the list.

To Jack Barry who serendipitously appeared in the pages of the *Cape Cod Times* recently, memorializing the life of his mother Geraldine Hill with a walk from Eastham to Race Point on the outer beach. As a result, I have received some important and previously lost details of the shack immediately west of Frenchie's that belonged to Esther Hill, Jack Barry's grandmother, and to her friend Josephine Ford. This shack was burned in 1970, presumably by vandals, without much retrievable information as to its background. I have now been provided some personal details and photographs of the shack by Jack, who has thus returned it to us with loving care.

To David Mayo for providing invaluable historic photographs of the life of the Peaked Hill Coast Guard Station in connection with the years his grandfather Frank L. Mayo served as chief of the station and for official Coast Guard information relevant to the text of this memoir. Not alone for this material evidence of the deep social ties between the back shore and Provincetown and Truro, but for the essential preservation of the connection from one generation to the next, David's personal love and family association with what the world of the dunes and the life of the sea represents as a continuing resource.

The description of the several "Lost Shacks" of The Peaked Hill Bars Historic District in Provincetown and in Truro in the area of the former Pilgrim Spring State Park, which existed prior to the creation of the Cape Cod National Seashore and whose presence, in many cases, continued for a certain tine after the establishment of the Seashore, is intended to contribute to the overall dimension of the historical perspective of dune shack habitation on the Great Outer Beach of Provincetown and Truro. The difficulty of recovering these shacks from near oblivion was not an easy task, but, with the assistance of a few dune dwellers and others whose valued memories and source statistics of the shacks' existence and of circumstances surrounding this extended community, we can retrieve a significant profile of their past life. Like the shacks still extant and now included in the Register of Historic Places within "The Dune Shacks of Peaked Hill Bars Historic District," their capsulated histories contribute significantly to the fuller profile of dune shack habitation.

The first number given in cataloguing these shacks is the number ascribed to the shack or to the location of the former shack as it was given at the time of the creation and processing of the Department of the Interior's aerial maps. These were largely compiled by Arthur L. Sparrow Co., Registered Land Surveyors, in South Orleans, Massachusetts, for the Department of the Interior, Northeast Region in August, 1964. The map number in parenthesis is the number of the large, overall section of land wherein the shack is located Most of the shacks were located in Truro, but not all.

11-8714 (Map 202-11)

The Shack of Tony Vevers and Family

(Dr. Graham Giese & Family; the Douglas Family)

After the establishment of the Cape Cod National Seashore and the incorporation of what was formerly the Commonwealth of Massachusetts' Pilgrim Spring State Park within its jurisdiction, the shacks built and still existing in that area of Truro, were subjected to a long, contentious, and difficult process in an attempt to eliminate them as quickly as possible, which process I have noted in Chapter 3 of this memoir. At the furthest and most easterly point of the area described on a map labeled "Cape Cod National Seashore Truro, Mass. .Schedule C, Tract 08-8628" by the National Seashore, which provides a series of numbers from 1 to 11, the shack of Tony Vevers can be identified as number 11. This shack was built in 1939 by craftsman Chet Pfeiffer of Truro and had been purchased by Tony Vevers on September 4, 1964. All transactions, deed, etc., had been properly recorded. In June 1967, the Vevers shack was burned to the ground by the Seashore.

In a letter to Mr. Lee Strange, Ranger for the National Seashore, the attorney for the Great Beach Cottage Owners Association Robert L. Meade, protested:

> In this regard, I have been informed by the Association that the cottage of one Mr. Vevers was recently burned to the ground deliberately by agents of the National Park Service without the consent or even knowledge of Mr. Vevers. If this allegation is true, I can only say that I hope Mr. Vevers pursues his obvious legal remedies vigorously, etc.

Attorney Meade continues:

> The legislative history of this act bristles with reference to the rights of owners in the area affected. Any actions that interfere unilaterally with their rights of ownership are unlawful and indeed could constitute crimes under Massachusetts law. [Mr. Strange was thought, correctly, to be the agent who burned the shack]

Two years later, Vevers himself described the act and the prior circumstances to the new attorney Samuel Angoff for the GBCOA on December 14, 1969:

> From 1964 to September 1966, the cottage was used by myself with my wife and two children and the Giese family with their five children, and the Douglas family with their three children. In 1966, our friends the Douglases bought a jeep so that they and we could have access to the cottage. It was in this jeep that we discovered that the shack had be burned down in June 1967. In summation, it seems clear that the rangers never checked the building during the summer when it was in use and when information could easily be found. I should add that every summer, as soon as possible, I used to write my name and telephone number on a shingle next to the door jamb so that an interested party or the Park Service could contact me about the cottage. The times when the rangers did inspect, then, must have been during the slack winter period when vandals had done their worst. Ranger Strange had just taken his position on the Cape and obviously knew nothing of the unique character of our situation. Certainly, no attempt was ever made by the Park Service to contact us at any time, either before or after the burning.

This accurately recalled history was never given the explanation that the Vevers family sought at the time nor ever explained to the Seashore Advisory Commission. It is important to detail the case of the Vevers shack, because it brings into sharp focus, the overall psychological and functional rationale which the Cape Cod National Seashore brought to the issue of the dune shacks on the Great Outer Beach and which reflected their conviction that, in spite of the legislation that stated forthrightly the protection of already existing private property, the aim of the Park should be to create "wilderness" where such a condition had never existed for the previous three hundred years. The burning of the Vevers shack, therefore, became a symbol for all the dune dwellers that has remained.

A fine artist and a respected art historian, Tony Vevers was a close personal friend of ours, and we were joined in many activities in the art community in the 1950s and 1960s. He died in 2008 at the age of eighty-two. His wife Elspeth Halvorsen is also an artist and sculptor and his daughter Tabitha carries on her father's painting legacy with distinction.

10-8651 (Map 203-10)

The "Red Shack" McCulley, Gushee, Bessay

The next shack designated on Schedule C as No. 10, moving in a westerly direction, was known as the "Red Shack" because it was, at some point, covered with red tar paper, This shack was destroyed in the same year as the Vevers shack in 1967. Prior to its destruction, it had an interesting and well-documented history.

It was located just west of the junction of High Head Road leading to the beach and the dune road following the contours of the foreshore, going in a westerly route. In the immediate vicinity of the shack was the High Head Coast Guard Station with surrounding structures, some of which can be seen in the photograph. Note also the communication tower in place. The history of the "Red Shack," beginning in c.1929, has been recounted as follows by its several owners:

In about the year 1929–1930, a couple by the name of McCulley either built or refurbished an already existing shack in this location. The daughter of Edward and Kathryn McCulley, Kathy Besag, from whom I have received a significant amount of primary source material, believes that it was a frame shack in its initial construction, which acquired the distinctive character associated with it for years when it was covered with red tar paper. In a note to me under one photograph of the shack, Besag surmises that the shack was probably originally built by the Coast Guardsmen, as it was immediately adjacent to the Coast Guard complex at High Head (see photo). There are no dates for this transition.

Kathryn McCulley was a painter and she studied with the artist E. Ambrose Webster in 1931 when he established his school in Provincetown. Her husband was a writer from California, and they occupied this shack until c.1937, when they returned to California. At the same time that Kathryn McCulley and Edward were in residence in the red shack, both summer and winter for a year or two, at least, they became acquainted with Loren MacIver, the painter, and her husband the poet Lloyd Frankenberg. Their friendships developed during that period and, according to Kathy Besag, her father assisted Frankenberg in the construction of their own dune shack, which they occupied between 1931 to c. 1941.

What emerges from these notes from Kathy Besag and from Anne Gushee Arsenault is that there was a nice camaraderie between these two couples who shared similar artistic disciplines. MacIver, of course, moved on to become one of America's "modernist" painters of note, whose works, some of which were painted on wood from her dune shack, were shown at the Museum of Modern Art. The year-round life of the McCulleys and Frankenbergs involved daily trips to Day's store on Beach Point and weekly, sometimes arduous trips to civilization to stock other provisions. Such excursions were characterized by Besag as part of the romantic and exhilarating way of life on the dunes her parents loved. By the late thirties, the McCulleys left the East Coast permanently and returned to California.

At this time, they passed the shack to their friend Charles H. Gushee with a quit claim deed. The Gushee family inhabited the shack from 1939 to 1957, and their daughter Anne Gushee Arsenault recounts moments of her early years spending summers on the dunes, as well as observations and reflections of a later time revealing both the spiritual and physical landscape which so influenced her life:

> As a child on the dunes, wandering alone, I remember the relief of being able to stop for a while and chat with a neighbor. (Remember back then when your mother said: "Go play and don't bother me." One autumn, I remember her saying, "Here is a recorder and a book on how to play it. Now go ahead and play it." I spent many days tooting this flute on the top of a sand dune.) I'm sure the neighbors became accustomed to seeing a tiny towhead at odd hours around their homes. My favorite person was a sculptor who kept his cement house cool for his work with clay. I would drop in unannounced, but never felt unwelcome. He would let me sit and watch him work, but once I had rested and cooled, I would be on my way because I didn't want to disturb his work. I still have that feeling about the importance of artists' work and never want to telephone anyone who might be working on their message to the world. Back then there were no phones and no electricity on the dunes, so all we had to adapt to was the natural world around us.
>
> But my heart would always lift when I saw the bright orange yellow nasturtiums he had planted around his shack, in dirt he had hauled in over the dunes. Such a feat seemed, to a child, so much work to create beauty, but well worth if you had the strength. The Armstrongs called this house "The Bunker," and I now have a picture of it. The owner had made a wooden frame which he covered with chicken wire and cement, It does look like a fortification, but it was a welcoming sight to a child.(see note at end of quote)
>
> The building closest to ours was owned by a writer, Stannard from New York City, according to the Armstrtongs. Since we had purchased our shack in the '30s and the Armstrongs didn't arrive until the '40s, it may be that the shack nearest to ours, owned by Mr. Stannard, was not yet there, or, perhaps, he did not want a child around and so I didn't visit him. I have no memory of his place. All of the pictures I have from that time concentrate on our shack and its visitors. According to tradition, anyone who wanted to could spend their vacation at the shack, and family and friends came when we were not there.
>
> Until family and friends gave me pictures of their visits to "the shack" I had not remembered the Coast Guard buildings, which were very close to us. My memory says that we were not happy being so near to the Coast Guard, because every summer we discovered that our shack would be vandalized and bullet holes found in the walls. The summer we discovered that all our Caruso records had been smashed was very painful. The Armstrongs told us about teenage vandals who might have done this and very likely were the cause of the shack burning down. That fits better with the reputation of the Coast Guard that I would like to have.
>
> For a while I thought it might have been a Coast Guard Rescue Station near us, but none of the pictures at the National Seashore looked familiar. Then the family pictures showed a building which stored life boats and a small communications building wit a telephone pole near it. And, of course, our outhouse. Those were the buildings near us that would identify where our shack had been once I am

Photo of Coast Guard life boat and communication buildings (c. 1940) see also photograph of half-way house Chapter 3. *Collection of Anne Gushee Arsenault*

gone. Now, I can find the site on the dunes with no help. I remember the path. And I recognize the reeds, which indicate where our water came from.

As a child of eight I roamed the dunes, often getting lost. One dune begins to look like another, like huge snow mountains which you have to go up and down As a person with no sense of direction, I often became afraid. I would sit and try to think. One thing has always given me direction, the ocean. The sound of its roar lulled me to sleep in the shack, a very comforting sound and I have always tried to live within the sound of the ocean. So I would walk toward the beach; the sand there was hard and flat, much more secure than the amorphous dunes which would change their shape with the wind. Then I knew that I had to walk either right or left, toward a shack or toward the cleft in the dunes which signaled home.

As I came over a dune, there would be home, a red tarpaper shack (I still have pieces of the tar paper) with a tall chimney which reminded me of a cat's tail. I called it "The Red Cat." We had planks across the front where we could sit and planks that made a short stair up to the porch. Of course everything was made of driftwood or it had bleached so much that it seemed part of the landscape. Inside we had a kitchen composed of a pump, a two-burner, and a refrigerator in the sand. The most important thing was the pump and we held our breath every summer until our priming brought up fresh water from the sand. Quickly, before it melted, we tied our butter securely in a rope and lowered it into the hole in the kitchen floor way down into the sand and coolness. Then we explored our bedroom, up an old ladder into the loft where we could see everything, especially the constant light from Highland Light, which flashed into our bedroom downstairs. We had wooden benches on either side of the room, a shelf with toys and games, a fireplace that I do not remember using, and perhaps a chair. We children were rarely in this room unless it was raining heavily, because the fun was outside.

What freedom. From the time I was nine years old and through the end of the war at the age of fourteen, I had two weeks of complete freedom. I had no chores, no school or camp, and no supervision. Once I was over a dune, no one knew where I was. No one even tried to monitor me. I still have that yearning to be alone, to think my own thoughts and to lead my own adventures. "You have such inner resources," people will say to me. I'm not quite sure I know what that means, but I think I learned it on the beach. Now that I am older, at the age of 75, I do have to be more careful, but I have trouble remembering that fact. Every once in a while, I find myself on the dunes in sandals, with no hat, water, or suntan lotion (which I've never grown used to)) just acting on a thought or emotion, a desire to

Early photograph, before 1930s, of the "Red Shack" showing proximity to U.S. Coast Guard buildings and communication tower just off High Head Road. "The original shack before my dad added the brick chimney and more windows. I think now that this is what they found and just remodeled." (quote from Kathy Besag). *Photo courtesy of Kathy Besag*

Photo of the "Red Shack" c. 1936–1937. "Kathryn McCulley and Edward McCulley beside the 'Red Shack,' now covered with red tar paper" (quote from Kathy Besag). *Photo courtesy of Kathy Besag*

investigate the dunes and the ocean. The last summer I did that, I was so distracted by seeing traffic on the dunes that I kept walking through the notch in the dunes to the beach. There was a trailer park on my beach; rows of RVs with awnings and patio furniture. I was horrified. Who was allowing such beauty to be so carelessly destroyed? (I was later told that this group had a strong lobby, another case of might making right).

As I walked the dunes, people came out of their trailers to welcome me. "Where did you come from? They asked in amazement. "How did you get here? When they realized that I had walked over the dunes, they offered the shade under their awnings and a drink of water from their refrigerators. I felt like a creature from another time trying to explain that I was walking to visit my old shack. We did not speak the same language. They were so proud of their fancy rigs that I could not explain the beauty of simplicity, or of quiet. The new residents of the dunes were listening to radios and yelling from trailer to trailer. I just wanted to escape and I've never been back. I'm fearful of erasing my memories of what living on the dunes is really like

First, it is about quietness, vast quietness under a large sky and a dome of stars. No better place to learn about the immensity of the earth and sky. I think I learned to observe the natural world around me, the footsteps in the sand of all the animals I shared my world with. I learned to love quiet. How else can you enjoy the sound of the wind and the waves, the natural sounds which are all around us? The radio, telephone, and cell phone have no place on the beach. Second, I did learn about the power of the forces of nature, a healthy respect for winds, tides, and undertows, electricity, and other natural forces. The only reason my mother felt safe in letting me

"Loren MacIver and Lloyd Frankenberg in front of their shack. They spent 10 years here in the summers, and stayed year-round twice. Their shack wasn't far from the Red Shack" (quote from Kathy Besag). *Photo courtesy of Kathy Besag*

roam the beach was that I agreed never to go in the water. I cringe when I see people getting close to high waves during a hurricane. I think they have been so isolated from nature that they have forgotten the force of nature. The lessons I learned from the beach, the dunes, the ocean, and the vast sky are those which have stayed with me for a lifetime. I learned deep lessons about God, the Force, the Spirit of the Universe, whatever you want to call the spirit which rules the world. When you are one very small child in an elemental world with a very large dome overhead, you come to believe that this great universe must have some director to make all this magic happen. And the world is magical on the dunes.

Now, I am the last person alive, so far as I know to have lived in a dune shack during the thirties and during the war, sharing my world with the war ships lined up just off the beach. What I would wish for every child is a time to live on the beach, learning the lessons of sea, sand, and sky, lessons that will stay with you for a lifetime.

—Anne Gushee Arsenault, January, 2007

In 1957, Charles Gushee gave the right of occupancy to the "Red Shack" to Grace Bessay as he and his family were no longer able to occupy it themselves. Grace carefully maintained it and used it until 1967 when it was burned and demolished at about the same time as the Vevers cottage. It has been assumed that the National Seashore burned it when they destroyed the Vevers cottage, but there is speculation that it might have been an act of vandalism. We do not have as clear a record in this case as we do in the case of the Vevers cottage.

10-8650 (Map 203-10)

The Howard Stanard (or Stannard) Shack

The shack owned by H. Stanard which is identified on the Schedule C map of the Seashore being used in the identification of positions in this survey of the eastern shacks, is numbered 9. We know almost nothing as to its profile or its background except that Howard Stanard, or Stannard, lived in Syracuse, New York, and the shack was sometimes referred to as "The New Yorker." In the archives of the GBCOA, notes of Grace Bessay, dated January 1981, mention that Stanard's son had called Andrew Fuller and told him that his father had received condemnation action papers from the government about a month before. There is no further notation on the action that was obviously being pursued to eliminate Stanard's shack at this time. Since four shacks were destroyed in the period between 1981–1984 in this area (Stanard, Joe Oliver's (Fuller-Bessay), the concrete shack of Fuller and Bessay ,and Charlie Schmid's), there is no reason to doubt that the Seashore swept up the Stanard shack at this time in the process of elimination. These other shacks were numbered 7, 6, and 4 and are discussed following No. 8, which follows in numerological order here, but not in geographical order on the map, as will be discussed. The Stanards were also members of the Great Beach Cottage Owners Association.

08-8646 (Map 204-8)

Grace Bessay's "Little Shack"

In this instance, we have come upon another enigma of identification, the resolution of which may not be possible with any finality, but which I shall attempt with a certain confidence in the fact of the fluid nature of back shore residency. It depended on numerous factors, the most frequent being physical jeopardy, but also a kind of placement subject to personal agendas and or projected hazards. In the preceding listing of shacks numbered in the Truro area of Pilgrim Spring State Park, we have moved from 11, 10 and 9 with security as to specifics of ownership, structure, site, etc. What we are discussing now is a small shack referred to as "The Little Shack" of Grace Bessay, which, on the map we are using for reference, Schedule C, Tract 08-8628 of the Seashore, has unexplainably been situated between numbers 5 and 4. I have not been able to ascertain a reason for this, except to conjecture that No. 8. was moved from its original position between 9 and 7

If one follows this conjecture, then we may begin to put together a few missing pieces of the narrative of these shacks during the 1930s, which, otherwise, is difficult to connect. Kathy Besag wrote on her photograph of the MacIver/Frankenberg shack "They spent ten years here in the summers, and stayed year-round twice. Their shack was not far from the Red Shack," meaning her parent's or McCulley's. shack. When Besag clearly states: "Their shack wasn't far from the Red Shack," she can't possibly mean it was almost a mile away, and yet, if we can now conjecture with good reason that this small shack was the same as "The Little Shack" of Grace Bessay which is shown as between 5 and 4, the distance between the two would have been more than a mile. This distance is verified by the acting superintendent of the Seashore Norton Bean in February 1969 in a letter to Andrew Fuller in which he discusses the shacks belonging to him, No. 6 and No. 7 as being 0.5 and 0.7 miles from High Head, or by inference, the "Red Shack" from the standpoint of this discussion. The "Little Shack" was even further away, and we may assume a distance of another 0.5 miles to the location of No. 8, or, representing at least one mile, if not more. This, of course, could not have been what Besag meant when she describes the MacIver/Frankenberg shack as "near." She meant near enough to have taken a picture of her parents with her baby sister in the same pose as the MacxIver/ Frankenberg couple in the pictures reproduced above.

The further comparison of the shack of MacIver/Frankenberf to the Bessay "Little Shack" may be made through two sources: The first is the reliable memory of Connie Armstrong who lived in proximity to the "Little Shack" after the Armstrongs bought their shack (No. 5) in 1948. Grace Bessay acquired the "Little Shack" at about the same time or a little later. Armstrong recalled Grace's shack to me with detailed recollection. It had a square window which Grace described as the "sunrise" window, which obviously faced in an easterly direction, and had a round hole in the opposite wall through where a chimney may have fitted. Both these physical markers are in place in the photograph of the MacIver/Frankenberg shack. Connie Armstrong also detailed communication between her shack and Grace's with a system of flags to notify each of them when in mutual residence. The possibility of actual corroboration of these two entities as one is furthered by comparing the overall architectural framework, clapboard siding, and size, especially with a photograph of the "Little Shack" in Benson & Clemons, *Traditional Dune Dwellers; etc. p.59.* Although this scenario of construction, use, and ownership is only my conjecture, and since the shack was destroyed sometime before November 3, 1981, when Park Ranger James A. Ebert inspected the site as well as the sites of others in the area, and found only: "a depression with two small pieces of wood and a section of bed springs." We will probably never be able to securely verify its lineage.

10-8649 (Map 203-10)

Andrew Fuller's Concrete Shack

The origin and construction of the original shack, No. 7 on the Seashore Schedule C map, which came to be known as the "concrete" shack seems, at this writing, to be unavailable; however, it may be one of Pat Patrick's several shacks built in the area, since Patrick is said to have built three or four, but we can probably only securely identify two at this time: the Armstrong cottage and Andrew Fuller's concrete shack, which Fuller acquired in 1960 from Thomas W. Shepard and Susan Shepard. From March 1960 to December, 30 1963, Shepard occupied the shack as a tenant, but, on June 22, 1968, the Shepards signed a release deed to Fuller. The circumstances of these arrangements seem to indicate that there was a mutual leniency as to occupation prior to the release deed. The cottage had already been cemented by 1960, and so we have no idea exactly what

Backshore Cottage (known as the "Concrete Shack") by Salvatore Del Deo, 1973; oil on canvas, 12" x 14"

it may have looked like prior to that time. In 1973, Sal painted the shack from a shoreward position looking toward Pilgrim Lake, or roughly north to south. The painting is pictured below and in Benson & Clemons, *Traditional Dune Dwellers,* p.58.

In a letter, which I cited in the discussion of "The Little Shack" No. 8 from acting superintendent Norton Bean to Andrew Fuller dated February 4, 1969, Bean suggests the ownership of the shack is not clear and cites Shepard and Bernard H. Rose as possible owners. The signed deed release of Thomas and Susan Shepard, however, removes the doubt. Bean then cites the distances of the concrete and Oliver shacks from High Head Road as has been noted in discussion of the "Little Shack." The next official correspondence with the Seashore is dated April 4, 1977, written by Thomas A. Coleman, Chief, Land Acquisition Division, commences the dialogue concerning condemnation proceedings: "In order to complete the acquisition of all property within the Cape Cod National Seashore, we would like to have your land appraised, etc." Fuller replied that the National Park Service had no authority to appraise it: "My land constitutes 'improved property' as defined under Section 4(d) of Public Law 87-126 and therefore you have no authority to appraise it." Coleman's official reply on May 19, 1977, was: "Your property does not meet the definition of improved property." This, of course was the central thesis to which the Park brought the life of every dune shack for judgment and eventual elimination in most cases. The future struggle for National Registered Landmark eligibility for the shacks was ten years away.

At about the same time, Seashore Superintendent Herbert Olsen posted a memorandum to the Regional Director of the Northeast Atlantic Regional Office about two shacks, identified as 10-8648 and 10-8649 on land tract 08-8628 under civil action 80-2425 C which were "potential safety hazards and aesthetic intrusions in the natural landscape." The case moved inexorably to the finish line: Andrew Fuller died in 1981, and Grace Bessay became the executor for both the concrete shack and the Joe Oliver Shack, Nos. 7 and 6, and on March 25, 1982, the District Court issued an order to remove all personal belongings from the shacks within thirty days. In the passage of months between this order and the shack's demolition, Grace Bessay waged an intrepid resistance, hiring substantial legal representation and making the case that the structure was historic: "This is an historic and totally unique structure. It was built before 1929. It is made of reinforced concrete shaped into a unique art form." This statement, by the way, is the only reference we have to the date of the concrete shack's construction. All protest was of little avail, however, and in December 1984, the concrete shack, No. 7 and Joe Oliver's shack, No. 6, were destroyed, and Grace, as the executor of Fuller's property, was given a bill for the cost of demolition.

10-8648 (Map 203-10)

Joe Oliver's Shack

This shack was east of the Armstrong cottage and was identified on the Seashore map Schedule C as dot. 6. In a notarized statement dated November 10, 1971, Hilda Patrick, Pat Patrick's wife, states that the shack was built by Chet Pfeiffer in 1930 and sold to Patrick in 1938 for $75,00.* Pat Patrick then sold it to Fuller prior to January 1959, as stated in a letter to the Land Acquisition Chief Thomas Coleman from Fuller dated April 20, 1977. Fuller wrote, "I am the owner of the shack, having bought it prior to 1959." In a notarized statement from Hilda Patrick, noted below, she claims, however, to be the sole owner of the shack after the death of her husband in 1964. After Andrew Fuller died in 1981, Grace Bessay became the inheritor and executor of this shack, as she was of the concrete shack. She came to its defense and brought her legal case through lawyers James Hughes and William Homans, who were lawyers for Fuller's estate, before the U.S. District Court on November 6, 1981. A year later, in November 1982, Grace was ordered to remove belongings from the shack in preparation for its demolition. The letter was addressed to both Bessay and Mrs. Patrick, which would indicate some confusion on the part of the Park Service. Though we cannot unravel, at this distance, the conflicts of the case, it would seem that the Park took the official position that Grace was the owner, since they presented her with the bill for demolition which she eventually paid.

Two views of the Joe Oliver's (Grace Bessay-Fuller) shack taken February 1, 1983. *Courtesy of Peter Clemons and Marianne Benson and the archive of the Great Beach Cottage Owners' Association*

During the period in which Grace Bessay had attempted to save both shacks as being of historic value, she provided her lawyer James Hughes with reinforcing information to that effect in October 1982: "This shack is historic and unique with a curved roof from lumber collected on the back shore, possibly collected from shipwrecks as was much of the lumber used to build the shacks. The building has great value because of its historic nature." In connection with the building of this group of shacks, and others, and with the information about lumber from shipwrecks which Grace Bessay emphasized were the materials frequently used to build shacks on the back shore, the following account given to me by Robert "Bobby" Patrick in connection with his father's activity on the back beach in the late thirties and early forties, especially, is both interesting and historically important.

Before World War II, between the years 1930 and 1938, Pat Patrick would go out to the back beach almost daily to collect "monkey wood," as it was called, for various building projects. One of these was the construction of his famous restaurant, "TheFlagship" which Jesse Meads, a Provincetown carpenter, built almost exclusively from such lumber. Later, during the war, Bobby joined his father on numerous back shore trips to help collect great quantities of found wood, which was often soaked with oil because the wood came from destroyed convoys of ships on their way to England, which had been torpedoed by German submarines. Bobby said that sometimes the bodies of the members of the crew would be scattered among the wreckage washed up on the shore, and he emphasized the fact that there was often so much lumber and other debris,such as rubber, on the beach that one couldn't see the water beyond the shoreline. Jimmy Thomas, a local builder of bulkhead construction fame, was almost always part of these trips as well, and his name appears, therefore, in the recounting of activities with the various caretaker responsibilities of other dune shacks and with the Peaked Hill Station, as has been noted elsewhere in this survey. All the transportation of wood was done with Pat's Model A pick-up, the more rugged and impervious progenitor of the dune 4-wheel drive vehicle of today. According to Bobby Patrick, his father built, on speculation, several shacks just after the war, but he cannot identify them at this distance of time. What we do know is that several are, or were, in the eastern section, but their lineage is subject to personal conjecture still, with the exception of the Armstrong cottage and possibly the cement, or concrete shack. Regardless of a broken or a less-than -perfect shack genealogy there is enough in the narration of the life of those who chose to dwell on the dunes and in the abodes which sheltered them to cast a permanent shadow of their former presence on the wall of history.

*This notarized document of Hilda Patrtick's is in the archives of the author.

08-8645 (Map 204-8)

Charlie Schmid's Shack

This shack is dot 4 on the Schedule C map and was west of the Armstrong cottage, dot. 5. It seems to be the accepted notion that there was some sort of structure in place, upon which Charlie constructed his dune shack, but there is no verifiable evidence of this. Charles Schmid, who arrived on the lower Cape c.1961, was a "wash-ashore" from Tennessee, as most non-natives were called who came to the Cape and laid claim, eventually, to residency. He was seriously depressed after the loss of his wife and at odds with the world. He sought the peace and quiet of the dune life and quickly became absorbed with the natural environment of the back shore. He did odd carpentry work in Provincetown and was a member of those eccentric crews of skilled and unskilled residents, composed of a few true carpenters together with artists, writers, bon vivants, and scattered sojourners. Sal had a crew, at that time, that fitted this description, of which Charlie was a part. The lure of the back shore became ever more compelling for Charlie, however, and he began to spend most of his days studying the dune swallows, who were his nearest and dearest neighbors. In the course of time, this study became a consuming passion, and he spent almost two decades documenting their patterns of behavior and keeping records. After many years, he was invited to share his observations with a gathering of international ornithologists in Switzerland and he attended the meeting with his many journals in hand.

As the years wore on, Schmid's shack was successively overwhelmed with sand, and so, as necessity dictated, he built progressive overlays of his original dwelling This lego set of a structure is very well pictured in Benson & Clemons *Traditional Dune Dwellers* on p. 59. I have also drawn a verbal portrait of Charlie and his shack in my collection of Provincetown Portraits called *Compass Grass Anthology*, 1984, in which I dubbed him "Dune Charlie-Bird-man." Charlie Schmid was a devoted, if eccentric, dune dweller, and he was remarkably sensitive to his dune dwelling friends and other members of the dune community, as evidenced by his devotion to Peg Watson ,whom he tenderly assisted at every turn as she grew increasingly enfeebled by age and arthritis. He was a staunch member of the Great Beach Cottage Owners Association, fighting for his shack with the rest of us and with determination to save our mutual way of life.

Charlie Schmid died in 1982, and his shack was bulldozed to the ground by the Cape Cod National Seashore several days after his death. In the chapter entitled "The Temples," I have given a very concise and thorough philosophical discussion of what this act of vandalism on the part of the Seashore meant to the dune shack community, both in terms of the single incident and the wider implications. It need not be replicated here, except, perhaps to reiterate a core concept of this memoir: that the "new challenge" for the Department of the Interior, as represented by the Cape Cod National Seashore, should have been, and should be in the future, to accommodate long established residential and non-intrusive use and habitation within the confines of environmentally sensitive areas and to regulate them in conjunction with each other in order to assure the beneficial survival of both.

The survey of "Lost Shacks" which were in the eastern section of the area of Provincetown and Truro, variously known as Pilgrim Spring State Park in Truro and the "Dune Shacks of Peaked Hill Bars Historic District" in Provincetown and Truro is completed with the foregoing inclusions. To make the discussion of the category as complete as possible, however, I am including the description of three more shacks that were in the central section of the "Dune Shacks of Peaked Hill Bars Historic District." There were a number of others that disappeared, some defined as outbuildings, etc., of the old Peaked Hill Life Saving Station complex, but the three I am citing here had a retrievable life history.

The shack of Frank L. Mayo, Chief of the Peaked Hill Coast Guard Station

Chief Mayo has previously come to our attention in this survey, most notably in the account of Zara Ofsevit as regards the circumstances of the storm of January 1931 and its consequences. In that graphic discussion of what was done in relation to the cottage of Chief Mayo in order to save it from going over the edge of the dune into the sea, the episode is made graphically plain: It was inadvertently destroyed in the rescue process. that was intended to keep it together for moving out of danger. All that remains here is for us to account for its position next to the boathouse of the Coast Guard Station as No. 3 on Hazel Hawthorne Werner's diagrammatic map No. 1, 1920 and her later map of 1933 which confirms its demise. The photograph (left) of the shack gives us a record of its structure as it appeared in an era when such shacks provided a welcome respite from daily routines for Coast Guardsmen and their families and friends.

The shack of Chief Frank L. Mayo, Peaked Hill Bars, c. 1928–1930. *Photo courtesy of David Mayo*

08-1046 (Map 201-8)

Esther Hill & Josephine Ford's Shack

The shack known to us as Josephine Ford's shack has, at this writing, to be discussed in terms of a more complicated lineage and ownership. In 1953, when Sal and I first visited Frenchie's shack as newlyweds, it was evidently owned by Esther Hill. Peg Watson mentions Hill in her letter to Annabelle Jones in 1962 as having notified the Coast Guard of the wreck of the Greek freighter *Eugenie* on September 7, 1953, after or during Hurricane "Carol." In that same letter she describes the role of the dune dwellers in their rescue and resuscitation of shipwrecked sailors. Esther Hill was very definitely, it appears, responsible for the construction of the original cottage on the premises, as I have now secured ample photographic proof from her grandson of the presence of the Hill family on the dunes, dating from 1951 to 1970. Several of these photographs are included below. This revelation of joint occupancy by both Hill and Ford remains unclear but not doubtful. It is a clouded background only because we can no longer determine the exact

The Geraldine and Esther Hill and Josephine Ford shack, 1952, facing the Atlantic (same view as Sal's drawing of Ford shack, 1954). *Photo courtesy of Jack Barry*

Above: Geraldine Hill Fraser at the shack, 1951. *Photo courtesy of Jack Barry*

Left: Grandfather Gerald Hill surveying the ruins after the shack burned down, 1970. *Photo courtesy of Jack Barry*

date of ownership, transfer, or of mutual agreement as to use and occupancy. What is known, however, does clarify how deeply the grandson, Jack Barry of Ashfield, Massachusetts, felt when he was moved on September 24, 2012 to honor his recently deceased mother, Geraldine Hill Fraser, by walking the 20 miles between Eastham and Race Point. Geraldine Hill spent summers in the early fifties at the Hill/Ford shack which was close to Frenchie's and where Jack himself, as a teenager encountered the extraordinary woman, Frenchie, who left such a lasting impression on his life. The Ford shack was burned down in 1970 on Labor Day, the work of vandals, it may be assumed. (See Chapter V). It was a shack like so many other beloved dune shacks, daring the sea and sand with minimal architecture but strongly held together by a wealth of innovative reinforcements and spiritual resources.

Alan Dodge's Cement Shack

According to architect Alan Dodge, he built the cement or "Bubble" shack, as it was referred to by some, in 1959 with the help of his friend Betty Mastenson, an artist, who, like himself, had studied at the Rhode Island School of Design In building this cement shack they enjoyed an experience quite unique among all the several examples of vernacular dune architecture, even that of the Fuller concrete shack, which originally may have been a frame structure built by Pat Patrick and which later wound up being covered in cement.

The Dodge-Mastenson effort was entirely a different approach in that it was carefully engineered, from its inception, to exist as a structure conceived and executed for strength using cement as its chief exterior building material overlaid upon a structured wire network which shaped the interior elements, including windows and a chimney. The unusual black and white photograph [page 206] reveals that process and the end result which appeared much like a cement igloo mistakenly inhabiting the landscape of the back shore. In describing the building process, Alan remarked that there were some interesting technical challenges. For instance, the sand he originally used to mix the cement for the roof was only beach sand and, therefore, could not hold in the cementing process. He quickly learned that one had to use what is known as "sharp" sand, because the particles stuck to each other and made a cohesive cement.

The location of this cement shack was slightly to the west of the Snail Road trail as it wound along to the outer beach. This road eventually exited on the shore just west of the Margo cottage, and so it was familiar to the central group of cottages both to the west and east, such as the Champlin and Tasha cottages, as one notes in Benson &

The completed cement shack by the sea (persons unidentified). *Photo courtesy of Alan Dodge*

View of the cement shack's under-structure of wire netting. *Photo courtesy of Alan Dodge*

Clemons *Traditional Dune Dwellers*, pp. 36 & 58. In 1961 or 1962, Alan Dodge gave the shack to artist Carl Tasha, who used it for several years until he went to college. At some point after that, the Seashore put it on the list of shacks to be eliminated; however, the construction of the shack evaded the normal methods of destruction, either burning or bulldozing. The only alternative, therefore, was to blow it up with dynamite, which the Park did in a last-stand effort to restore the "natural landscape." Today, nonetheless, thanks to Alan's carefully kept record of the construction process, we have ample evidence of its former existence, something melding both art and architecture with an ingenious deference to both.

Endnotes

Chapter I

[1] Frenchie was impressed with the exotic nature and picturesque aspect of the Haitian population on a trip to Haiti: (date unavailable).

[2] John Bell, "Alongshore," *Provincetown Advocate*, Thursday, July 2, 1970.

[3] See Appendix, p. 159, "The Dune Cottages at Peaked Hill Bars A Survey, 1986," {Revised, 2011).

[4] Adrienne Schnell ("Schatzi"); Letter to the Cape Cod National Seashore, Chapter 10, p. 154.

[5] William Brevda, *Harry Kemp The Last Bohemian*, Bucknell University Press, London and Toronto, 1986, (passim).

[6] William Brevda, (ibid, above) Chapter 13, "The Poet of the Dunes," p. 196: referring to"The Poet's Pilgrimage," a portion of which was published in *Provincetown Tideways, A Miscellany:* Volume 1: No. 1& No. 2, 1947; Volume 2: No.1, 1948, and Volume 2: No.2, 1950 (Privately printed by Harry Kemp through the Provincetown Publisher).

[7] William Brevda, (ibid, above, Chapter 13, pp. 200, 201).

[8] Sheila Burlingame, sculptor, resident of Provincetown, c. 1950 to c, 1970.

[9] *Mayflower II, Official Souvenir Book;* National Publishing Co. New York, (passim)

[10] William Brevda, *Harry Kemp, The Last Bohemian*, Bucknell University Press, "Afterword," p. 217.

[11] Harry Kemp, *Poet of the Dunes, Songs of the Dunes and the Outer Shore with Others in Varying Modes* "Fishertown," p. 21; privately printed by The Advocate Press, 1952.

Chapter II

The notes in this chapter largely refer to the material and notes in Chapter XV of my biography entitled: *Figures in a Landscape, The Life and Times of the American Painter Ross Moffett, 1888-1971* (The Donning Co, Publishers, Virginia Beach, Virginia, 1994) which source is referenced throughout as MB Moffett biography.

[1] "Cape Cod: Its Indians and Its Archaeology," published in the *Bulletin of the Massachusetts Archaeological Society,* October 1957, MB, Bibliography, p. 431; "Prehistoric Americans;" lecture given at the Provincetown Art Association and at the Cape Cod Art Association, Hyannis, summer, 1953; "Cape Cod and the Massachusetts Mainland; an Archaeological Comparison," Archaeological Society in Andover, April 12, 1952 (typescript), MB, Bibliography, pp. 431,432; See also, Chapter X1, "Archaeology and Art; Constants and Changes," Note 5.

[2] pp. 320, 321, MB.

[3] p. 344, Note 9: Legislative Council Report on Legal Background of the Province Lands, etc. MB.

[4] See Chapter IV, Troubled Times, p. 51 of this book..

[5] p. 344, Note 10: *Cape Cod, A Proposed National Seashore Field Investigation,* Report United States Department of the Interior, etc., 1958, MB.

[6] p. 344, Note 11: Ross Moffett Statement before the Subcommittee on Public Lands of the Committee on Interior and Insular Affairs, House of Representatives, Eastham, MA, Dec. 16 & 17, 1960, MB.

[7] p. 344, Note 12: Hearings Before the Subcommittee on Public Lands of the Committee on Interior and Insular Affairs, U.S, Senate, etc. First Session on S. 2636,etc, Eastham, MA, December 9 & 10, 1959 MB.

[8] p. 344, Note 14, Miriam DeWitt, "Testimony Before the Subcommittee on Public Lands of the Committee on Interior and Insular Affairs in support of S. 2636," etc. June 20, 1960, Ross Moffett Estate, MB.

[9] p. 325 & Note 15, p. 344: "Plan Pictures Elaborate Future—Report Delivered in July Gets No Publicity," *The New Beacon*, September 21, 1960, MB.

[10] p. 326, MBA.

[11] p. .326, MB.

[12] p. 344, & Note 18, MB.

[13] p. 327, 328, & Note 19, p. 344, MB.

[14] p. 330, MB.

[15] p. 331, MB.

[16] p. 331 & Note 24, p. 344, MB.

[17] p. 332, MB.

[18] p. 333, MB.

[19] p. 333 & Note 27, p. 345, MB.

[20] p. 334 & Note 28,.p. 345, MB.

[21] p. 334 & Note 29, p. 345, MB.

[22] p. 335 & Note 30. p. 345, MB.

[23] p. 335 & Note 31, p. 345, MB.

[24] p. 335 & Note 32. p. 345, MB.

[25] Ross Moffett, *Art In Narrow Streets, The First Thirty-three Years of the Provincetown Art Association, 1914-1947;* Chapter 10 "Brighter Days—1945–1947," Kendall Printing Co. Falmouth, Massachusetts, 1964, p 99.

Chapter III

[1] Herman A. Jennings, *Provincetown, or Odds and Ends from the Tip End,* Peaked Hill Press,Provincetown, Massachusetts, 1890, "Early History," p. 19.

[2] (See reference in Footnote [3], Chapter II of this work).

[3] George Goode Brown, *The Fisheries and Fishing Industries of the United States*; Prepared through the cooperation of the Commissioner of Fisheries and the Superintendent of the tenth census of the Fish and Fisheries, Stephen F. Baird Government printing office, Washington, D.C., 1887 Archives of the Provincetown Heritage Museum; Article 482, Sheet 202, File D (Gift of George Bryant).

[4] *Cape Cod Fisheries in 1862; Autobiography of Captain Nathaniel Atwood,* pp. 146–168, Archives of the Provincetown Heritage Museum: Article 482, F. Appendix, Sheet 202, File D (Gift of George Bryant).

[5] Jean Louis Rodolphe Agassiz, 1807–1873, " Swiss naturalist, teacher, author, Professor at Harvard, curator of the Agassiz Museum at Cambridge, Massachusetts, founder of the Marine Biolological Laboratory at Woods Hole, a fluent writer on geology and zoology..." *The Reader's Encyclopedia, Second Edition, Volume One,* Thomas Y. Crowell Co., New York, 1965, p. 14.

[6] "Hunting on the Back Shore," collection of ten photographs and text: Archives of the Provincetown Heritage Museum, Article No. 815, Sheet 521 of Photogrtaphic archive, (Gift of Dan Towler).

[7] Frances L. Higgins, *Drifting Memories—The Nauset Beach Camps on Cape Cod—South Beach—North Beach Chatham*, Lower Cape Publishing Co. 2004 Orleans, 2004 (passim).

[8] M.C.M. Hatch, *The Log of Provincetown and Truro on Cape Cod, Massachusetts,* "The Coast Guard," Fidelity Press, Boston, Massachusetts, 1939, p. 59.

[9] J.W. Dalton, *The Life Savers of Cape Cod,* Barta Press, Boston, Massachusetts, 1905, p. 35.

[10] Estate of Randolph & Annabelle Jones, Archives of the Provincetown Heritage Museum, Article 729, Sheet 434, (Gift of the Historical Commission).

[11] National Register of Historic Places, National Park Service, Determination of Eligibility Notification, EQ11593—*Dune Shacks of Peaked Hill Bars Historic District,* Cape Cod National Seashore, Barnstable County; Carol Shull, Keeper of the National Register, May 12, 1989.

[12] Donald Lee, Regional Director, Region Five, National Park Service; policy statement concerning the proposed Cape Cod National Seashore, December 1960, p. 3.

[13] Charles Foster, H.W., letter to Massachusetts State Representative Allan Jones, August 29, 1962, Archives, Great Beach Cottage Owners Association, 1962–1978.

[14] Allan Jones, letter to Charles H.W.Foster, Massachusetts Commissioner of Natural Resources, October 4, 1962, Archives of the Great Beach Cottage Owners Association, 1962–1978.

[15] Tony Vevers, letter to attorney Samuel E. Angoff regarding history of the burning of his dune cottage by the Cape Cod National Seashore in 1967 dated December 14, 1969, Archives of the Great Beach Cottage Owner's Association, 1962–1978.

[16] Charles Schmid, newspaper article concerning his dune cottage entitled "Author tries to capture spirit of dune dweller," by Peter Howard; *Cape Cod Times (New Bedford Standard Times),* July 1982.

[17] Andrew Fuller, letter to the Secretary of the Interior Stewart Udall regarding the rights of cottage owners, etc. August 27, 1965, Archives of the Great Beach Cottage Owners Association, 1962–1978.

Chapter IV

[1] *Provincetown Advocate,* Tuesday, June 3, 1966, page 1.

[2] Ibid, p. 12.

[3] "Provincetown Forfeits 41.5 Acres of Marsh To the Seashore as 19-Year Option Expires," *Provincetown Advocate,* Thursday, February 1, 1973, p. 1.

[4] Josephine C. Del Deo, *Beginnings-The History of the Fine Arts Work Center: 1964–1969,* Three Dunes Press, 1999, passim.

[5] Persons referred to in the text: Arthur Cohen (painter); Victor De Carlo (painter); Adelaide Gregory (pianist); John Gregory (etcher, lithographer and photographer); Tony Pereira (fisherman).

[6] Letter from Tony Vevers to attorney Samuel E. Angoff, counsel for the Great Beach Cottager Owners Association, December 14, 1969; Archives of the Great Beach Cottage Owners Association.

[7] Letter from U.S. attorney Paul F. Markham to George H. Thompson, Land Acquisition Officer, Dept. of the Interior, December 12, 1967; Archives of the Great Beach Cottage Owners Association.

[8] Archives of the Great Beach Cottage Owners Association; passim.

[9] Josephine Del Deo, personal journals, entry, June 4, 1968.

[10] Letter from Andrew Fuller to Robert L, Meade, February 6, 1968; letter from Grace Bessay to attorney Meade, January 18, 1968; Archives, GBCOA.

[11] Robert J. Wolfe, *Dwelling in the Dunes: Traditional Use of the Dune Shacks of the Peaked Hill Bar Historic District of Cape Cod;* final report for the Research Project "Traditional Cultural Significance of the Dune Shacks Historic District, Cape Cod National Seashore" (No. P4506040200) Supported by the National Park Service, U.S. Department of the Interior, August 2005; Chapter 1, People Living on the Edge, Map No. 4, p. 8.

[12] Letter from Superintendent Leslie p. Arnberger, Cape Cod National Seashore to attorney Samuel E. Angoff, Angoff, Golden, Manning and Pyle, Boston, Massachusetts, dated October 20, 1969; Archives Great Beach Cottage Owners Association.

[13] (See note 6 above): letter from Tony Vevers to attorney Samuel E. Angoff, counsel for the GBCOA, dated December 14, 1969: History of the Pfeiffer cottage; copy of deed to Vevers from Chet Pfeiffer dated September 4, 1964; date of construction of cottage -1939, etc. (6 pages-GBCOA Archives).

[14] Chase, Alston, "Unhappy Birthday," *Outside,* December, 1991, p. 36.

Chapter V

[1] Croswell Bowen, *The Curse of the Misbegotten,* McGraw Hill, New York, London, 1959, pp. 110–151 passim.

[2] Gail Cohen, twentieth century American theater specialist: Director of the Hedgerow Theater Collection: Archive of Selected materials pertaining to the Hedgerow Theater company and to the Provincetown Playhouse on the Wharf (personal archive of the author).

[3] Gail Cohen, (See note 2 above).

[4] Ibid.

[5] Ibid.

[6] Archives: Great Beach Cottage Owners Association (GBCOA).

[7] Ibid.

[8] Archives: Andrew D. Fuller & Grace Bessay.

[9] See Appendix I: pp. 186–189.

[10] See Chapter III, p. 45 and Notes 13 and 14.

[11] Archive: Andrew D. Fuller & Grace Bessay: Grace Bessay's notes regarding discussions with Attorney Samuel Angoff and Asst.U.S. Attorney James Gabriel dated February, March & April, 1971.

[12] Archives: Andrew D. Fuller & Grace Bessay.

[13] See Appendix: Del Deo, Josephine C.; *The Dune Cottages at Peaked Hill Bars, 1986, Updated & Revised* Construction dates, ownership, location, etc. of shacks, also article by John Bell: *Provincetown Advocate,* "Alongshore," July 2, 1970.

[14] Archives: Great Beach Cottage Owners Association (GBCOA).

[15] Ibid.

[16] Archives: GBCOA: Letters from Andrew Fuller to: David Armstrong; Randolph Jones; Charlie Schmid; Nick Wells, April 28, 1977.

[17] Thomas and Sibylle De Carlo: the son and wife of the painter Victor De Carlo, lifelong friends.

[18] Provincetown Historic District Study Committee: Appointed in 1973 by the Selectmen: Mary Avellar, John Bell*, George Bryant*, Alice Cook,* Josephine Del Deo, Claude Jensen, Phyllis Temple, Edward Allodi (architectural consultant). *=resigned—Paul Mendes, later replacement.

[19] The Provincetown Historic District as a local historic district protected by local zoning was approved by the town in 2003 at the recommendation of the Provincetown Historical Commission under the chairmanship of Eric Dray. This concluded a twenty-six year effort to establish such a district; a National Registered District was approved by the Massachusetts Historical Commission in 1989 due to the effort, at that time, of Preston Babbitt and others. Thus the long trajectory, beginning with the 1977 presentation of such a concept proposed by our original committee and rejected by the town then, was finally and successfully achieved.

[20] The artist Elizabeth Howland Caliga was the wife of I.H. Caliga,(1857–c.1940), a well-know Provincetown painter. Ruth DeWitt was Elizabeth's sister, and these two sisters were our first landlords in Provincetown in 1954.

[21] See Chapter IX, p. 141.

Chapter VI

[1] William Shakespeare, *Shakespeare's Sonnets*, J.M .Dent and Co., Aldine House, W.C. London, 1906, Sonnet LXIV.

[2] Notification of National Register Acceptance by the Secretary of the Commonwealth, Paul Guzzi and the State Historic Preservation Officer , Elizabeth Amadon, to Josephine Del Deo, November 19, 1975: Date Center Methodist Church entered in Register: October 31, 1975.

[3] History of "*The Provincetown Heritage Museum 1976*" by Josephine Del Deo, Curator, July 4, 1986, "The committee,the first board of trustees, (see Note 4) powered the effort to secure the vote to acquire the building at a special town meeting on November 12, 1975, and arranged to purchase the property from the First National Bank of Provincetown on March 15, 1975."

[4] First Board of Trustees: Josephine Del Deo, Chairman, Salvatore Del Deo, Adelaide Kenney, Joseph Lema, Cyril Patrick, Jr.

[5] Edie Clark, "Another Rose for Provincetown," *Yankee Magazine,* January, 1989, Dublin, NH, pp. 68–74 & 120–127.

[6] William Marlin, "A Cast of Characters for a Playhouse on Cape Cod," *Architectural Record,* March 1979, McGraw Hill, New York, Volume 165, No. 3, pp. 129–138.

[7] Photograph of The Provincetown Playhouse on the Wharf interior c. 1970. Postcard to Josephine Del Deo from Catharine Huntington dated Monday, July 26, 1971: "Dear Josephine—Now there *is* a swimming pool. It is like 'Alice in Wonderland' what goes on. Last night a great geyser rose from the Harbor and poured into the tank. Just keeping you posted. Catharine Huntington."

[8] George Goodman, "Edwin Dickinson Dies at 87; Noted Representational Artist," *The New York Times,* Sunday, December 3, 1978.(Tim) Attorney Timothy H. Everett-grandson of Provincetown painter Mary Hackett (1906–1989).

[9] Josephine C. Del Deo, *Figures In A Landscape, The Life & Times of the American Painter Ross Moffett: 1888–1971;* The Donning Co., Virginia Beach, VA, 1994; Part II, Chapter II, "The Man, the Time and the Place," p. 19.

[10] Ibid: Notes for Chapter 11: Note 3, p. 31: "Diaries of Edwin Dickinson 1916–1919, Archives of American Art, Smithsonian Institution, Microfilm Rolls, D 93 & D 96.

[11] Alice Hoyt Palmer, 1910–1984: editor, McGraw Hill Publ. Co.; Textbook Publishing Advisor, U.S.A.I.D., South Vietnam, Indonesia & Brazil; artist (maternal aunt of Josephine Del Deo).

[12] Frank Byron Couch, 1868–1928: Adirondack landscape painter who studied at the National Academy of Design and The Art Students' League and exhibited widely in New York City and on the East Coast (father of the author).

[13] Reference to photographs taken by George Bryant, Provincetown historian, depicting the aftermath of the destruction of Charlie Schmid's shack by the Cape Cod National Seashore .

[14] Osma Palmer Couch (Gallinger Tod), 1895–1983: national authority on weaving and basketry; author of numerous books and articles on weaving and related crafts; author, teacher, lecturer and musician (mother of the author). Francis S, Del Deo, 1914–1983: born in Forio d'Ischia, Naples, Italy; resident of Rhode Island; publisher of periodicals; journalist, linguist & teacher (brother of Salvatore Del Deo).

Chapter VII

[1] Talilla Schuster, daughter of neighboring dune dweller Lawrence Schuster and Genevieve Martin.

[2] Frank Milby, Provincetown painter and frequent resident of the Ofsevit shack: "Art Costa founded his beach taxi business with the commitment to the "way of life" on the dunes equal, in many respects, to the dune dwellers he loved and assisted for so many years He never tired of telling the stories of the dune shacks, their occupants, and their histories to his clients riding the dunes in his beach taxi which he drove daily in the summer months. His motto painted on the doors of his several vehicles was the clue to his enthusiasm: "You gotta have Art's."

[3] Stanley Kunitz: American poet and teacher; Pulitzer Prize winner in 1959 for his collection entitled *Selected Poems;* founder of the writing program of the Fine Arts Work Center in Provincetown, Massachusetts, a resident community for young artists and writer.

[4]NARO—North Atlantic Regional Office of the National Park Service; Division of Cultural Resources: "Historic Structure Inventory, Cape Cod National Seashore," prepared February 1987.

[5] Dr. Julie Schecter, "Description of Pilot Project to Establish the Peaked Hill Trust" together with a draft proposal. Correspondence between Dr. Julie Schecter and Josephine Del Deo: November 11, December 9 and December 12, 1985.

[6] Letter from Dr. Julie Schecter to Peaked Hill Trust members; July 22, 1988.

[7] The National Preservation Act of 1966 amended and updated and published in the Federal Register on Februaary 18, 1988, containing Section 110: Guidelines, "The Section 110 Guidelines—Annotated Guidelines for Federal Agency Responsibilities under Section110 of the National Preservation Act."

[8] Letter to James Bradley, chairman of the Massachusetts Historical Commission, from Josephine Del Deo and Norman Mailer, July 14, 1988.

[9] Harry Kemp, *Poet of the Dunes; Songs of the Dunes and the Outer Shore with Others in Varying Modes and Moods* 1952, Provincetown Publishers, Advocate Press, p. 29.

[10] Josephine Del Deo, statement to the Massachusetts Historical Commission regarding the dune cottages at Peaked Hill at the hearing in Provincetown, August 26, 1988, typescript, pp. 7 & 8 (accompanying letter to Chairman James Bradley).

Chapter VIII

[1] Civil Action No. 67-988: United States of America, Plaintiff, Certain Land located in the county of Barnstable, Commonwealth of Massachusetts, E. Bennett Beede, et al.,' Grace Bessay, executrix of the Estate of Andrew D. Fuller, Jr., Defendants, Grace Bessay Individually, Defendant, Sept. 15, 1988; Nelson, D.J., Archives of Andrew D. Fuller & Grace Bessay.

[2] *Congressional Record,* September 3, 1959, p. 1.

[3] E.O. 11593: Determination of Eligibility Notification, National Register of Historic Places: National Park Service; Name of property: "Dune Shacks of Peaked Hill Bars Historic District," 5/12/89.

[4] Massachusetts Historical Commission: Media Advisory; Date, January 20, 1989; "Area of Interest; Dune Shacks; National Park Service Recommends Against Dune Shack Eligibility—Connolly and MHC Promise Fight for Preservation of Shacks".

[5] News Release: U.S. Department of the Interior, National Park Service: "NPS To Consider Retention of Cape Cod Dune Shacks; National Register Keeper to Make Determination" (4 pages), Dated 12/11/88.

[6] See statement by Grace Bessay contained in a letter to the Secretary of the Interior Manuel J. Lujan, Jr., May 26, 1989, on page 3 of her statement (pp. 120–121 of this chapter).Archive of Andrew D.Fuller-& Grace Bessay.

[7] Joyce Johnson, "Building Continues in Cape Cod National Seashore," April 14, 1989; "Call Town Officials to Meeting on Seashore Building," Sept. 8. 1989;

"Explaining Act Shows How Park is Hamstrung," Sept. 15, 1989; "Truro Takes the Lead in Moving to Curb Building in Seashore," Sept. 22, 1989. *The Cape Codder* (all articles).

[8] See Note 1 above and: "In the Supreme Court of the United States October Term, 1989: Grace E. Bessay, petitioner v. United States of America: Petition for a Writ of Certiorari to the United States Court of Appeals for the First Circuit, Statement of Case, pp. 12, 13, 14, especially. Archives of Andrew D. Fuller & Grace Bessay.

[9] See Note 8 above, especially pp. 16, 17, 18, & 19.

[10] Alston Chase, "Dismantling Civilization Is Expensive," Creators Syndicate, Inc, November 15, 1993.

[11] Alston Chase, "Unhappy Birthday," *Outside* (magazine), December 1991, pp. 33 et al.

[12] Josephine Del Deo, letter to Manual Lujan, Jr., U.S. Secretary of the Interior, Sept. 13, 1990.

[13] Settlement Agreement: David W. Adams and Marcia C Adams, Plaintiffs v. United States of America, Defendant; Civil Action No. 84-1193-S. Archives of Andrew D. Fuller & Grace Bessay.

[14] Joyce Starr, "Sands of Time: Deal Gives Woman 25-Year Use of Dune Shack," *The Cape Cod Times,"* October 3, 1990.

[15] Francis F. McManamon, "Laying the Foundation, Ross Moffett and Cape Cod Archaeology," *Bulletin of the Massachusetts Archaeological Society,* Volume 69 (1), spring 2008, pp. 2-5 Seiser, Beth, "The Cape's first real archaeologist also was one of its great painters," *The Cape Cod Voice,* Volume 1, No. 15, November 22–December 5, 2001.

[16] Judith B. McDonough, Director, State Historic Preservation Officer, Massachusetts Historical Commission: letter to Gerald Patten, Regional Director, National Park Service, North Atlantic Regional Office, October 31, 1991.

[17] Josephine Del Deo, "The Status of the Grace Bessay Cottage and Others," statement to the Seashore Advisory Commission, November 10, 1991, p. 2.

[18] Jeff McLaughlin, "Case shifts sands under Provincetown Refuge," *The Boston Globe,* November 16, 1991.

[19] Grace Bessay, statement to the Seashore Advisory Commission, January 31,1992 (4 pages). Archives of Andrew D. Fuller and Grace Bessay.

[20] Photo courtesy of Benson & Clemons: *Traditional Dune Dwellers—A Way of Life on the Backshore of Provincetown and Truro,* 2011, p. 20

Chapter IX

[1] The several challenges Chairman Philbrick proposed we solve: Bringing to the Commission a full option of proposals; need to reach for feedback from owners and users; need to bear in mind the Peaked Hill Trust and their role; the question of

access-extent and method; does the method adequately recognize the unique nature of these shacks? (plus the three items I have listed).

[2] United States Department of the Interior, National Park Service; Annual Review, June 27, 1989, five pages plus Part 18: (18-1-18-13) Leases and Exchanges of Historic Property.

[3] 36 CFR Part 800: Protection of Historic Properties Regulations of the Advisory Council on Historic Preservation Governing the Section 106–Sections 800-1 and 800-9, Effective October 1986.

[4] Murray Zimiles to Chairman Philbrick, Dune Shack Subcommittee April 17, 1992.

[5] Report of the Dune Shack Subcommittee to the Cape Cod National Seashore Advisory Commission, May 29, 1992

[6] Reference as above in note 5.

[7] See Chapter VIII: p. 102 ff. and Note Numbers 8 and 9.

[8] The Wood End Station in Provincetown was built in 1896 as part of the several Life Saving Service stations constructed in the "Duluth" style, as was the Old Harbor Station in Chatham built in 1898. The Chatham station was moved, at great cost, from its location in Chatham to the environs of Race Point in 1978. It is hard to understand why the Wood End Station was burned, since it represented the identical period and design as its replacement. (Information as to the date and style of the two stations by Cape Cod National Seashore Historian William Burke).

[9] "A Retrospective Exhibition, Salvatore Del Deo, Selected Works 1953–1993," Provincetown Art Association and Museum, May 28–June 28, 1993. "Manuel, Doryman," 1968, oil on canvas, 32"x 22", *Collection of Provincetown Art Association and Museum.*

[10] See above Note 9, page 14.

[11] Marilyn Miller, "Seashore Planners Get Earful of Complaints," *The Advocate,* Thursday, November 11, 1993, pp. 1 & 28.

[12] Lawrence Schuster, year-round dune dweller in the Braaten cottage since 1984 (See Appendix: Dune Cottage History).

[13] *Bolts of Melody—New Poems of Emily Dickinson,* Edited by Mabel Loomis Todd and Millicent Todd Bingham, Dover Publications, New York, 1969, "Vital Light," 432. p. 227

Chapter X

[1] Lorenzo Ghiberti, Italian sculptor who executed the bronze doors for the Baptistery in Florence; between 1425 and 1472. They were designed in a sequence of ten sections representing scenes from the Old Testament.

[2] Personally given to the author by Father Thomas Ryan, art consultant and historian for the building project of the Church of the Transfiguration, Orleans, Massachusetts, dedicated in the year 2000.

[3] See Chapter V; "Eugene O'Neill Doesn't Live Here Anymore" pp. 69–71. See also: Bowen, Croswell, *The Curse of the Misbegotten*, McGraw Hill, New York, Toronto & London, 1959, pp. 110–151 passim.

[4] Letters submitted to Superintendent Maria Burks in regard to comments sought by the Seashore Advisory Commission for a third Dune Shack Subcommittee appointed in 2003 from dune shack residents All letters quoted date as follows: Mildred Champlin, 4/03/03; Sue Pomerantz, 5/01/03; Murray Zimiles, 5/05/03; "Schatzi," Adreienne Schnell, 5/14/03; Dawn Zimiles, 6/06/03 .

[5] Personal conversation: Joyce Johnson with the author in 2011.

[6] Letter to Chairman Brenda Boleyn, Advisory Commission, Cape Cod National Seashore; SUBJ Dune Shack Subcommittee Report from: The Provincetown Board of Selectmen, Mary-Jo Avellar Chairman, May 14, 2003. This plan, undertaken by the CNSS General Management Plan Implementation Advisory Commission (IAC) for the Selectmen, had been researched and formulated by attorney John Thomas, a writer and composer and an occasional dune shack inhabitant, which had given him a valued perspective of the dune shacks and the way of life they represent. Research for this report was largely undertaken by the chairman of the CCNS General Management Plan Implementation Advisory Committee for the Provincetown Board of Selectmen, John W. Thomas. The report of the IAC was extensively researched and formulated under the direction of Co-chairman Thomas, whose experience as an attorney and whose interest in the dune shacks and the way of life of the dune dwellers had been a personal and primary interest for many years, contributing to his creative career as a musician and a writer.

[7] Letter from Dawn Zimiles to Superintendent Maria Burks (Subject described as in Footnote 4 above), 6/06/03.

Appendix Part I

[1] The Foreword to the original 1986 Survey is presented in full on pages 102 and 103, Chapter 7, "Defining a Way of Life."

[2] Dr. Robert J. Wolfe; *Dwelling in the Dunes; Traditional Use of the Dune Shacks of the Peaked Hill Bars Historic District, Cape Cod,* Final Report for the Research Project, Traditional Cultural Significance of the Dune Shacks Historic District, Cape Cod National Seashore (No P4506040200). Supported by the National Park Service, U.S. Department of the Interior, August 2005 (hereafter referred to as DITD) Chapter 3, "Dune Shack Safety," p. 67.

[3] Division of Cultural Resources, NARO Historic Structure Inventory; Cape Cod National Seashore, Feb, 1987.

[4] Marcia Adams/Sally Adams: key documents regarding dune shack history, December 26, 2011.

[5] Date of official placement on the National Register of Historic Places of the Dune Shacks of Peaked Hill Bars Historic District, September 14, 2011.

[6] Marcia Adams: key document regarding Champlin, Villemain, etc., December 03, 2009.

[7] Information from Mildred Champlin by phone to the author in September 2012.

[8] Division of Cultural Resources, NARO Historic Structure Inventory, Cape Cod National Seashore, Feb. 1987.

[9] Josephine Del Deo: "Statement Delivered to the Cape Cod National Seashore Advisory Commission Regarding the Status of the Grace Bessay Cottage and Others," Nov. 10, 1991, pp. 1, 6, 7.

[10] "Request for Proposals: Dune Shacks of Peaked Hill Bars, Cape Cod National Seashore, Provincetown and Truro, Massachusetts, September 10, 1993" (Leases awarded January 10, 1994.

[11] Personal knowledge of the author. See also Ross Moffett; *"Art In Narrow Streets," The First Thirty-Three Years of the Provincetown Art Association,"* Kendall Press, Falmouth, MA, 1964.

[12] Dr. Robert J. Wolfe, DITD, Chapter 2. "The Roots of Tradition," p. 23.

[13] The Malicoat property is listed on the December 12, 1985, Inventory of the Cape Cod National Seashore and, therefore, was eligible for inclusion in the National Register of Historic Places: however, the Malicoat family chose not to be listed in the "Dune Shacks of Peaked Hill Bars Historic District" when the nomination became official. I have, nevertheless included the shack as an integral component of the constellation of dune shacks discussed in this memoir.

[14] Josephine Del Deo; *The Dune Cottages at Peaked Hill Bars, A Survey,* 1986, p. 4.

[15] Material provided by William Burke, Historian, Cape Cod National Seashore: typewritten statement from Cora Holbrook regarding the sale of her cottage to Hazel Hawthorne Werner and typewritten statement from Hazel Hawthorne Werner regarding the moving of the cottage named "Euphoria" from its shore-ward position in 1952.

[16] See MAPS of this Appendix: Hazel Hawthorne's drawings of dune shack, locations p. 4 (1939–1949) and p. 6. (1950–1960).

[17] Josephine Del Deo, *The Dune Cottages at Peaked Hill Bars, A Survey, 1986:* Appendix pp. 31, 32. "Hearings for the Cape Cod National Seashore Park before the Subcommittee on Insular and Interior Affairs House of Representatives, Eighty-sixth Congress, Second Session, Eastham, Mass, Saturday, December 17, 1960 (*Congressional Record*).

[18] Edmund Wilson, *The Thirties*, Washington Square Press New York, 1982; William Brevda, *Harry Kemp, The Last Bohemian,* Bucknell University Press, London and Toronto, 1986.

[19] Dr. Robert J. Wolfe, DITD, Chapter 8, "Cultural Traditions II, The Edge of

America's Art Colony," pp. 187–200 passim.

[20] Josephine Del Deo, *The Dune Cottages at Peaked Hill Bars, A Survey, 1986* (afterward referred to as DCPHB), p. 5, Note 6.

[21] Dr. Robert J. Wolfe, DITD, pp. 187, 188.

[22] DCPHB, p. 5, Note 7.

[23] DCPHB, Appendix: letter from Congressman Gerry Studds re: building of Coast Guard Station, p. 36; Photo and dates of construction, p. 38.

[24] DCPHB, p. 7, Note 19.

[25] DCPHB, pp. 9 & 10: See also: Crosswell Bowen, *The Curse of the Misbegotten,* McGraw Hill, New York, London, 1959, p. 110.

[26] DCPHB, p. 7 See also Edmund Wilson, *The Thirties*, Washington Square Press, New York,1982, pp. 18–42 passim & p. 194.

[27] See Ofsevit in this survey and reference to Frank Mayo shack.

[28] DCPHB, See Rose Tasha shack, pp. 11, 12.

[29] DCPHB, p. 8, & Note 13; telephone conversation with John Corea, October 29, 1986, and also p. 9.

[30] DCPHB, p. 8 and Note 12, interview with Philip S. Packett, October 29, 1986.

[31] U.S, Coast Guard information from U.S. Coast Guard Motor Life Boat Station, Chatham, MA, four pages dated 1933, scanned 9/21/2012, and made available to the author by David Mayo, grandson of former Chief Frank Mayo of the Peaked Hill Coast Guard Station:

The following information excerpted from the above report is an expansion of the information provided to me by Philip S. Packett in 1986 as noted on p. 8 and Footnote 12 of my 1986 survey:

> Provincetown, January 1933: More than 100 officers and men are on duty in the 12 Coast Guard Stations of the Cape which are affected by the recent reorganization of the Coast Guard life saving service... Next Jan. 15, the office of the Coast Guard District Headquarters, in Provincetown,will be closed permanently by order of the government. Consummation of this edict will give an entirely new aspect to Coast Guard affairs on the Cape .The 12 Coast Guard Stations which have been under the direct supervision of the Provincetown office, while their officers-in-charge have maintained almost daily a close personal contact with their district commander, will in the future report to the Third District headquarters in Wakefield, R.I. ...It will be the first time in 61 years since the U.S. Life Saving Service established headquarters on the Cape that the "men on watch" will get their orders from an office located off the Cape.
>
> In 1871, this district was created with headquarters in East Orleans. Then there were 32 stations in the district from Plum Island south and including Nantucket and the adjacent islands. Now the district is composed of 22 stations from Rockport to Monomoy Point. The U.S. Life Saving Service was in operation until 1915 when the U.S. Coast Guard took over the duties of protecting this dangerous strip of coast. Second District headquarters were reestablished in Provincetown in 1904...

The establishment of the headquarters here meant considerably more to the Provincetown men in the service than appeared on the surface.... Numerous keepers of the various stations are Provincetown men...Local men won these coveted places because of their intimate contact with the district commanders here. It was not due to favoritism that they were chosen, but because each man chosen for an important job was known personally to the headquarters chief who had ample opportunity to judge the caliber of the man before recommending him for promotion Taking the office out of Provincetown meant a loss of thousands of dollars to the community.....Coast Guards on the Cape in these days give aid. Since July, the Second District stations have responded to more than 1,000 calls for assistance mostly fishing craft, freighters, coasters and pleasure boats. The Wood End station alone has answered 154 of these calls. This station and the Monomoy Point station are regarded by headquarters as the two most important stations in the district." The report goes on to list the personnel in each of the 12 Cape Stations In the case of the Peaked Hill Bars listing, every one of the names, except one, of the ten Coast Guard personnel of the station are noted in this memoir as having been associated with the building of, maintenance and or ownership of a dune shack in the Peaked Hill area. These were: Boatswain's Frank L. Mayo, officer in charge; Boatswain's Mate 1st Class. Joseph A. Morris; Surfmen: Manuel F.Silva; John F. Cook, Joseph Medeiros, Louis H. Silva, Raymond A. Brown, Morris F. Worth, Philip S. Packett, Warren L. Ellis.

[32] See text of this memoir, "Chapter 10, p. , Note 4. Letter from Murray Zimiles to Maria Burks, May 5, 2003.

[33] Mary Heaton Vorse, *Time and the Town,A Provincwetown Chronicle,* The Dial Press; New York; 1942, p. 124.

[34] William Brevda, *Harry Kemp, The Last Bohemian*, Bucknell University Press, London and Toronto, 1986, Chapter 13: "The Poet of the Dunes," pp. 190, 203.

[35] See Tasha survey. See also Hazel Hawthorne Werner dune cottage diagrams for 1920, 1933, and 1933–1939.

[36] See Margo survey.

[37] The distance moved was in line with the Coast Guard Station distance moved, or approximately 660 feet.

[38] See Hazel Hawthorne Werner's diagram for 1939–1946 (map 4) explaining watch tower position.

[39] Ibid, p. 2 1933. See also references in this survey to Bessay-Fearing and Thalassa. Of these two cottages built, the transfer is definite: Brown to Fearing, Silva to Hawthorne Werner. The disappearance of the third cottage referred to by Werner as #10, however, is explained in her 1946–1950 diagram, p. 5 as " abandoned and fallen over."

[40] Josephine Del Deo, DCPHB, 1986: p. 8 and Note 12. Packett's description of fate of the Peaked Hill Station from 1931 to final destruction in late fifties.

[41] Edward Denby, ballet and dance critic for the" *New York Times*."

[42] Josephine Del Deo; archive pertaining to the work of the Dune Shack Subcommittee of the Seashore Advisory Commission; material received from Stanley E. fowler and Laura Fowler.

[43] Ibid.

[44] Peter Clemons and Marianne Benson: "History of the Stan and Laura Fowler Dune Shack;" provided to the author.

[45] Hazel Hawthorne Werner's diagrammatic sketches of dune shacks at Peaked Hill, 1933, p. 2.

[46] Material provided to the author by Peter Clemons and Marianne Benson: "History of Bessay/Fuller Dune Shack," December 2009.

[47] John Bell, "Alongshore," *The Provincetown Advocate*, Thursday, July 2, 1970.

Also: Hazel Hawthorne Werner's diagrammatic sketches of dune shacks, 1939–1946, p. 4.

[48] See also Boris Margo/Jan Gelb in this survey and DCPHB, 1986 p. 16.

[49] Josephine Del Deo: DCPHB, 1986, p. 7, Note 11.

[50] Josephine Del Deo to William Burke, Historian, Cape Cod National Seashore, regarding material for preparation of National Register listing of dune shacks, Nov. 15, 2011: Dates of Thalassa construction and photocopy of statement by Louis Silva confirming sale date to Werner. Also photocopy of Werner's confirmation of moving Thalassa in 1949 to present location. Photocopies provided to the author by William Burke.

[51] Ibid.

[52] See Hazel Hawthorne Werner's diagrammatic sketches, 1939–1946, p. 4 showing watch tower of the Coast Guard Station, which had been moved back from the shore in 1931. She indicates the number of the watch tower on the map as 17, and the position corresponds to the position of Thalassa described by the National Register of Historic Places Form 10-900 as the former site of the watch tower which Werner says was destroyed by fire in 1946 (see Note 4. of Ofsevit in "Notes" of this survey).

[53] Josephine Del Deo: DCPHB, 1986, p. 20.

[54] Information from Gordon Spingler & Lawrence Schuster.

[55] National Register of Historic Places Form 10-900 regarding "Dune Shacks of Peaked Hill Bars Historic District."

[56] Gail Cohen, "Dune Shack Report to Maria Burks, Superintendent Cape Cod National Seashore," March 17, 1997, pp. 5, 6, 7.

[57] Survey of legal status of the dune shacks by Grace Bessay, p. 14, GBCOA Archives.

[58] See Note 4 above and also Dr. Robert J. Wolfe, DITD, p. 125.

[59] Dr. Robert J. Wolfe, DITD, pp. 125, 126.

[60] Josephine Del Deo, DCPHB, 1986, p. 20.

[61] Notice of decease: "*Cape Cod Times*" and "*Provincetown Advocate*," March 28, 1972, GBCOA Archives.

[62] Information from GB COA.

[63] Letter from Miriam Hapgood DeWitt to Superintendent Herbert Olsen, Cape Cod National Seashore, January 5, 1986: Josephine Del Deo, DCPHB, Appendix, p. 34.

[64] Dr. Robert J. Wolfe, DITD, Chapter 11 "Shack Management and Protection," pp. 235–243 passim.

[65] Josephine Del Deo DCPHB, 1986, p. . 21.

[66] Ray Wells diagrammatic sketch of dune shacks at Peaked Hill Bars,GBCOA Archives. Also "*Provincetown Banner*, August 4, 2011, p. 21.

[67] *Provincetown Banner*, August 4, 2011, p. 21.

[68] Josephine Del Deo, DCPHB, 1986, p. 21.

[69] Ibid, p. 22.

[70] Provincetown Heritage Museum Inventory; Provincetown Public Library, Josephine C. Del Deo Archive: Article 729, Sheet 434, history of Jones occupancy of shack .

[71] See page 1, from above history and also National Register of Historic Places Form 10-900 for attribution of builder.

[72] Correspondence with Peg Watson, various, 1962–1963.

[73] Survey of legal status of dune shacks by Grace Bessay, p. 17. GBCOA Archives.

[74] Dr. Robert J. Wolfe, DITD, Chapter 4 "Social Formation," p. 99.

[75] D. Robert J. Wolfe, DITD, Chapter 1 "People Living on the Edge, Dune Shacks in the Eastern Group," p. 8.

[76] Conversation with Connie Armstrong, September-October, 2012.

[77] Ibid.

[78] Dr. Robert J. Wolfe, DITD, Chapter 2. "The Edge of Nature and Society," p. 214.

[79] See Note (13) under Malicoat Notes.

[80] Dr. Robert J. Wolfe, DITD, Chapter 11, "Shack Management and Preservation," "Minimal Infrastructures," pp. 234, 235

Notes

Frenchie's Shack at Peaked Hill, 1990, oil on canvas, 11" x 20"